TURNED ON TO JESUS

D1428620

TURNED ON
TO JESUS

by ARTHUR BLESSITT
with WALTER WAGNER

WORD BOOKS
LONDON

Paperback edition—1st printing March 1972
2nd printing April 1972
Published by WORD BOOKS, London, a division of
WORD (UK) LTD, Park Lane, Hemel Hempstead, Hertfordshire.

Printed and bound in Great Britain by
Hazell Watson & Viney Ltd,
Aylesbury, Bucks

For Mom, Dad, and Sherry, who helped the most

Contents

If any man be called to preach, don't stoop to be a king.

—PHILLIPS BROOKS

The team went in a huddle;
The captain raised his head.
They all got together,
And this is what they said:
"Jesus saves!"

—SHERRY BLESSITT

Therefore, if any man be in Christ, he is a new creation;
old things are passed away; behold, all things are become new.

—2 CORINTHIANS 5:17

TURNED ON TO JESUS

Calvary in California

THE BUILDING at 450 North Crescent Drive in Beverly Hills, California, swaggers under the smog-leaden sky, its hundred feet of perfectly manicured greensward swimming up to a rococo, palm-fronted, broad-shouldered edifice that houses the municipal court of the world's toniest suburb. Here justice is dispensed in the most golden of America's golden ghettos.

Though it boasts ten churches of every major faith within its tiny 5.69-square-mile radius, on the blistering hot morning of June 26, 1969, I was skeptical that Jesus Christ would find justice in Beverly Hills, for it was surely Him, not myself as one of His ordained ministers, who was the defendant in the trial slated to begin in a few moments.

Beverly Hills, the Everest of Establishment enclaves, was playing reluctant host to several dozen members of my congregation, most of them under thirty—hoods, bikers, dopers, pushers, runaways, teeny-boppers, strippers, topless dancers, hippies, male and female prostitutes, pimps, homosexuals, and two Syndicate soldiers who between them had committed five murders. They were a gaggle of unlikely interlopers, white and black, tie-and-suited, bearded and beaded, mini- and micro-skirted, blue-jeaned, leather-jacketed, turtlenecked, bare-footed, jackbooted, some unwashed, many, for all I knew, concealing acid, uppers, downers, chains, knives, and guns in their pockets and brassieres.

They all had come unbidden, a spontaneous turnout of my pariah parishioners whose only house of worship was His Place, my combination church and gospel nightclub located in the heart of the Sunset Strip.

Despite their bizarre appearance and powder-keg mood, they were well-behaved and respectful as they filled virtually all the spectators' seats in the snug, richly paneled courtroom where the majesty of the law worked its Monday-to-Friday wonders, protecting due process and freedom of speech, of assembly, and of religion.

His Place was in dire jeopardy, and my outcast flock shared my skepticism that straight society would allow our unorthodox church to survive on a notorious public thoroughfare where every conceivable perversion and sin is for sale, where Satanic merchants who call themselves legitimate businessmen cater to the full range of human weaknesses, providing the price is right.

Stripped of legalese, the issue about to be decided in court boiled down to a single, vitally important question: *Was there room for Jesus Christ on the Sunset Strip?*

The prosecution's answer was no, at least not on the premises of 8913 Sunset Boulevard, where His Place occupied a nine-room building under the terms of a $400-a-month lease.

I had been brought to court to face a civil action following my refusal to obey my landlord's eviction order. I could do nothing else but refuse—I knew from wearying experience that no other property owner on the Strip would rent to me. Now, if the case were lost, there would be no haven for the young people of the Strip who more than anything else needed Christ in their lives. That was the whole point of His Place and the reason I would make whatever sacrifice was necessary to prevent its being crushed by the power-brokers who ruled the Strip.

I smiled to myself remembering the first clash I'd had with my landlord only a few days after we moved in. He sent me a letter requesting that I remove a sign from the front of the building that he termed "offensive." The sign, which I did not remove, read: "GOD IS LOVE." Who, except someone encoiled by the Devil, could find the thought embodied in those three words offensive?

Now the trial was underway and the prosecution began to build its case. One witness testified that His Place attracted "degenerates and people of destitute condition." Another said that those we ministered to were filthy in dress, speech, and manner. Then one of the private security guards in the pay of a Strip merchant who runs a particularly unsavory bar swore under oath that he had seen "twenty to thirty couples locked in fond embraces on the floor."

The clincher was my landlord, who claimed that the existence of our House of God had led to an increase in his fire insurance rates, that people streaming in and out of His Place caused street congestion, and that when the building had been rented to us, he was unaware it was going to be used as a "religious center."

Several members of my Team took the stand to refute the charges. Dale Larsen, normally the most unexcitable of young men, snapped that kissing and dancing much less "fond embraces on the floor" were strictly against the rules at His Place. That "twenty to thirty couples" could engage in such behavior without attracting the attention of a staff member would be impossible. His Place was not a brothel, but a sanctuary of God as sacred as a cathedral.

Ed Human, the dark-haired father of three children who had given up a $15,000-a-year engineer's job to work full time in my ministry, pointed out that the young people who crossed our threshold committed no public outrage comparable to the foul-mouthed curses of the weaving, drunken men and women in alligator shoes and mink stoles who emerged from Sneaky Pete's and The Galaxy, the restaurant and nightclub on either side of His Place. The only difference was that parking attendants poured these well-dressed, well-heeled, staggering straights into Lincolns and Cadillacs. Few who came to His Place had more than a chopper or a flower-decorated Volkswagen and their clothes didn't come from Saks or I. Magnin.

The attorney for the prosecution did his best to make Dale and Ed appear as kooks and freaks who dealt only with other kooks and freaks. Yet Dale, the strong right arm of my ministry, is a deeply dedicated Christian who has won hundreds to the Lord. Ed, an ordained minister, has preached often in some of the country's largest churches.

I strode to the stand impatiently when my name was called. I was no stranger to a courtroom. I had been busted and tried three times and to me the witness box was a pulpit—a marvelous opportunity to quote at least a few passages of Scripture. No telling who might be reached: the bailiff, the court stenographer—even the judge.

The prosecution's lawyer couldn't have been more helpful. He seemed an unwitting messenger direct from the Lord as he pursued a line of questioning that would soon give me a wonderful opportunity to preach, a temptation I am incapable of resisting under any circumstances.

Holding one of my tracts in his hand, he asked, "Do you acknowledge that you pass out these pieces of paper on the sidewalk in front of your building?"

"Yes, sir. I pass them out on the sidewalk, and I also pass them out in a lot of other places, everywhere I can. I especially like to place them between the covers of pornographic magazines in all those dirty book stores on Santa Monica Boulevard."

A wave of laughter swept the courtroom.

"What does this paper contain?"

"It's a gospel message I call 'The Big Question.' "

"And what may I ask *is* 'The Big Question'?"

That was a tactical error. I had written the tract myself, knew it by heart, and was joyful at the chance to inform everyone in sight of its exact contents.

" 'The Big Question,' sir, and you should consider it yourself, is: If you died this minute, do you have the assurance you would go to Heaven?"

He looked startled. I raced on quickly, anxious to get as much of God's Word as possible into the official court transcript.

"The Bible says there are four things a person must know to reach Heaven. It's all in the Book of Romans."

I ticked off the verses, adding a sentence of explanation for each passage.

"One: 'For all have sinned, and come short of the glory of God.' This means we all have sinned and we fall short of Jesus, God's glory.

"Two: 'For the wages of sin is death.' Our sin has earned a wage and that wage is death or separation from God in Hell.

"Three: 'But God commendeth his love toward us in that, while we were yet sinners, Christ died for us.' Even in our sin God loved us and sent Jesus two thousand years ago to die on the cross for us.

"Four: 'For whosoever shall call upon the name of the Lord shall be saved.' An indication of God's concern that the gospel should be preached worldwide, and that salvation awaits all who accept the teachings of Jesus and the apostles."

Nobody in the courtroom was shouting "Hallelujah," but everyone, including opposing counsel, was paying rapt attention. I paused to catch my breath and in the absence of any objections I continued.

"Now, how do you bring Christ into your life as Savior? Simple. Talk to Him."

I bowed my head, I closed my eyes, and prayed the life-changing prayer:

"Dear Jesus, forgive me all my sins and save my soul. I repent of all my sins and ask you to come into my heart and be the Lord of my life. Take control of my life, for I give myself to Thee. Thank you for hearing my prayers and saving my soul. In Jesus' name, I pray. Amen."

Reverence was on every face when I opened my eyes. And utter silence. I moved on quickly.

"What does a child in Christ do after committing his life to Jesus?"

Slowly and carefully, I spelled out the six critical steps that buttressed the newborn Christian in his faith. A few people were taking notes so I added chapter and verse from the Bible.

"Pray daiy. One Thessalonians, chapter five, verse seventeen; Luke, chapter eighteen, verse one.

"Read the Bible daily. Acts, chapter seventeen, verse eleven; Psalms, chapter one, verse two.

"Witness for Christ daily. Acts, chapter one, verse eight, and chapter five, verse forty-two.

"Confess Christ openly and be baptized. Matthew, chapter ten, verse thirty-two, and chapter twenty-eight, verses nineteen through twenty; Acts, chapter two, verse forty-one.

"Attend church where the Bible is preached and Christ is honored. Hebrews, chapter ten, verse twenty-five.

"Keep Christ's commandments. John, chapter fourteen, verse fifteen."

I was only beginning, merely laying the groundwork to show how the message of Christ related to our work at His Place. I was surprised, therefore, when I was interrupted by *my* attorney, Bruce Margolin, a brilliant, socially conscious advocate who, under the aegis of the American Civil Liberties Union, had fought for many unpopular causes and defendants. Apparently concerned that I had been centerstage too long, Bruce said, "Your Honor, please instruct the witness just to answer the question."

Judge Leonard S. Wolf, thin-faced, in his early forties, was a pleasant, fair-minded man. I had appeared before him in my three previous trials, and we knew each other well.

"You have answered the question sufficiently," he said mildly.

After Bruce examined me at some length, I left the stand, grateful for the chance I'd had to preach, but with a sinking feeling in my stomach that I had not sufficiently emphasized the heart of the matter: the life or death of His Place. Lost in my preaching, I had perhaps diverted the attention of the court. Unfortunately, Blackstone, not the Bible, would decide the case.

Now I found myself on my feet before Judge Wolf, properly forbidding in his black robes, who peered down at me from his throne-high chair.

"Mr. Blessitt, what I am about to rule on here has nothing to do with you as a person, because I know that your ministry is very commendable, that you are doing the best and only job that is being done for the young people on the Sunset Strip. But my hands are tied."

The words were civilized, temperate, complimentary, but they also were a foretaste of the stern, uncompromising, heartbreaking verdict.

"You signed the wrong kind of lease, Mr. Blessitt. And I will have to rule on the lease as written."

Since I'd been unable to rent a building in the name of the Arthur Blessitt Evangelistic Association, I had asked a friend, Bill Harris, a converted nightclub drummer now working as an insurance agent, to lease a location in his name, then sublet it to me. Subleasing is a common practice on the Strip. One millionaire uses subleasing to keep his ownership of a lucrative lesbian hangout hidden and to protect his reputation and avoid taxes (easily accomplished in an all-cash business). Cosa Nostra chieftains pocket the profits from a number of spangled sex palaces, but these clubs are in the names of front men. And there are prudent men who run such enterprises as barber shops, hamburger stands, motels, and clothing stores who insist on a sublease clause for protection should their businesses fail. They then have the option of installing a new tenant to avoid continued payment of high rents for periods of five years or more under their original leases. This is accepted practice all over the country.

Our building, at the time Bill rented it, had been a lemon; only one tenant had occupied it briefly in two years. The landlord was delighted to fill his vacant space, even when Bill told him he was going to sublet it. He even gave Bill permission to strike from the lease a clause that said the building couldn't be transferred without the consent of the owner. The landlord was concerned only that Bill would be the nominal tenant.

The reason he subsequently pressed for our eviction was due to the heavy pressure he was under. From the moment His Place opened its doors, the income of the adjoining spots plummeted. Many straights obviously felt uncomfortable patronizing establishments that abutted a church. The Galaxy had been forced to reduce its minimum from three dollars to fifty cents. Patronage at Sneaky Pete's and Whisky-A-Go-Go a few doors away was also down. So the alliance against us was forged. The instrument used to bring us to court was the fine print in the lease that defined the building rules, the most important of which said that no tenant could create an atmosphere that was not similar to or in concert with that of other buildings in the immediate area. Therefore, a church on the Strip was as welcome as martinis at a WCTU meeting. An acceptable tenant undoubtedly would have been a topless dive, a psychedelic nightclub where drugs would be openly pushed, a dirty book store, or a gay bar. Certainly Jesus rated equal space with any of these sinkholes!

"The charges are sustained!" Judge Wolf declared. "Taken one by one you have not violated the rules of the building, but taken as a whole you are in violation."

Thus we were going to be evicted on the most tenuous of legal technicalities despite the judge's affirmation that we had a moral right to be on the Strip.

"I will stipulate that this is Thursday and you are supposed to be out today," the judge added. "But I won't sign the papers until Monday, so this gives you five days. You are to be moved out completely at that time."

An angry murmur of protest went up from the kids. Only a word would trigger bedlam, but I turned and flashed the peace sign with my fingers.

Tears welled in my eyes. They were bulldozing us out of existence, plowing Jesus under. All the ferocious effort that had gone into giving Christ a foothold in the Babylon that was the Strip was being washed away. My tears were for the thousands of His Place regulars, swelled each night by new faces, who now would have no contact with Christ. The Establishment churches had failed resoundingly to reach these young people, none of whom would be caught stoned or clean, dead or alive, in the comfortable pews of air-conditioned, high-ceilinged, stained-glass-windowed sanctuaries presided over by clergymen who couldn't or wouldn't tell it like it was, who didn't dig the youth scene, who failed completely to communicate with a generation in rebellion against the questionable and hypocritical religious and moral values of its elders.

After his ruling, the expression on Judge Wolf's face was sorrowful. I think he felt as much anguish as I did. He was standing now, ready to move toward his chambers, and he said, "Mr. Blessitt, surely there is someone who will rent you a building on Sunset Strip."

In a breaking voice, I answered, "No, your Honor, *no one seems to really care.*"

The judge dropped his head and took out a handkerchief to dry the tears I was certain I saw in his eyes. "My hands are tied," he said, and so the skepticism that my flock and I had brought into the courtroom proved justified. The majesty of the law and freedom of religion could be invalidated by a virus-sized legal trifle, a trifle that had brought down our church.

The kids crowded around me as I started to leave, their mood subdued, shouting brave but unconvincing words of encouragement.

Bruce was in shock—he had taken the ruling very hard. I accompanied him out of the building with my arm around his shoulder to the lot where his Porsche was parked. Bruce was of Jewish ancestry and a professed agnostic. Since the day we had met I'd been trying to lead him to the Lord. I fell on my knees beside his car and prayed, asking him to let Jesus into his life.

"Not now, Arthur," he said, gunning his motor and driving off somberly.

Watching his car melt into the traffic, the full emotional impact of the punishing verdict hit me.

His Place had been assassinated.

It would take only a few hours for the word to be passed along the Strip, and the merchants of Mammon would rejoice and thrive once more without competition from Christ.

The smog was still lead-heavy in the sky. Looking up, I searched in vain for a patch of blue as my mind wrestled with a hurricane of bitterness bordering on hatred.

Then suddenly I recalled the dreadful but cleansing and redeeming lines from Luke 23:33–34:

"And when they were come to the place which is called Calvary, there they crucified him. . . . Then said Jesus, Father, forgive them; for they know not what they do."

Christ, after the nails had been riveted into His body, had risen again.

Could His Place also rise again?

2

At the Cross

THROUGH THE ANGUISH that had all but engulfed me while I listened to Judge Wolf's portentous verdict, a vision appeared before my eyes, clear as a full moon.

The inspiring words of Genesis 15:1 rushed to my mind: "After these things the word of the Lord came unto Abram in a vision, saying, Fear not, Abram: I am thy shield, and thy exceedingly great reward."

Visions may be unfashionable and suspect in the nuclear age, but there it was nevertheless: without doubt a revelation from Christ.

I didn't see Him in the courtroom, though I felt His presence. Jesus would not absent himself from a trial in which He had been found guilty!

The vision he inspired was not an abstraction; it was practical as a safety pin and detailed as a snowflake.

Strong and insistent, its main elements were: a cross . . . a chain . . . a lock . . . a telephone pole . . . and myself sitting in the midst of the Strip, praying and witnessing, until someone rented me a building or until He returned!

I was stunned by the vision. For a moment I considered the possibility that my terrible disappointment in court was somehow causing me to hallucinate, inducing phantoms like those that chase and torture the brain of an acid freak on a bad trip. And I remembered in the Old Testament that false prophets feigned visions and were denounced by Jeremiah and Ezekiel. Yet the visions of Isaiah, Hosea, Micah, Daniel, and John were part of the cherished history of Christianity. And in Joel 2:28 the Lord said, "Your old men shall dream dreams, your young men shall see visions."

That was good enough for me. No, I wasn't hallucinating—the vision was real. Now as I drove from the courthouse parking lot toward the Strip for breakfast at The Gaiety I knew I had to thrust into motion what had been revealed to me.

I was certain of Divine help. He had said to Abram and He was saying to me as well, *I am thy shield, and thy exceedingly great reward.*

The more I thought about chaining myself to a cross for the purpose of rescuing His Place from the oblivion to which it had just been consigned, the more excited I became.

Because what had to be done was wild, daring, and unprecedented (and would in the eyes of some be considered the scheme of a crazy man), I was reluctant for the time being to tell anyone. I postponed calling my wife, Sherry, who was resting at her parents' home in Bogalusa, Louisiana, following the birth two weeks before of Joy, our third child. Nor did I call one of my closest friends, Jack Taylor, pastor of Castle Hills First Baptist Church in San Antonio, Texas, and as avid a soul-winner as I knew. Jack had given me wise advice on many occasions and he was one of the most ardent supporters of my ministry. There were many people I could have contacted, other ministers and close friends. But a vision is gossamer, difficult to explain, more difficult for the hearer to believe. Moreover, I felt everyone would try to talk me out of my planned vigil at the cross. I didn't want to hear the well-meaning, prudent counsel of caution, compromise, and common sense. The Bible is filled with the glory of giants who sacrificed everything for their beliefs. If Jesus had been cautious and offered compromise and a "common sense" alternative to Pilate, how different the history of the world would be, how empty Heaven would be.

Over scrambled eggs and toast, I realized the complexity of the plan. I had been shown the way and the light, but had not been told what the result would be. Going to the cross had to be an act of faith. His Place *must* find a new, permanent home, this time with a lease in my name, a lease that couldn't be broken by the Supreme Court.

The stakes were enormous, the opposition would be formidable.

The moment the word spread along the Strip grapevine that I was making a public protest because His Place was dead as a functioning church, I would be in conflict with four power blocs:

1. The heavy-handed, cynical potentates with cash registers for hearts who own the biggest clubs on the Strip. This was the second time we had been evicted from a location on Sunset Boulevard. I wasn't given to paranoia, but it was obvious there was a confederation of men, riddled with fear and living outside the grace of the Lord, who would gladly pass the hat to pay my expenses for life had I suddenly announced I wanted to be a missionary in Africa. That would be their friendliest gesture. At worst, a number of them were capable of ordering my murder in cold blood. I had been offered bribes and my life had been threatened in vain attempts to get me off the Strip. Therefore, an intelligent precaution would be to station a member of my staff to stand guard during those hours I would have to sleep at the cross.

2. The Sheriff's Department. I had a love-hate relationship with the gold-shirted officers who patrol the Strip. I did not believe with Dickens that "the law is a ass, a idiot" but agreed with Lydia Maria Child that "law is not law if it violates the principles of eternal justice." Several times I had called for the assistance of sheriff's deputies on those embattled nights when things got out of hand at His Place, and I had cooperated with the department in many other ways. Yet our relationship was far from smooth. I recalled three occasions when handcuffs were snapped on my wrists and I'd been hauled to jail on charges of violating the impossible no-loitering statute in force on the Strip. At the cross the odds were overwhelming that I would be busted again under the no-loitering ban. And it wouldn't take the efficient men in gold shirts an hour to burn through the metal of my chain with an acetylene torch. If my protest was met with such swift retaliation, I felt it would be a humiliating defeat for Jesus. Strategy was called for, and the Bible suggested the approach in Matthew 10:16: "Behold, I sent you forth as sheep in the midst of wolves; be ye, therefore, wise as serpents, and harmless as doves." If I was blitz-busted, I had to be ready. I would call a bail bondsman friend and arrange to have him on standby to spring me immediately. Then I'd go right back to the cross. If necessary, I was ready to be busted twenty, thirty, a hundred times. If they finally locked me up and threw the key away, I would wait for my ultimate release

and return to the cross, refreshed and strengthened. "But they that wait upon the Lord shall renew their strength; they shall mount up with wings like eagles; they shall run, and not be weary" is the promise of Isaiah 40:31.

3. The West Hollywood Chamber of Commerce. These men, good men and true by their own lights, were terror-stricken over the declining prestige of the Strip and the drop in land values that had resulted since the invasion of the various subcultures of young people they lumped together and called hippies. The Chamber contended that His Place attracted even more outlaw kids to the area. But the influx was a reality long before I came to the Strip. I had seen this roaming, questing, stoned river of rebels, godless and unchurched, and, so massive was their need for Christ, I had heeded a call to minister to them. That was the genesis of His Place. My work actually meshed with the desire of the Chamber to banish the kids from the Strip. The first thing I did after winning a young soul for Christ was to urge him to find a new scene, away from drug-drenched Sunset Boulevard. But it wasn't only the young people who'd brought the Strip to its knees in shame, made it a notorious tenderloin famous around the world for its anything-goes atmosphere. B ame that on the righteous city fathers who so freely licensed the hellholes that peddled sex, perversion, and watered booze. The kids were speed and acid freaks, but they didn't have the bread or inclination to patronize the bars and the topless-bottomless joints. These were the playgrounds of the straight freaks who leered at undressed girls, supported the army of prostitutes, paid high prices for endless rounds of drinks, yet were the first to cast stones at the troubled, bedraggled, long-haired kids. Sinners condemning sinners, two houses infested by plague. Although our ministry was responsible for the disappearance of hundreds of kids from the Strip, I'd failed to win the trust and confidence of the Chamber. They refused to realize or were incapable of understanding that the Strip they once knew would never return. They noted only the ever-rising influx of kids from all over the country, and marked not the fact that my ultimate goal was to reverse the tide and see every kid leave the Strip. Then I would be free to minister to all the straights who needed Jesus in *their* lives. I knew that the conservative, short-sighted men who made up the membership of the Chamber would resent my presence at the cross.

4. The real-estate brokers. The young people who had captured Sunset Boulevard were bad for business. As the chic of the Strip eroded month after month, so too did the commissions of the brokers. There were dozens of empty locations along the Strip, barren, paint-faded shells of once-prosperous businesses that had moved on. The thicket of angry, frustrated brokers who held listings on these buildings had repeatedly refused to rent to me at any price. They, too, were dreaming of a has-been past, and none of them would come to the cross and declare for Jesus by offering me a new location. If Christ Himself returned and asked for a building on the Strip, he undoubtedly would be refused. ("Cut your hair, shave your beard, wash your feet, throw away that robe, wear a two-button suit and then maybe we can find suitable quarters for you. When you look like a 'real' Christian, we'll have lunch and talk business. Do you like your martini with or without an olive?")

So would the battle against the four prongs of the Establishment be joined—direct, pure confrontation and challenge.

I was ready to go down to the wire against the opposition. All they had was money, guns, influence, intimidation, and jails.

I would have a New Testament in my hand, a cross at my back, and Christ at my side.

I couldn't lose.

Waiting for me when I arrived at His Place were five members of the Team, Dale, Ed, Marsha Edwards, our pert and pretty secretary, Jesse Wise, a black and beautiful Christian, and stocky Dan Peterson, known the length and breadth of the Strip as "O. J." for the orange juice he perpetually drank since his conversion after years as a boozing nightclub piano player.

They all looked as if they were suffering the travails of Job, as indeed they were. His Place was as important to them as it was to me.

This was the obvious moment to put my toe in the water and share my plan for the first time. When I outlined what I was going to do, I was thrilled that no one raised an objection. They did not counsel caution. They all understood immediately. The defeated looks on their faces were replaced by broad grins, new hope, and cries of "Praise the Lord." In a moment they were laughing, slapping each other on the back, shouting, all talking at once. Above the tumult I heard Ed say, "I'll get the chain."

After the euphoria died down, I said, "I feel Jesus also wants me to fast while I'm at the cross."

As one given to ravenous hunger pangs when mealtimes roll around, the thought of fasting scared me to death. But did not Jesus fast for forty days in the wilderness?

Soon a mood of quiet contemplation settled in the room. It was time for prayer.

"Dear Jesus," I said, "give us the strength for this witness in Thy name.

"You have opened the door and we are about to enter.

"We will hold firm in our resolve to stay at the cross until a heart is filled with compassion and Thy house is restored on this most evil of streets so that we may continue Thy ministry to those thousands in desperate need of Thy message.

"Arm us with the will to maintain our vigil, no matter what the consequences.

"You have guided us to this place as Thy servants. We know Thy will is for us to remain and that the journey on which we now embark is a test of our commitment.

"We ask mercy and blessings, confident that triumph and light will emerge from this passing moment of darkness.

"Amen."

We decided that I would go to the cross the next day. Tonight His Place would be open as usual.

The crowd that evening was unusually large. The word had floated into the crash pads and the kids poured in, a sea of boiling mad, hurt, puzzled, resentful, confused partisans. Though the bulk of them were unsaved, they all loved His Place with fierce passion. It was a way-station where they could rap freely among themselves, always find a sympathetic ear among the staff, listen to the gospel rock of our musicians, and fill their stomachs with free sandwiches, coffee, and soft drinks as they came down off their trips and their appetites returned.

I preach at least twice every night at His Place, and this night there was no question what my sermon would be about. As I told them we were going to make our stand at the cross, I was interrupted by ominous shouts from a few hotheads.

"Let's riot."

"I'm for tearing the Strip down."

"We'll do nothing like that," I answered quickly to block the outbursts of the frenzied few who could whip the crowd into a stampede the like of which the Strip had never seen. Gandhi freed a nation of four hundred million with passive resistance. Martin Luther King learned from him and won victory after victory for his people with nonviolence.

"Christ means peace. 'Seek peace, and pursue it,' Jesus said. I want no riots, no demonstrations, no provocation of The Man."

The kids calmed down, the turbulence nipped in the bud. They promised there would be no trouble.

It turned out to be one of the most inspiring nights we ever experienced at His Place. We usually do not close until four in the morning, but because of the next day's emergency we shut the doors at midnight. I had greeted hundreds of kids who came in throughout the evening, all wishing me well and pledging their support. By the time I turned the key in the lock, seventeen had been saved!

I was home at one-thirty and fell exhausted into bed. Yet sleep eluded me. Alone in the dark, a wave of second thoughts surfaced. Was I stark-raving mad? Could the watch at the cross really succeed? Would people respond? I was sick at the thought that I might be tagged as just another Strip "weirdo." The questions lingered, a drumfire of doubt pummeling my mind. I closed my eyes and found sleep, my anxieties gone, only after comforting myself with the wisdom of the Divine psychiatrist in the sixth chapter of Matthew: "O ye of little faith. . . . Therefore, be not anxious saying, What shall we eat? or What shall we drink? . . . For your heavenly Father knoweth that ye have need of all these things. . . . But seek ye first the kingdom of God, and his righteousness, and all these things shall be added unto you. Be, therefore, not anxious about tomorrow."

I woke early and made several phone calls. I shored up the financial support of my bail bondsman. I talked to a reporter I knew at the Los Angeles *Free Press*, the irreverent underground newspaper filled with obscenities and column after column of scatological personal ads in which the sick in soul brazenly advertise their perverse needs and whims. But the *Free Press* was the only paper that had published a story about our court case. ("Arthur Blessitt has been evicted for practicing what the Establishment preaches," the lead ran.) I told the reporter my plans. Delighted, he said he would alert the media.

I reached Sherry in Bogalusa, her voice on the line velvet and silk. "Yes, the children are fine. . . . . Everyone says the baby looks exactly like you. . . . I'm feeling wonderful. . . . If you really feel the Lord leading you to the cross, go ahead. . . . I'll be home soon. . . . Arthur, I love you. . . . God bless you."

. I dressed in the only black ministerial suit I owned. I normally favor the easy comfort of turtlenecks, bell-bottoms, and sandals, but today I wanted to look as dignified as possible.

Facing a long fast, I should have been wolf-hungry, but there was a tautness in my stomach and all I could manage for the last meal I would eat until who knew when was a bowl of cereal.

I was at His Place at ten, busying myself by helping to clean up last night's debris. A shower of kids were on hand: bikers with mean swastikas blazing from their jackets, several chicks in serapes, a knot of Black Panthers in leg-hugging Levi's playing and harmonizing soul at the piano. Some were stoned, having already devoured their morning quota of downers. But most were clean and had turned out simply to show by their presence that they were behind me. I got on my knees several times in our prayer room, repeating my entreaties for strength. Between prayers I wandered from room to room, talking to the kids. Gloriously, I led two to Christ, a sixteen-year-old runaway girl from Indianapolis, and a marine AWOL from boot training at Camp Pendleton, near San Diego. The girl agreed to return home to her "drunken old man" and take care of her bed-ridden mother. The marine said he'd go back and risk a court-martial for slugging his sergeant.

Then I went to the rugged, wooden His Place cross, which dominated our main room. I ran my hand across it lovingly. Eighty pounds heavy, six feet in width and ten feet long, it was going to be my constant companion during the foreseeable future.

Now Ed came bustling in with the chain.

"You ready, Arthur?"

"Yes."

We looped the chain around my left wrist, and up and through the intersecting bars of the cross, attached the lock and clicked it shut. The chain felt wonderful, each link binding me to Christ.

It was precisely high noon, June 27, 1969. Could it be only some twenty-four hours since I had first been told to manacle myself?

With Jesse shouldering one end of the cross, we moved down the flight of fifteen steps. At the bottom, I hesitated. Despite all the reassurances of Christ and Scripture, I didn't know whether I was stepping into a folly that would discredit me completely as a minister or into the most important victory of my life.

Waiting for me in the street was my first surprise: half-a-dozen television cameramen, their equipment already whirring. Several TV, wire service, and radio reporters began hurling questions at me.

After moving a trash can aside and laying the cross against a telephone pole, I gave a statement to the press, explaining why we had been evicted, what our purpose was now. I was amazed at the outpouring of the media and thankful that the news of our witness would shortly be spread around the world.

The cameramen were loading their gear and the reporters preparing to leave when two of my friends—Tim Mallory, a young man I'd recently helped get right with the Lord, and his pretty, blond fiancée, Jodi, dressed in a knee-length wedding gown—appeared.

I had completely forgotten that this was the day I was scheduled to marry them.

I apologized to Tim and Jodi and offered to perform the wedding as soon as I got off the cross.

"Why don't you marry us right here?" Tim asked.

Startled, I said, "Are you sure?"

They both nodded their heads.

The cameramen hastily unpacked their equipment and the reporters rushed back for what I guess was the first marriage ceremony ever held on a Sunset Boulevard sidewalk.

Tim and Jodi joined hands. Traffic in the street rolled by slowly, the curious peeking out of their car windows. Passers-by stopped and listened as I preached briefly on the sanctity of marriage, how the bringing together of man and woman is ordained by God, that man without woman is empty as man without Christ. Then I recited the marriage vows, pronounced them man and wife, and signed the wedding certificate. Someone in the crowd even had some rice, which was thrown at the bride and groom as they kissed.

The wedding, despite its unusual geography and atmosphere, wasn't a circus. It came off beautifully, as sacred and reverent as the taking of the vows in a church, perhaps more so. At least, the mother of the bride wasn't counting the house and the father of the bride wasn't worriedly toting the tab. I find it appalling that church weddings cum embellishments not infrequently cost five thousand dollars or more. Are such couples being married in the sight of God or Mammon?

Tim and Jodi hugged me and ran off, the press hurried on to file their stories, the crowd melted away. The staff was now spread out along the sidewalk, witnessing to pedestrians.

I was suddenly alone, the initial excitement of the interviews and the wedding over.

The first long afternoon in the baking sun yawned ahead. The heavy material of my suit added to the discomfort engendered by the heat. I wished I had thought to bring an umbrella. And now, all of a sudden, I was hungry. My stomach ached for a two-inch steak.

To the few strollers out in the heat, I called, "Jesus loves you." Many ignored me; a few came over to talk, their reaction to my stand at the cross ranging from respect to condemnation. One elderly woman, anger exploding from eyes bordered by crow's feet, declared, "You couldn't be a minister. If you are, you're a disgrace to the name of Jesus." She had forgotten as she trumpeted the "sensible" Christianity that she practiced every Sunday from 10 to 11 A.M. in a "sensible" Methodist church that the apostles were rebels, too, and that Christ once made an epic journey to a cross.

I spent the next several hours dealing reds, Strip argot for one of the barbiturates that immobilizes body and brain, causing the user to walk around in a state of wakeful sleep. Straights get their reds or other types of downer by prescription from their family doctors and psychiatrists, and millions of successful, high-income Americans can unwind from their anxieties only with these pills, which sledgehammer them into unconsciousness. By prescription downers cost about $1.50 for thirty pills. The price for users on the Strip is astronomical in proportion, usually three for $1.00, sometimes higher, depending on the supply at any given time.

The reds I deal, however, aren't pills. They are stickers the size of a half-dollar that have proved to be an extremely successful advertisement for our ministry. I've seen them pasted on the dressing-room mirrors of strippers and topless dancers, in johns, and outside almost every club, psychedelic shop, and bar throughout West Hollywood. At out-of-town revivals I have them passed out to everyone who comes to hear me preach.

The vivid orange-red stickers bear my name and are bisected by a cross thrusting up from the familiar peace symbol:

Many a Strip habitué has been startled when ⅃ approach and say, "I'm dealing reds." Interest is immediately galvanized. "But these reds can turn you on to Jesus. It's a far, far better trip, man." It's a wonderful way of breaking the ice with a stranger and of spreading the gospel so it gets to the kids.

One straight friend of mine told me that while driving down Santa Monica Boulevard he spotted a hippie hitchhiker. Hair matted and long, dressed raggedly, he didn't exactly look as if he had a pad in Bel-Air. But pasted to the hitchhiker's jacket was one of our reds. My friend slammed on the brakes and gave him a lift.

"Your sticker," he told me, "made me trust that kid. I knew he was one of yours. That's the first hitchhiker I've picked up in fifteen years. The kid was on his way down the street to apply for a job at a gas station. I hope he got it. I talked to him for only five minutes, but I liked him. I realized for the first time that you can't judge a person by the cut of his clothes and hair."

The reds do their work in many ways: they've been the seed that has led to numberless conversions, they bind people together in fellowship and remind the troubled and despairing that there is a spiritual oasis called His Place.

At 6 P.M. Dale arrived with several hundred copies of "An Open Letter," a position paper I had written to pass out to people who were curious about our purpose in being at the cross. We gummed a copy to the telephone pole with a four-sided border of our reds. It said:

The famed Sunset Strip is a United Nations of people from every background, race, and religion. There seems to be room on the Strip for everything—topless and bottomless clubs, drugs, bars, dirty-book stores, pornographic movies—except Jesus Christ and His Place.

I ask, "Why is the Strip Establishment afraid of Christianity?"

The first His Place was located at 9109 Sunset Boulevard until the owner refused to renew our lease due to pressure from the community and the Sheriff's Department to "clean up" the Strip. The "cleaning up" produced the replacement of His Place with a club featuring nude dancers!

We have now been evicted from the second His Place for similar and misguided reasons. And due to an organized conspiracy we are unable to find a new location.

Millions of dollars are being spent to eradicate the use of drugs in America. I have heard solutions offered by supposedly learned men and so-called experts who say the way to cope with the problem is to legalize pot, dry up the sources of drugs, hire thousands of additional policemen and narcotics agents, build hospitals and clinics and expensive rehabilitation facilities for drug addicts.

I have heard every solution except the only one that is lastingly effective—the spiritual regeneration of the user!

Turn the addict on to Christ and with his new birth he will have no need for pot, reds, whites, LSD, speed, or any other artificial mind-bender.

. Jesus Christ *is* the only answer. I know this is true because I've seen it work. We have helped thousands hung up on drugs. They've been saved and are now on a real trip, hooked on Christ.

We have seen the power of Christ change the lives of people from every walk of life here on the Strip.

His Place, which is absolutely free—no charge and no collections —is a ray of hope in this area of hopelessness. It is the only place on the Strip with a waiting line throughout most of the night.

His Place offers peace, love, God.

The young people want and need it.

All we ask is the freedom to have a church on the Strip available to anyone who wants to come. We don't look up or down our noses at you, count your coins, or consider your dress.

We just love people.

The hearts of men must be changed before their lives are. We are dedicated to this. And we ask your help.

Leading religious leaders throughout the world have endorsed this ministry. Stories of our work have appeared in *The New York Times*, the Los Angeles *Times*, and hundreds of other newspapers.

Teen magazine, *Christianity Today, World Vision, Christian Times,* and *Christian Life* have published articles of praise. I have appeared on countless television and radio shows and told of the lives that have been restructured through His Place. Not a word of criticism has been leveled against us in the media. In fact, we have almost been embarrassed by the superlatives and praise we have received.

The only criticism comes from the Establishment that controls the Strip.

They want us out.

But I will remain chained to this cross twenty-four hours a day until we are again part of the Strip scene.

We invite you to call friends to join in prayer and come to the Strip, if possible, and make this commitment your own.

By late evening the first signs of support began arriving at the cross in a cascade of telegrams. The word had indeed been passed and people all over the nation were responding. The telegrams became a yellow ribbon of unending encouragement, and my heart leaped with the arrival of each one.

From W. A. Criswell, president of the Southern Baptist Convention and pastor of the First Baptist Church in Dallas, Texas, the largest Baptist church in the world:

PRAYING THAT GOD WILL GIVE YOU AN OPEN DOOR FOR A GREATER WITNESS

The Reverend Duane Stenzel, of Louisville, Kentucky:

I AND MANY ROMAN CATHOLICS HERE ARE BEHIND YOU WE ARE PRAYING WITH YOU AND FOR YOU MAY WHAT YOU ARE DOING FOR THE LORD JESUS REACH THE ENDS OF THE WORLD

From the First Baptist Church, Van Nuys, the largest church on the West Coast, pastored by a man on fire for God all his life, Harold L. Fickett, Jr.:

PRAYING THAT YOU WILL FIND ANOTHER PLACE ON THE STRIP

Owen Cooper, of Yazoo City, Mississippi, an influential businessman, dedicated Christian, and a man who's been crucially important in my life:

ALL AMERICA PRAYING FOR YOU SECURING NEW MEETING PLACE

Gwin Turner, my own pastor at First Baptist Church, Mar Vista:

I AM FOR YOU AND WITH YOU ALL THE WAY I AM PRAYING THAT GOD WILL MOVE UPON SOMEONE'S HEART TO LEASE YOU A BUILDING ON THE STRIP

A friend from Louisville, Wayne DeHoney, pastor of Walnut Street Baptist Church:

CITY SHAKEN BY YOUR FAST WE ARE PRAYING FOR YOU

Ned H. Brown and the congregation at Gardena (California) Baptist Church:

HAVING SPECIAL PRAYER FOR YOU UNDOUBTEDLY THE LORD HAS A PLAN DON'T GIVE UP

Unsigned from New York City:

PRAYING FOR YOU PSALMS 34 AND 37 ["He teacheth my hands to war, so that a bow of bronze is broken by mine arms. I have pursued mine enemies, and overtaken them; neither did I turn again till they were consumed."]

Signed "An apostle of Christ," from Chicago:

JESUS WILL HELP YOU TO HELP OTHERS

L. T. and Onie Robertson, friends from Mar Vista:

TAKE COURAGE AND BE STRONG IN GOD

Roy Buckelew, pastor, Tate Springs Baptist Church, Fort Worth, Texas:

PRAYING FOR YOU AND THE REOPENING OF HIS PLACE

Mr. and Mrs. John McPheeters, Kalamazoo, Michigan:

ASSURE YOU OF OUR PRAYERS FOR HIS PLACE WE KNOW CHRIST
CHANGES LIVES

Anonymous from Cleveland, Ohio:

I KNOW GOD IS LEADING YOU IN YOUR WITNESS AND SACRIFICE HE
WILL KEEP AND STRENGTHEN YOU I PRAY HE WILL SOON SOMEDAY
OPEN THE HEART OF THOSE WHO ARE PERSECUTING HIS SERVANT

Pastor L. Kenneth Balthrop, of Albuquerque, New Mexico:

THE 2000 MEMBER HOFFMAN TOWN BAPIST CHURCH IS PRAYING FOR
YOU AND WISHES TO EXPRESS ITS SUPPORT FOR YOUR WORK WE PRAY
YOU WILL HAVE CONTINUED OPPORTUNITY TO WORK AMONG THE
NEEDY PEOPLE ON THE STRIP

A group of "Teen-age Bible students" in Minneapolis:

GIVE EM HEAVEN ARTHUR BUT SCARE THE "HELL" OUT OF THEM OUR
PRAYERS ARE BEHIND YOU

From "3,000 Christians" in Portland, Oregon:

PLEASE KNOW THAT WE ARE CONTINUING TO PRAY FOR YOU AND
YOUR ONGOING WORK FOR THE LORD YOUR FRIENDS IN CHRIST
ISAIAH 12:2 ["Behold, God is my salvation; I will trust, and not be
afraid; for the Lord, even the Lord, is my strength and my song; he
also is become my salvation."]

One of my youngest supporters, Diane Wagner, a brown-eyed,
cherub-faced nine-year-old, of nearby Toluca Lake, California:

DEAR MR BLESSED [sic] HOW ARE YOU I AM PRAYING FOR YOU I'M
SORRY I CAN'T COME TO THE CROSS BUT I HAVE A COLD I HOPE THE
CHAIN DOES NOT HURT TOO MUCH

The chain didn't hurt at all. It was lightened by the prairie fire
of national support from concerned people, more support than I
thought possible. Each telegram was added encouragement. Not
for a moment would I doubt again that I had been led to the right
decision.

By two o'clock in the morning the last straggler from the comfortable red booths inside Sneaky Pete's had split for home or an after-hours joint to guzzle yet more booze.

The Strip was settling down. Soon the garbage trucks would thunder by.

I spotted an unmarked sheriff's car cruising past, a plainclothesman staring out at me. Apparently the decision had been made not to bust me, at least for the time being. Maybe the law had decided on a war of nerves, a silent clash of wills.

Three o'clock in the morning, and the sky was clear. The stars were shining boldly and except for Dale, who had the first night's guard duty, there wasn't a soul in sight. Even the traffic had dwindled to only an occasional car.

My first fifteen hours at the cross were behind me. I felt relaxed, but not tired enough to sleep.

There was leisure now to think about all the days that had brought me to this moment of my life. The future was uncertain, but, as with all men, my past, with its victories and defeats, was frozen.

I was only twenty-eight years old, but there was much to remember.

3

The Making of an Evangelist

GREENVILLE, MISSISSIPPI, where I was born on October 27, 1940, was the hub of the Delta, populated by some thirty thousand souls. The farmers in Big Mac overalls hauled their long-staple cotton into town and sold it for about two hundred dollars a bale. Then they loaded their wagons and old Fords with groceries and went down to stare at and lovingly touch the gleaming, efficient farm machinery that was beginning to revolutionize the land.

Greenville was part of that all-but-vanished Deep South that still voted Democratic and listened to and believed the flowery Fourth of July oratory of gallus-snapping politicians who harangued at election time in front of the courthouse. As for the blacks, they ruled the town in numbers only: They comprised 75 percent of the inhabitants.

The white minority took its main pleasure at the annual county fair but the real core of social life was the Methodist and Baptist churches, which offered, in addition to Sunday morning services, midweek prayer meetings, socials, and revivals featuring circuit evangelists preaching old-time religion.

I didn't care much for the evangelists. Most of them were fat, dissipated, rheumy-eyed men who seemed more interested in Hell than Heaven. Even then I sensed that religion should tell of the abundant joy that Christianity offered, the wonder of living for Jesus. The sinners should be preached into Heaven, not threatened with damnation.

Mary Virginia Campbell Blessitt, my mother, saw to it that my sister, Virginia, and I attended Sunday school at the Methodist church. Unfortunately, I had a habit of causing all sorts of mischief, the least of which was turning up with frogs in my pocket. Finally the exasperated teacher got to the point where she let me take charge of the class just to keep me out of trouble. I made up stories about un-Christian monsters and moonmen, but, under her watchful, accusing eye, I put a happy ending on the tall tales. The monsters and moonmen always ended up saved.

The most exciting day of my life came when Mom, Virginia, and I went down to the station to greet my dad, home at last from the war. Captain Arthur O. N. Blessitt, wearing a chestful of medals and a big smile, scooped us all into his long, powerful arms. Dad hadn't seen me since I was six months old. He was only 135 pounds but extremely well muscled and deceptively strong for a man who stood a mere five feet four. But to me, he looked ten feet tall in his beribboned uniform. We headed for home happily, a whole family again.

But our happiness was short-lived. Dad was one of those men who came back from the war seared by the fighting and butchery he'd seen in the Pacific and the Aleutians. For him, it had been a hard, nearly fatal war. He came eyelash-close to death on at least two occasions.

He and eighteen buddies were assigned to scout an atoll, but the mission turned into a disaster. All but Dad and one other man were killed in a Japanese ambush. They were spirited off the rock in the nick of time by submarine. Dad's second escape came over the Aleutians when a plane in which he was flying was shot down. Every one of the nine other men aboard was killed. Dad's injuries kept him in the hospital for four months. Only through the Red Cross did we learn he was alive.

I was too young to measure the intensity with which he wanted to forget the war. After a heated argument in school one day about whose father had been the biggest hero in the fighting, I rushed home to Dad and said, "How many Japs did you kill?" He looked hurt as he answered softly, "Son, I went through a lot and I'm not proud of it. I had to do it, but I'm not going to boast about taking the lives of others, even if they were enemy soldiers."

It was impossible for Dad to forget the war. He turned short-tempered, unable to excise all the horrible memories. A church-loving Baptist who had once felt but ignored God's call to preach, he was now a man in search. But he was searching in the wrong place—at the bottom of a bottle.

I recall several trips to town during which Dad would tell me to wait while he went into a bar. On one occasion, after two hours of lingering in the sun, I got thirsty and walked inside, hoping I could get a Coke. I arrived at precisely the moment when Dad was squaring off against seven men, several of them with knives in their hands.

"Son, get the lug wrench."

I ran out to our truck and hurried back with *two* wrenches, though I didn't think the extra would do much to even the 7 to 1 odds.

But I had never seen my dad really angry. Neither, apparently, had the men confronting him. Dad's eyes and manner were savage, and I'm certain he could have reduced the pack of them to screaming, bloody pulp if they had moved in on him. But it never came to that; after muttering threats and curses, the men lost their nerve and backed off. I never did find out what started the argument.

Shortly after this incident, we were in town again when a towering, bull-shaped man accosted Dad and without preface accused him of being a tinhorn hero.

"You and all your damn medals, you don't look that tough to me."

Dad was ready to kill him, but caught his temper and walked away. When we got home, he threw every one of his medals into the trash.

During his tough period of readjustment, Dad had the added burden of not being able to find a decent job. Finally, he gathered us together and said he was going to New Orleans to look for work. It was a body blow, the family being rent asunder so soon again.

But he did find a job on the docks and then a better one at a steel mill. We moved to New Orleans and joined him. Dad was earning good money, but he was still drinking, still restless, and for the most part uncommunicative.

"It's too hard to save, and I don't like the city," he announced one day. "Anyway, kids should be raised in the country."

We moved to a small farm near Oak Grove, Louisiana. If Dad wanted to be as far from civilization as possible, he succeeded. The nearest gravel road to our place was ten miles away, reached only by a dirt trail under an arch of low-hanging moss trees, which Virginia and I were certain hid panthers and cottonmouths.

Though we were living in perhaps the most remote backwoods refuge of the sixteen-hundred-member community, we weren't entirely cut off from contact with the outside world. There were several shopping excursions a month to town and an occasional gossipy neighbor would find his way to our door "to set and jaw a spell." But our major tie to Oak Grove came via the bumpy Sunday morning rides to church, the Blessitts, of course, decked out in their best finery.

One Sunday our pastor, Brother Dewey Mercer, announced that a brush-arbor revival was going to break out the following week. An evangelist from Texas would be the preacher.

Something in me stirred. I was only seven, but I knew I was a sinner. "For all have sinned," I remembered from Romans 5:12. I also knew I was in rebellion against God, however slight my boyish transgressions might have been. ("Know ye not that a little leaven leaveneth the whole lump?" it said in I Corinthians 5:6.) And in the eyes of God sin wasn't measured in degrees. According to John 8:34, "Whosoever committeth sin is the servant of sin."

My mother set me an inspiring example. Always fervent in her belief, she had been saved in the Methodist church. I wanted the ecstasy of the Lord, too. I also felt guilty about cursing, lying to my parents, and not taking Sunday school seriously.

We arrived for the first night of the revival to find a makeshift church: The old Baptist building had been torn down and was in the process of being rebuilt. We found seats on the right-hand side of the parking lot where the service was going to be held. Sawdust covered the dirt, and the pulpit and piano had been moved out from the church. We sat under a roof of boards, tree limbs, and brush held in place by a dozen slim poles, each topped by a naked light bulb, flashpoints of glare that looked like giant fireflies. I was certain the Lord didn't mind that His word was going to be preached from a parking lot.

And preached it was, fast, furious, forceful, ending with a call from the evangelist for sinners to step to the pulpit and be saved.

I started to get out of my seat and go forward, but my mother caught me by the shirt.

"You're cutting up, son," she said.

She wouldn't let me go. And I couldn't blame her. I had wiggled all through the service, but it was the wiggling of impatience and excitement rather than boredom or inattention. No one had ever been more anxious to get up and be counted for Christ, but I couldn't convince my mother.

"Hush," she ordered.

The service over, I looked with envy at the two dozen or so who had given themselves to Christ.

On the ride home I asked Mom, "Why wouldn't you let me go up to the front with the others?"

"Why did you want to go?"

"I wanted to be saved!"

"We'll be back tomorrow night, and the same fellow will be preaching."

"But I want to be saved *tonight!*"

Dad, who'd been unresponsive up to now, suddenly screeched our truck to a halt in the middle of the road. He shifted into reverse, backed up and wheeled toward the brush arbor. I knew that ribbon of road was leading me straight to Christ. It was too dark to see the expression on Dad's face and he didn't say a word as the miles flicked by, but he had felt my need!

Dad, I couldn't quite bring myself to say out loud, I love you.

Brother Mercer and the evangelist were still in the parking lot, several people gathered around them. Dad and I hopped out of the truck. I waited while he marched up to the two preachers and began talking to them. Then Brother Mercer and the evangelist came over to me.

"All you have to do, son, is ask Jesus into your heart," the evangelist said. "Accept him as your Savior and know that He died on the cross for you. Then you can be saved, right here, right at this moment."

"I'm ready."

We fell to the ground and I repeated each line of the brief prayer offered by the evangelist.

"Dear God, I know I'm a sinner."

"Dear God, I know I'm a sinner."

"I ask Jesus to come into my heart. . . ."

"I ask Jesus to come into my heart. . . ."

"And live in my life forever."

"And live in my life forever."

"Make my home Heaven."

"Make my home Heaven."

"Thank you, Jesus."

"Thank you, Jesus."

A knot of people had formed around us during the prayer, and when I rose from my knees everyone was smiling and silent except for one man who said loud enough for me to hear, "I don't believe that little fellow is saved and I don't think he knows what he's doing."

I didn't trouble to answer, to say that I knew exactly what I was doing, that in the eyes of God I was now as saved as anyone. I was right with the Lord, and too happy to argue the point.

That moment of coming to Christ, my bridge to Heaven and eternal life, didn't cause me to shout, clap my hands, or dance in the air; it was a private feeling of quiet contentment.

I don't remember the ride home, or if Dad, Mom, or Virginia said a word. I do remember that truck was as a golden chariot pulled by a band of angels.

Sin washed away, paradise gained, I went to sleep knowing that now Jesus was my best friend and that He always would be.

And He always has been.

My last thought as I closed my eyes was that I wanted to win others for Him.

Before breakfast next morning, I began witnessing to Virginia. "Christ is in my heart, and He should be in yours, too." I witnessed to her all day, the torrent of His words and majestic logic leaping easily from my lips, and when we went back to the revival that night Jesus won another victory. Virginia stepped up to be saved and cried all through the prayer.

Soon afterward, Mom, Virginia, and I were all baptized. But Dad still wasn't right with the Lord. He was drinking hard as ever. He wouldn't let me get too close to his innermost thoughts, but there were moments when we would talk and I'd implore him to give his life to Christ.

"There'll come a time when I'll be ready," he predicted. "Right now I can't seem to find the strength."

It took four frightening, bewildering incidents over the next several years for Dad "to find the strength."

At the general store one day, a barrel-chested, unshaven man walked in. I had never seen him before, and I watched with horror as he swept to the hardware counter, picked up a double-edged ax and headed straight for Dad, intent on slicing him down the middle.

"Look out!" I hollered.

Dad whirled in time to block the arc of the descending blow. He wrestled the ax away from the man, and using the handle like a battering ram, he shoved his attacker to the floor. The tables had been quickly reversed, and Dad could have claimed, successfully, self-defense in any court in the land had he turned the ax on the man.

Cowed though he was, the man threatened, "I'm gonna kill you."

"Why?" Dad asked quietly. "I don't even know you."

"I'm gonna kill you just the same."

He got up and headed for Dad with bare knuckles. Dad threw the ax aside and swung at him—two powerful, jaw-breaking punches. The man tumbled to the floor in a heap.

The sheriff, summoned by the store clerk, finally arrived. He misjudged the situation and he misjudged Dad. Taking out his handcuffs, he asked Dad to extend his wrists.

Dad said, "I'm not really mad yet. I'll go along with you, but not in handcuffs. If you give me any trouble, I'll take your gun away from you so fast you won't know what's happening."

Chastised, the sheriff put the handcuffs away. When Dad finally got a chance to explain what had happened, he was released from custody.

We never discovered the stranger's motive for wanting to kill Dad.

On another occasion, Dad, two friends, and I were hunting quail. We stumbled on a covey almost at our feet, and the birds took off with a furious beating of wings. We all emptied our five-round shotguns at the fleeing quail . . . but only fifteen shots were fired. I turned and looked at Dad. He was lying on the ground, his face in the dirt, his gun unfired. He couldn't bring himself to kill so much as a bird. The war had completely expunged his instinct for killing anything or anyone.

One night Dad came home late, the odor of whiskey strong around him. He walked to his gun rack, grabbed his rifle, and strode out of the house. I was awakened by the sound of a shot. The terrible thought crossed my mind that Dad had become so mired in despair that he had committed suicide. But we found him sitting on the front porch, the rifle resting between his legs. He never said why he had sent the shot up.

After that none of us ever went to bed with an easy thought, and Mom didn't close her eyes until Dad arrived home and settled in for the night. Frequently, when he came home, he was drunk.

The three of us prayed continually for him, offering our supplications to the Lord to strengthen and lead him.

Our prayers remained unanswered until, driving alone one night, his car weaving dangerously, Dad was arrested for drunken driving.

He pleaded guilty and was fined four hundred dollars, all the money the farm had earned in a year.

"Son," he said when we got home from court, "get the Bible out."

I handed it to him. He placed it on the couch, went to his knees, and called on God for deliverance from his sins.

Facing us without shame, he confessed, "I've failed you all. And I want to ask your forgiveness. I've tried to stop drinking, but couldn't, until now. Tonight I'm giving my whole life to Jesus Christ and I'm asking God to make me a new man with a new heart. I'm going to need your help, but mostly I'm going to need the help of God.

"From now on, we're going to have Bible study and prayer in this house every night."

I felt indescribably uplifted, free in a way I never was before. Dad's been good as his word. Since that day he's never touched another drop of liquor. His belief in God has been the sustaining force of his life, particularly since he contracted emphysema several years ago. He's an invalid now, and my mother spends most of her time nursing him. But, despite his illness, Dad finds the God-inspired power to face the world day by day, even in those terrifying moments when he gasps for air.

Dad's commitment to Christ came when I was thirteen, and in the six years since I'd been led to the Lord my own commitment had never wavered. It grew with each day, and I became a modest soul-winner, bringing one person, mostly young friends and field hands, to the Lord for each of my thirteen years.

I was fully conscious of the difference between good and evil and that each man's soul is a battlefield in which God and the

Devil contend for supremacy. So every chance I got, wherever I was, I witnessed for Christ, leading more to Him every week until I was fifteen years old.

Then came a crisis. On a Tuesday night in August, 1955, as the moon shimmered outside my window, I felt uneasy and began praying for serenity. But it wouldn't come. God seemed to be dealing with me in a way I couldn't decipher. I prayed harder— perhaps in God's view I wasn't really saved. I asked Jesus to come into my heart again, forgive me for my sins and be my Savior once more.

Then He told me to rest and be at peace with myself, and He gave me direction, a focus and a mission for my life: He was calling me to preach.

The idea of becoming a preacher had been on my mind since the night I was saved. I'd hide in the fields and dream that I was preaching before an enormous crowd at the Sugar Bowl in New Orleans, that I was an evangelist with the power to proselytize millions throughout the world.

But cold reality was another matter. I felt timid, doubtful, unsure of the call I had heard.

I brought my doubts to Mom.

"I think the Lord's calling me to preach," I said. "What should I do about it?"

"Wait for Him to give you the determination and the power."

I knew one thing for certain. If I did surrender to spread the gospel, I didn't want to be like most of the other preachers I'd heard. They didn't seem consumed by God, nor did they preach with the conviction of the apostles.

The next day I met with the Lord again in prayer. The call this time was sweet and clear and loud and long and unmistakable.

The mighty injunction from Luke 9:60 rang out commandingly: "Go thou and preach the kingdom of God."

An unbelievable peace came into my soul.

I'd always been close to my mother's dad, Robert Campbell, and when I told him I was going to become a preacher, he took me on a ride through the fields near his farm.

"Grandson, when I was a young man, God called me to preach, too. But I didn't have the dedication and the love. I'll tell you a secret, never mentioned it to another soul. All these years I've preached to the cotton stalks, the corn, and the trees, but never to people. Your granddad failed God. I'm going to be dead soon, but I want to ask the Lord to keep you inspired."

He stopped the car, laid his hand on my head, looked upward, and said, "Dear God, give him the strength to do what I never had the nerve to do. Let him work among the needy in mind, body, and soul for the rest of his days."

Granddad's prayer has always stayed with me, and it strengthened both of us.

I was in college when word came that Granddad was dying. He had asked to see me. When I arrived at the hospital, the doctor told me Granddad hadn't said a word to anyone in days and that he was so weak he might slip away at any moment.

I walked into his room and whispered in his ear, "Granddad, it's Arthur. I'm here."

There was life and courage in him still. He looked at me and smiled. "My preacher," he said. Then he sat up in bed and put his arms around my neck.

We talked for a few moments, and his last words to me were, "Remember, my prayers are with you."

He died a few hours later.

Members of the family told me that after I left he said the Lord's Prayer—twice. Then he sang the hymn that has warmed Christian hearts for two hundred years. The first thing I'm going to do when I meet Granddad in Heaven is sing that hymn with him. The harmony might be off-key, but I don't think anybody will mind.

> Amazing grace! how sweet the sound
> That saved a wretch like me!
> I once was lost, but now am found,
> Was blind, but now I see.

Granddad's voice had broken as he struggled through the last verse:

> Yea, when this flesh and heart shall fail,
> And mortal life shall cease,
> I shall possess, within the veil,
> A life of joy and peace.

He made it to the end. Seconds later he went to spend his first ten thousand years with the Lord.

4

That His House May Be Full

THE STEEL DOOR of the bullpen at the county jail in Jackson, Mississippi, clanged shut behind me with an echoing bang.

I was alone in the cavernous holding facility with more than one hundred men, all black, charged with everything from jaywalking to murder.

Here certainly was a captive audience for the message of Christ I was there to preach.

I moved tentatively toward the center of the giant cell, Bible in hand, and looked for a friendly face.

I might as well have been invisible.

The men were sleeping, playing cards and checkers, reading newspapers and magazines, and a television set and radio were blaring simultaneously. A few were staring at the ceiling, wondering perhaps what kind of justice would be meted out to them in Jackson's tough, no-nonsense courts. Segregation was still officially sanctioned in the city, though thousands of Jacksonians were privately against persecution of the Negro.

I had agreed to stay locked in with the prisoners for forty-five minutes, and the time yawned ahead of me. Surrounded by indifference, I wondered, Lord, what am I going to say, what am I going to do, how am I going to reach anyone for Thy glory?

It was worse than I had thought it would be. A few hours before I'd been sitting in my room at the dorm when a fellow student, Johnny Dollarhide, walked in and said, "Five of us are going down to the jail. Want to come along?"

"What'll I have to do?"

"Witness and preach."

"I wouldn't know what to say or do. I've never witnessed in a jail. Can I just stand around and watch and listen?"

"Fine," Johnny said.

As soon as we arrived the others fanned out quickly to various parts of the jail—solitary, the juvenile section, and the individual cells of men already convicted and sentenced to death awaiting transfer to state prison.

I found myself alone with Johnny in the corridor between two huge bullpens, one for whites, one blacks.

"Which do you want?" Johnny said.

"Neither. I told you I just wanted to watch and listen."

"Well, Arthur, you *have* to take one of them. Make up your mind."

Before I could protest further, Johnny added, "If you want to let one group of these men die and go to Hell, then you can come and watch me. If you want to try to save souls, then you'll go into one of these bullpens."

I happened to be standing closer to the black pen, and after a hesitant glance at Johnny, I told the jailer, "I'll go in here."

Thus my unheralded entrance and my dilemma. How could I capture the attention of these oblivious men?

"We're going to have a preaching service," I announced in a tinny, unsure voice.

Nobody heard or if they did they couldn't have cared less. From the nearby white bullpen I could hear Johnny's loud, confident voice. He was preaching up a storm.

I tried again. "I'd like you all to gather around and listen to the message of Jesus."

No one moved.

I was desperate. I had to do something. I decided to emulate Johnny and began to shout at the top of my lungs from John 3:16.

" 'For God so loved the world, that he gave his only begotten Son, that whosoever believeth in him should not perish, but have everlasting life.' "

A few heads turned in my direction, faces mirroring mild interest.

Nervous and unsure, I flipped furiously through the Scripture, quoting passages at random from Genesis through Revelation. At last three or four men came over and sat down in front of me. The television and radio were still shouting their afternoon inanities, so I pitched my voice as high as I could and began to preach. It was the longest sermon I had ever delivered, a ragged, rambling jack-rabbit of a sermon skipping from point to point without coherence or continuity.

I preached about everything I knew until I ran out of things to say. Then I began repeating myself.

My efforts were a total disaster.

Finally, I called out, "If anyone wants to be saved, come up here, stand beside me and let me pray for you."

One thin man in a tattered shirt, brown eyes twinkling from an onyx face, stepped forward. "I'd like to be saved, preacher," he said.

As I brought that man to the Lord there wasn't a happier soul-winner anywhere in the world. After the prayer, the newly saved man said, "Thank you. Maybe it doesn't look like it, but we all appreciate your being here. A lot of these men are good Christians, and the rest of them will get right with the Lord one day. Come back again."

One man saved among more than a hundred. I hadn't exactly set Jesus' torch to that bullpen, but at least that one man had been spiraled into Heaven.

Each Thursday from then on I returned to the jail to witness. On every visit I led at least one prisoner to the Lord, white and black men scheduled for execution, lifers, others sentenced to ten-, twenty-, fifty-year terms.

These witnessing missions were the most exciting part of my life at Mississippi College, where I had enrolled because I knew I would meet others who wanted to spend their lives doing God's work. Of the two thousand-member student body, about two hundred of us planned to go on to seminary.

I was interested and did well in some of my courses—Bible study, history, political science, and speech. But I was a washout in foreign languages. As the semesters rolled by I flunked Spanish three times and French twice. It really wasn't important to me that *casa* meant house and *plume* was the word for pen. It seemed stupid to waste my time on such trivia when there was a world of people outside that needed Jesus.

The school, founded in 1826 and one of the oldest in the United States, was coeducational and controlled by the Mississippi

Baptist Convention. It dominated the small town of Clinton, which was only a short bus ride to sprawling Jackson, the county seat.

Jesus commanded his followers to seek and save the lost on the highways and hedges in order that "my house may be full." So in addition to the regular Thursday visits to the jail, every chance I got I went into Jackson to witness and fill the house of God with saved souls from among the lost I found on the streets and in the bars and nightclubs.

One evening Bill Mosley, another student who'd become a good friend, went into Jackson with me. We headed straight for Capitol Street, the main drag.

As we walked along we passed out tracts and talked to people about Christ. Then I spotted a young Negro leaning against a building, an inviting smile on his face.

"How're you doing, brother?" I said, stepping over to him. I shook his hand and introduced myself and Bill.

"I want to share with you the most important and wonderful experience in the world," I continued. "It's not something temporary. I'm offering an eternal home in Heaven. Have you ever received Jesus Christ in your heart as your Savior?"

"No," he answered, after listening to me intently. "But I've been thinking about it for a long time. It's just that I'm not fit; I'm not good enough."

I turned to Matthew 10:32–33 and read, " 'Whosoever, therefore, shall confess me before men, him will I confess also before my Father, who is in heaven. But whosoever shall deny me before men, him will I also deny before my Father, who is in heaven.' "

He was genuinely interested and, I'm certain, on the verge of coming to Christ when I saw his face suddenly become a mask of fright. He was no longer hearing me and his eyes were staring at something behind my back.

I turned and saw two police officers striding toward us. Three squad cars were parked at the curb about fifteen feet away. As the officers approached, the Negro ran off quickly.

One policeman grabbed Bill, the other shoved me roughly against the building and let loose a stream of invective.

"We ought to beat hell out of you nigger lovers," he said.

"Let's take them in," his sidekick suggested.

Handcuffs were snapped on our wrists, and we were pushed into separate squad cars. On the ride to the station, I kept asking if we were under arrest, but I was answered only with more curses.

At headquarters the handcuffs were removed. Bill was shunted into one office and I was led to another. A plainclothesman came in and identified himself as a lieutenant. He was a tall, beefy man with tired eyes.

"Why did you shake hands with that black s.o.b.?"

"Is that why we're here? For shaking hands with that man?"

"You bet. You just can't shake hands with blacks on the streets of Jackson. You one of them damn northerners coming down and causing trouble?"

I was surprised at the question. My southern accent was as pronounced as his.

"I was born in Mississippi and I'm a student at Mississippi College."

"What does your dad do?"

"He's a farmer."

"What do you think he would say about you shaking hands with a nigger?"

"My dad would beat me half to death if I didn't respect a man enough to shake his hand. I was on the street sharing with people the love of God. I meet a man and I naturally shake his hand. Why wouldn't I? We're going to spend eternity together in Heaven, so I'd just as soon be friends with him down here. I love every man, and maybe a handshake isn't much, but it's something. Jesus saved me and I wanted to save that brother. And I would have if your men hadn't come along and messed it up."

"We're going to call your dad."

"Go ahead. He's not going to like it one bit your arresting me for shaking hands."

"Then I'll call the college and see if you're really a student there."

"You do that and if you tell them that you arrested me for shaking hands with a Negro on the street, you're going to open a hornet's nest because a big percentage of our students don't think like you do. They'll be down here protesting and marching."

He calmed down a bit after that and in honest puzzlement he asked, "But *why* would a white man shake hands with a nigger?"

"Because he's as good as I am, as good as you are, maybe better than both of us. By the way, sir, are you saved?"

"Shut up and answer *my* questions!"

"You've been questioning me long enough. All I want to talk about now is *your* relationship with God."

He was angry again. "I'm going to book you."

"You can book me, beat me, but when you're in Hell, and, man, that's where you're headed, you'll be sorry."

He turned and loped out of the room. He was back an hour later and had simmered down some. "All right," he said, "we're going to let you go. But you have to give me your word that you won't shake hands with any more niggers in downtown Jackson."

"No, sir, I can't do that. Because when I get out of here I'm going right back to Capitol Street and keep witnessing. I'm going to shake hands with any man who'll talk to me, black or white. And maybe, if he comes to the Lord, I'll shout and kiss him."

"Listen, somebody driving by and seeing you shake hands with a nigger might just shoot you to death."

"I'm willing to die for what I believe."

He chewed me out some more, but with less enthusiasm. I think I had shaken him more than he'd shaken me. He ordered me into the hall, and there was Bill with the two officers who had arrested us.

"We'll drive you back to your car," the lieutenant said.

"No, sir. Unless I'm still under arrest, I'm not going to ride in your car. We'll walk."

"It's a long way."

"Fine. That'll give us a chance to witness to lots of people."

The lieutenant conferred with the two officers for a moment and then said, "Remember, I warned you. Now get the hell out of here, the both of you."

Bill had been subjected to similar intimidation, and when we reached the steps outside the police station we had a prayer meeting right there.

I felt wonderful. For the first time in my life I had really taken a stand for what I believed in, for what I knew was true and right, unafraid to face any consequences for my principles. But it made me sick to see the hatred of the police and realize that they were so fearful of us and what we were doing.

Bill and I did witness all the way back to our car. And I continued to witness in Jackson as long as I was in college. I was never troubled by the police again, though other students from school who also felt the need to street-witness were often picked up and harassed as Bill and I had been.

To cleave a soul to Christ I would go anywhere, do anything, for that continued to be more important to me than my classes.

I craved the excitement inherent in my commitment to Jesus. Winning souls and helping people was the name of the game. Let others devote their lives to splitting theological hairs; I knew myself well enough by now to realize that I would spend my life as a Christian activist. The world needed the gospel in practice, not in theory.

I hungered for action, and it was not long in coming. The story of my treatment at the hands of the Jackson police had spread around the campus. Opinion was divided: Half the students understood my feelings about racial equality and my zeal for Christ, the others thought it necessary to conform to local social customs and tagged me a fanatic.

But many people were curious to see what manner of preacher had tangled with the police, and I began to get requests to speak in Jackson. I didn't turn down a single invitation, and I was soon spreading the word at rescue missions, convalescent homes, hospitals, and the nearby Oakley reform school for Negro juvenile delinquents. Among these youngsters, the reaction was especially encouraging. Several dozen of them made decisions for Christ in response to my call.

The experience I was gaining was more precious than diamonds. I was honing my style and learning to structure my message. By now I had lost all fear of addressing an audience.

Then, unexpectedly, I was asked by a girl at school to preach at a church. Naturally, I agreed, never foreseeing that I was being led to my first pastorate among a roiling congregation.

Toss a giant net from the quadrangle at Mississippi College and you snare a Baptist church at the summit of every clay hill and in every black-soiled valley within a hundred-mile radius. Lodged in this area are scores of towns, running an unlikely gamut from tiny to small. Some of these microdot communities had two or three contentious Baptist churches, each believing that it alone was the path to God, that it alone was the alpha and omega.

Pastors and parishioners fussed and fretted over Bible doctrine, impervious to the reality that not every *t* could be crossed and *i* dotted to the satisfaction of all.

Pastors feuded with their congregations.

Pastors feuded with pastors.

The congregation of one church feuded with the congregation of a church down the street.

In almost every congregation there was a doctrinal feud among the members. They chose sides and came out slugging.

The result, of course, was chaos.

Seemingly every time you turned around there was a new Baptist church being built. Where the people should have come together and massed their strength, they dissipated their force by forming more and more splinter groups.

Where was the true love of Christ in all this?

East Lincoln Baptist Church, where I had been asked to preach, was in Brookhaven, a superficially quiet town of almost ten thousand on Highway 51, some sixty-five miles from Clinton.

I drove down in my rickety car and found a congregation of twenty members! It was a tiny splinter church that had been doggedly meeting for a year in a schoolhouse. Not one new member had been added to the congregation in the twelve months of its existence.

The members seemed to respond well to my sermon; they not only invited me back, but asked me to become their pastor. I suggested that they reunite with their parent church, but they adamantly refused.

Therefore, I accepted their offer as a challenge. They offered to pay me $80 a month, enough to replace the 60 cents an hour I was earning washing dishes at The Wigwam, the school cafeteria.

But there was a roadblock to my becoming a preacher: I hadn't been ordained.

A Baptist ordination board does not usually issue a minister's certificate to a fledgling in Christ, but will do so in cases where a church is in dire need of a pastor and makes a formal request. So the members of East Lincoln voted to request my ordination from my home church at Indianola, Mississippi, where my family had moved before I entered college. I'd attended the Second Baptist Church there for more than two years.

A twenty-five member ordination board convened for my oral examination. They quizzed me meticulously on Bible doctrine and interpretation. I answered all the questions to their apparent satisfaction. Then, like a baseball pitcher deciding to confound the opposing team after seven innings of serving up hard, clean fast balls, they threw me a curve.

"Mr. Blessitt, if you were sitting on an ordination board, would you vote to ordain a divorced minister?" a deacon asked.

There was that old Baptist nitpicking again.

"It would depend on the circumstances," I answered. "For example, if a man married at seventeen, was divorced at eighteen, went into the Army, got converted after his discharge and felt the call to preach, I wouldn't consider his former marriage a reason to vote against him. But if a man divorced his wife because he lusted after another woman, I'd feel that wasn't right."

Then my interrogator said, "Don't you know that you're not supposed to ordain a divorced preacher under any circumstances? The Bible is very clear on the point. The Book says specifically that a minister shall be the husband of only one wife."

More than half the board nodded their heads in agreement, and I thought I'd had it.

Then Dr. Harry Kellogg, a veteran minister, rose and asked me, "Mr. Blessitt, are you married?"

"No, sir."

"Do you plan to be married before the ordination?"

"No, sir."

I was ready to hug that man. I could see what he was leading up to.

Dr. Kellogg turned to the board. "The Scripture indeed says a minister shall be the husband of only one wife. So since Mr. Blessitt is not married, technically he doesn't qualify for ordination!

"However, you are asking this young man to answer a question that I, after many, many years as a pastor, could not easily answer. I would have to say exactly what he has said. I would have to fall on my knees and pray for Divine guidance. Then, and only then, would I be able to judge the particular case."

Now Dr. Kellogg dropped the bomb.

"Since Mr. Blessitt does not qualify, I hereby move that this ordination council be dissolved!"

It grew so quiet you could have heard the footfalls of the wise men on the road to Bethlehem.

The chairman finally found his voice and politely asked me to leave the room.

I wasn't certain which way the vote would go, and I sweated out every second, boring holes in the face of my watch as time crawled by. I never learned what went on in that room while those twenty-five men debated my fate, but after a long, long forty-five minutes my pastor came out and told me the board had ruled favorably!

Mom, Dad, Virginia, and Grandma and Granddad Blessitt were in the packed church at the formal ceremony of ordination. As I knelt before the congregation, each member of the board laid a hand on my head and said a word of prayer. ("Then laid they their hands on them, and they received the Holy Spirit. . . . Saying, Give me also this power, that on whomsoever I lay hands, he may receive the Holy Spirit." Acts 8:17 and 19.)

Now, in the words of my Certificate of Ordination, I was "solemnly and publicly set apart and ordained to the work of The Gospel Ministry."

It was a moment of gold and silver.

The next day I barreled my car back to Brookhaven, my colors flying for Jesus.

Since I was still in college, the members of East Lincoln had agreed that I would serve as pastor from Friday night to Sunday night. Only forty-eight hours a week of pastoring was a handicap but if I crammed every moment with activity, there would be time to accomplish much. In fact, I could hardly fail. There was no way to go but up with a church that had come to a grinding halt.

I set two immediate objectives. The first, obviously, was to increase membership. I told my twenty-member congregation that there were undoubtedly some families in town who entertained more people at Sunday supper than we had in our church. Yet Jesus had begun with only twelve. No one raised an objection to adding members, but a unanimous wail of dissent greeted my second statement, "We're going to construct a new building."

Everyone agreed it was impossible, the money just wasn't available. "We don't have the price of one two-by-four," somebody said.

"If you vote to build, we'll get it built somehow." I responded. "For now we'll proceed on faith."

After much discussion; they reluctantly went along. I was given the responsibility for overseeing the construction of a building no one believed would get off the ground. I couldn't but chuckle at the thought that the only things I had built in my life were two utilitarian structures—a chicken coop and an outhouse.

I mulled over how to get the building started. The solution presented itself only after I surmounted my initial crisis as a pastor.

After preaching my Sunday morning service I called on two men, sitting on opposite sides of the room, to take up the offering. After a moment of reluctance, both rose and passed the plates.

Later a wizened member in his eighties took me aside. "Preacher," he said, "you've made your first mistake."

I looked at him blankly.

"Jeffrey Haynes and Claude Lynde, the two you asked to take the offering, hate each other's guts. They haven't talked in twenty years. They both pack guns, and have threatened to shoot one another a hundred times. They live within shouting distance of each other, but let one of their dogs stray on to the other's property and they're ready for murder."

Until this moment I'd been unaware of the feud. I knew only that Jeffrey Haynes, tousled-haired and craggy-faced, and Claude Lynde, a stoop-shouldered six-footer with hooded eyes, were considered the leading men in the congregation. Coincidentally, both were professional contractors and carpenters, and I was counting on them to do the lion's share of the work once we raised enough money to start building the church.

I soon learned that the reason for the feud was lost in the mists of time. The families had been warring for more than forty years, but no one remembered how it all began. They were still feuding only out of habit.

Not only did their feud jeopardize construction of the building, but it was un-Christian. To bring the men together, I decided on the most direct course. I called on Jeffrey Haynes first.

"What's this I hear about you and Claude Lynde?" I asked.

He thereupon went into a twenty-minute monologue, ticking off his grievances, which appeared to me to be more imagined than real. All of them didn't amount to a pig's oink. It was merely a question of foolish pride.

When he was finished at last with his parade of lusty insults, I said, "Are you saved?"

"Sure I'm saved."

"Are you really saved?"

"I said I was."

"Then let's pray right now. I don't care what Claude's done to you, or what you think he's done to you. I want you to forgive him. If he should walk in that door and shoot your wife, I'd expect you to forgive him. The Bible says forgiveness is the giving up of resentment. And the Lord's Prayer speaks of forgiveness, too. How can you call yourself saved and not forgive your enemy?"

I wasn't reaching him. "No, I won't forgive. Never!"

It went much the same when I talked with Claude, but I did manage to drag him over to Jeffrey's house. "I'll do it for you as a personal favor, Pastor, but if he so much as blinks at me the wrong way, I'll go for him."

The moment they saw each other you could taste the hatred with a spoon.

"I'm going to say only one thing," I told them. "If you two don't get together, I'm going to ask the church to vote you both out, or dismiss me as pastor."

Jeffrey said, "How are you going to put up the building without us? We're the only carpenters in the church."

"We don't need a building if we're going to have people like you in it. Now you both either get right or get out."

Thus challenged, Jeffrey's and Claude's attitudes seemed to soften. I asked them to pray with me, and I sought the aid of God to rid them of their anger and bind them together in love and brotherhood.

It was a short prayer, but as soon as it was over the miracle happened. Jeffrey and Claude looked at each other and their faces were wreathed in smiles. They shook hands and were soon in animated conversation, each claiming the feud was the fault of his own family.

Now that Jeffrey and Claude were joined in friendship, they agreed to work side by side without charge on the new church building. But first we needed funds to buy the materials.

It was decided that every fourth Sunday's offering would go into the building fund. More was raised when members sold a cow or a pig and contributed the proceeds. The kids sold eggs. The ladies baked cakes and pastries and put them up for sale. Some gave as little as a few ears of corn to the Lord, but it all added up. Soon we had almost three hundred dollars, enough for a beginning. We drew up the plans, then dug the foundation. Because they had full-time jobs during the week, the men in the congregation could work only on Saturdays. Progress was slow but steady, and the Lord met all our needs as they came along. When the foundation was completed, we raised enough money to purchase the concrete. Then we got enough for the two-by-fours, then the roof, the pulpit, the altar, the cross. Eventually everything down to hymn books was provided.

With the building underway, I moved toward my other objective. I got a map of the town, and in red I marked the houses of all the members of our church, in blue I marked those of members of other churches, and in black I marked the houses of all who were lost and not members of any church.

I went from house to house, door to door, through gullies and dirt roads, and into the remotest hollows. To those who answered my knock, my first question was always the same: "Are you planning to enter Heaven?"

One day I was driving down a road with a member of our congregation. He pointed at a house and said, "That's the Saunders' place. No use trying to win Howard to the Lord. He's the meanest man in these parts."

I wrote the name of Howard Saunders at the top of my prospect list. I'd already discovered that the worst sinners are the easiest to convert. They're hungry for God and lonely living outside His kingdom. Underneath their bluff, gruff exteriors they're aching to be saved. The problem is that most preachers give up on such sinners without trying. I was confident Howard Saunders could be reached. All I had to do was talk to him.

"I'm going to witness to Mr. Saunders," I told my companion.

"If I don't make church one Sunday 'cause I'm sick in bed, and Mr. Saunders shows up, you call me and I'll come, even if I'm on my deathbed. I'll want to see that," he said.

Mr. Saunders wasn't home when I visited his house the next day, but I witnessed to his wife and four children and led them to the Lord. They were all in church the next Sunday.

But I hadn't caught up with Mr. Saunders. One Friday night as I hit town from Clinton, I went to his house, unannounced. He had a roomful of company, so I asked him to step outside.

I stuck out my hand and said, "I'm here to talk about your soul and about making God a part of your life. I'm aware you aren't saved. Would you like to be?"

"I'm lost and I know it."

"God loves you, and Christ died for you. Why not come to Him right now. You can be a new man, a new father to your children, a new husband to your wife."

It took only a few moments to bring him to the Lord.

Then he went back into the house and declared to his family and friends: "I'm saved! I'm going to church from now on and live for the Lord." His wife and children were ecstatic, and we all had a good, old-fashioned cry-in, weeping tears of joy.

No one ever again called Mr. Saunders "the meanest man in town." He did change, Christ's promise fulfilled. He became friendly, giving, warm, helpful, and a pillar of our church.

All six members of the Saunders family wanted to be baptized. Since we had no baptismal facilities of our own, I arranged for the immersion rite to be held at another church. Then it occurred to me that I had never baptized anyone. I wasn't even sure how the ceremony was supposed to be conducted. I decided just to do my best—no one had ever taught me how to pastor a church, either.

It was a freezing November morning when I stepped into the large baptism tank at the borrowed church. It took only a second to discover that somebody had forgotten to warm the water. My teeth started chattering immediately.

Waist-deep in the water and chilled to the bone I read the passages in the second chapter of Matthew describing the baptism of Jesus.

One by one I lowered Mrs Saunders and her four children into the tank, immersed them, and said over each, "In obedience to the command of our Lord and Savior, Jesus Christ, I now baptize you in the name of the Father, the Son, and the Holy Spirit." They all braved the icy water in silence.

Then Mr. Saunders, smiling, hit the water with a confident splash. When he felt the cold he leaped up like a porpoise, thrashing water over half a dozen people in the front row.

"Man, that's cold," he shouted. The congregation roared.

It was so cold that Mr. Saunders wouldn't go all the way under. I had to keep pushing him down. When he emerged from the tank, purple-faced, he said, "Does the Bible say a man's got to be baptized or frozen to death?"

Another roar of laughter swept the church.

It was probably the most inept baptism ceremony in the history of Christendom. I made a mental note that in the future I would at least check the temperature of the water.

At the end of a year, through personal witnessing, the congregation had been built up to 120, and the new building was almost ready for occupancy.

The church now had grown to the point where a full-time pastor was needed, which, I explained in my final sermon, was the reason I was resigning.

I felt that a beginning had been made at East Lincoln. The new church was as imposing to me as the Empire State Building. It stood proud and beckoning where nothing had stood before. More important, East Lincoln was now a congregation of dedicated Christians worshipping in harmony and peace.

My old Ford sputtered back to the campus from my last trip to Brookhaven. But now I couldn't abide the thought that there would only be school to fill my time. I prayed that God would call me for further work in His name.

By the time I reached my room at the dorm, my prayer seemingly had been answered. Waiting for me was a scrawled message: "Phone Mr. Owen Cooper."

A call from Owen Cooper was a summons to the throne of Baptist power in Mississippi. What could one of the most influential and important men in the state want with me?.

5

The Town Too Tough to Crack

O WEN COOPER was a legend in the South, one of a rare breed, a multimillionaire and a fervent, dedicated Christian. A leading industrialist, he was president of two large chemical companies and director of a bank and a score of corporations. He had twice served brilliantly and conscientiously as president of the Mississippi Baptist Convention and was vice-president of the Southern Baptist Convention and director of the Pioneer Missions Committee. In the press he was often described either as "Mr. Mississippi" or "Mr. Mississippi Baptist."

Owen Cooper wasn't a man to waste time with small talk: He had a reputation for going to the jugular vein of a conversation. I couldn't imagine what door, if any, he was opening for an anonymous twenty-two-year-old college student doing his best to serve the Lord.

When I arrived at his office, his secretary said, "Mr. Cooper and a group of other men are waiting for you." I glanced quickly at my watch, found I was on time, and sighed with relief. Punctuality has never been one of my attributes.

In person Mr. Cooper matched his reputation. Six feet tall and 185 pounds, he radiated quiet power and forcefulness. He welcomed me cordially and smiled warmly as he introduced me to the four other men ranged around the room: Claude Townsend, president of the Jackson piano company bearing his name; Chester Quarles, executive secretary of the Mississippi Baptist Convention; Joe Odle, editor of the Baptist *Record*, the largest newspaper, secular or religious, in Mississippi; and the Reverend William

Parker, the area missionary in Montana for the Southern Baptist Convention.

These five men were waiting for me, the secretary had said.

But for what conceivable reason?

The suspense ended abruptly.

"We're looking for a college student to send to Anaconda, Montana, to start a new mission," Mr. Cooper said. "Would you like to go?"

Anaconda, Montana? It was only a half-remembered name from a high school geography book.

"Why me?"

"We've heard about your work in Brookhaven."

"I don't know anything about starting a mission. Who would train me?"

"There will be no training," Mr. Cooper said tersely. "You've already had it—at East Lincoln."

While I sat open-mouthed, the Reverend Mr. Parker—who knew Montana as well as he knew his Bible—explained that the Southern Baptist Convention had unsuccessfully tried for several years to carry its evangelical message into Anaconda. Two churches had been started and both failed, victims of indifference.

I wasn't sure what to say or how to react. My life was committed to serving God, but the offer, so surprising and unlikely, filled me with a foretaste of failure. How could I succeed where others with far more experience had been compelled to give up? I would be an alien in a strange land. Someone in the room mentioned that Anaconda was 2,300 miles from Mississippi, and I had never been out of the South.

I asked for time to think it over.

As I prepared to leave, Mr. Cooper said, "Before you decide, there's one more thing you should know."

"Yes, sir?"

Owen Cooper's voice was razor sharp. "I've been told Anaconda is a town too tough to crack!"

I left with mixed emotions and tried to sort my thoughts out by discussing the offer with everyone close to me.

Dad and Mom said no. ("People outside the South are different. Most of them are good people, but different nevertheless.")

My professors said no. ("Keep studying." "Why lose a year of school?" "Education comes first.")

Preachers I knew said no. ("Impossible!" "Anaconda, where's that?" "You won't convert enough people to fill a station wagon.")

The more "no's" I heard, the more I leaned toward going. I kept remembering Mr. Cooper's final words. But did he whip out that sentence as a warning to be cautious or a challenge to be courageous?

Only my friend Bill Mosley offered encouragement. "If you feel the Lord leading you to Anaconda, then go."

Two incidents clinched it for me. Walking by the post office in Jackson one day, I saw the famous World War I recruiting poster that had been revived—Uncle Sam pointing a stern finger and saying, "I want you." I gazed at the poster, transfixed. Finally, it seemed it wasn't Uncle Sam but God saying, "I want you." Then a day or so later, while I was still pondering, I found a card with a prayer that someone had written on it in my wallet. I had never before taken the time to read the words: "O God, glorify Thyself today at my expense. Send me the bill—anything, Lord. I set no price. I will not dicker or bargain. Glorify Thyself. I'll take the consequences."

The signs were all pointing in one direction—Anaconda.

When I told Dad that I had decided to go, he didn't try to change my mind. Instead he gave me the advice that is still my standard, the simple, meaningful principles by which I live. No son ever received a more precious gift of wisdom:

"Always let God fill your heart with love.

"Look at every person as though he were a member of your own family.

"Think of every man as your father, except that he may be lost and needs Jesus.

"Think of every woman as your mother, except that she could need Christ to change her life.

"Look at every boy and girl as your brother and sister and consider them all candidates for the Lord's mercy and blessings.

"Never insult a man or a woman by look, word, or gesture.

"Love everybody. The good have already earned your love. The bad may give you love when you least expect it.

"Don't look up at anyone and don't look down at anyone.

"Consider every woman a lady, every man a gentleman.

"If you do this, you'll never mistreat anyone or pass them by without telling about God's power to save."

That is my code. To me a whore has always been a lady, a stumbling, incoherent drunk a gentleman. No matter what the provocation I've never answered a curse with a curse. I've attempted to treat everyone with the love and respect I would want for my own family.

In practice, Dad's advice has been priceless. It has soothed my anger, given me patience and understanding, forged friendships, and helped me win souls for Christ.

The semester at an end, I left on June 10, 1962, at 11 P.M. on a boiling hot and humid Mississippi evening. The transition in climate a week later would be stark. I was to learn that it snowed in Montana in June.

My blue '55 Ford limped along, radiator smoking, eating gas and oil copiously. The water pump broke in Raton, New Mexico. It cost twenty-two dollars to fix, which put a massive dent in my budget. I'd left Mississippi with one hundred dollars.

The snow fell as I rolled through Montana's 10,000- and 12,000-foot peaks. I'd never driven on snow before, and the more the car slid and skidded around the scythe-shaped curves above the yawning valleys below, the more I gave thanks that I was saved.

After seven days Anaconda loomed ahead. It is not the most beautiful city on earth. The first sight to hit you is an enormous, depressing mountain of slag, the unprocessable residue of ore. The ore is extracted from the mines at Butte, twenty-five miles away, and shipped to Anaconda, which has the world's largest smelter.

The city was tossed together in 1883 as a working duchy of the Anaconda cooper and zinc mines in Butte.

The mine owners imported both rugged men from the potato-famine counties of Ireland and persecuted peasants from the mountains of the Balkans in southeastern Europe to work in the shadow of the peaks ringing Anaconda.

The men brought their religions—Roman Catholicism, Lutheranism, and Serbian Orthodoxy—with them when they settled in the deep, fiercely cold Anaconda canyon.

Driving along Main Street I wondered if there was room in Anaconda for the sound of yet another drummer. "Too tough to crack"?

I'd find out soon enough.

I had three immediate needs—a place to stay, a church building, and a congregation.

I pulled up at the Marcus Daly Hotel, named for the principal founder of the Anaconda Company, and told the desk clerk, "I'm a preacher. I'm here to start a new church and I want the cheapest room you have."

He rented me four walls for only one dollar a day.

The bed was comfortable and I fell asleep a few moments after entering the room. I awoke at about 10 P.M., still tired and very, very lonely.

I began praying aloud for guidance. During the night God came and told me that I wasn't alone, and that I need not fear. If I knocked on enough doors, witnessed to enough people, and preached the Word, many lives would be changed.

I prayed nonstop till morning when I was totally confident of victory.

When I went down for breakfast the desk clerk, a charming, blue-eyed lady, signaled to me. She moved in close and confided in a low, almost conspiratorial voice, "A very wicked woman—in plain language, a prostitute—who's lived in the hotel a long time came down an hour ago with her bags packed and said, 'I'm checking out.' When I asked her why, she told me, 'I don't know where I'm going, but I've got to get out of here. I must be rooming next to a preacher. When I came in last night I heard him praying. I pulled a chair close to the wall and listened to him all night, crying and praying for people like me. I can't stand it.'"

I was sorry I never got a chance to witness to that lady, but at least she was under conviction.

A Baptist pastor in Butte had arranged for me to use the Seventh-day Adventist Church building for one Sunday. I placed an ad in the paper, optimistically announcing the formation of the First Southern Baptist Church of Anaconda. I expected the ad to draw something of a crowd, believers, nonbelievers, and those who might be curious to meet Anaconda's newest minister.

When the moment for the service came that Sunday I raced to the pulpit and preached an on-fire sermon titled "The Challenge Before Us." Never had I preached so fervently. I lost track of time and when I finally concluded I was out of breath and perspiring.

Then I issued the invitation to step forward and be saved and to join the First Southern Baptist Church of Anaconda. My eyes were riveted on a pleasant, dark-haired, neatly dressed middle-aged man in the front row.

He was the only one who had heard my sermon, the only Anacondan who responded to my ad.

And even he did not step forward.

His name was Roland Smathers and I did convert him a few days later. "Only reason I didn't make the decision that first day was that sermon of yours scared me to death," he told me. "Never heard a preacher carry on so."

My first service had bred my first conversion. That's how you start—with one, then two, then more, and yet more. A journey of a thousand miles still begins with a single step.

I began roaming the streets looking for a permanent meeting place. Across from the courthouse was a Salvation Army building. I tried the door but it was padlocked.

I called Army headquarters in Butte and a jovial captain told me it was for rent. The Army had closed out its work in Anaconda.

The rent was $30 a month, and when I entered the building the sight was beautiful. It was all there—organ, piano, carpeted floor, recreation hall, classrooms, heater, even a refrigerator.

I was elated. Finding the building was proof anew, if proof was needed, of the power of God.

But when I looked at those empty classrooms my heart ached. Then it occurred to me that since it was summer, why not start a Vacation Bible School for Anaconda's children? "Those who seek me early shall find me," Proverbs 8:17 counseled. And in Proverbs 22:6 was the clear mandate, "Train up a child in the way he should go and, when he is old, he will not depart from it."

That night, while I was still considering the challenge of starting the school, I heard a knock at my door. A crinkly eyed, smiling old woman introduced herself, and told me she'd learned through the Pioneer Missions Board that I was in town.

"How can I help you?" Mom Anthony asked.

Well into her nineties, Mom Anthony was cheerful, amazingly spry, and independent, an altogether remarkable senior citizen. She had the tireless energy of one fueled by a passionate love of the Lord. At an age when others thirty or more years her junior were huddled in retirement and convalescent homes, Mom indefatigably traveled the world, spreading a shower of good works wherever she went. For more than twenty years, she'd been a missionary and Christian troubleshooter.

"After my husband passed away," she said, "I asked myself: What am I going to do with the rest of my life? Just sit around, waiting to die and go to Heaven?"

Mom decided she would earn her place in Heaven a hundred times over. I spent the night listening to her tell story after story as mesmerized as the Sultan of Persia hearing the tales spun by Scheherazade.

My favorite was her experience during World War II. Shortly after Pearl Harbor, she was courageous enough to open her house in Texas to a number of students of Japanese ancestry. These young Nisei had slipped through the cordon thrown up by panic-stricken California authorities who were herding all the yellow-skinned men, women, and children they could find into primitive, barely habitable camps. Despite the loud disapproval of her neighbors and community pressure, Mom kept those young, blameless Japanese-Americans with her until the end of the fighting.

She was tough as well as good.

Mom said she'd help me recruit pupils for our Bible school. Together we piled into my car the next day and bumped our way over the dreadful unpaved streets outside town. "Worse roads than I saw while I was a missionary in Nigeria," Mom declared disapprovingly.

We stopped at random at house after house and knocked on doors. On some of these forays we traveled two hundred miles a day throughout the county to sign up the kids. One week my oil bill alone was nine dollars.

But the kids came, their high-pitched laughter filling the building. And through the summer, they learned the things of the Lord. For most of them, it was their first encounter with Christ.

Fifty-eight youngsters, all under fourteen years old, completed the course, and nineteen were saved.

Mom and I shared a wonderful victory through those children. There would have been even more youngsters in the class, except for parental opposition to an evangelical ministry.

One nine-year-old boy who dropped out in mid-summer told me, "My folks said I can't come to your church again, and you can't come to our house any more. I like you and when I get big, I want to come to your church."

Even more poignant was a letter I received from one of my former pupils, a thirteen-year-old girl. "Dear Arthur," she wrote on a lined piece of composition paper, "I don't think you had better come to get me on Sunday because mother will not let me go. I'm very sorry. I love my mother very much and I don't want to hurt her more than I already have by going to your church and believing in Christ. Since I was saved my life has been changed. I want to get baptized, but Mom won't let me. I promise that when I get older I am going to be baptized. I know Christ understands, and I hope you do, too."

I thought of those misguided parents and the words of Jesus in Matthew 19:14, "Suffer little children, and forbid them not, to come unto me; for of such is the kingdom of heaven."

Still the kingdom of Heaven had been breached in Anaconda, and our first impact had come through the children.

When Bible school ended, Mom took off for her next assignment for the Lord in a cloud of confident good humor.

How I hated to see her go, though I knew her call to leave was as loud as mine to stay.

By now I had seen enough of Anaconda to realize how many were bereft of the hope of God. It was a hard place to earn a living, a cruel, mountainous spot where, as I would discover during the approaching winter, temperatures went down to forty degrees below zero. I wondered what made so many of these aimless Anacondans fight so ferociously for survival. They were nowhere—and going nowhere except to Hell once the hell of their lives on this earth was ended.

I rededicated my heart to winning new souls for Christ.

On Main Street one morning as I was passing out tracts and looking for prospects, I saw a small down-at-the-heels building and walked in. It was a combination greasy spoon and pool hall. About a dozen teen-age boys were hanging around, some at the tables, a few at the two pinball machines.

"Have you got Christ in your hearts?" I asked in a loud voice.

Every head turned toward me.

Then they laughed and cursed. One of them snarled, "Take your damn Bible and take off. You're not our kind. You don't belong in a place like this."

"Don't any of you have guts enough to listen to me?"

Then I heard a strong voice behind me, "What's going on?" A tall 195-pounder with big arms and red hair stepped over.

"Hey, Tiny, this guy's some kind of religious nut," one of the kids said.

"What do you want?" Tiny asked.

"I want to talk about Jesus and what Christ can mean in your lives."

"You stand there like a man," Tiny said. "I'm a man, and I'll listen to you and all my boys will listen. You s.o.b.'s sit down and let's hear what the man has to say."

The command was obeyed immediately, and I now had, thanks to Tiny, their undivided attention.

"I want to show all of you how to be saved. We're all sinners—me, too. I can read your faces and see in your eyes that not one of you is happy fooling around this place, wasting your time playing pool and pinball."

"I'm happy," roared one of the young lions, "happy as hell!"

A look from Tiny that could almost kill turned the "happy" protester into a meek kitten.

"Let him finish," Tiny said through clenched teeth.

"I say you're not happy. The Bible says you're not. Jesus *knows* you're not. Because if you don't have Christ in your heart, you can't be happy. He's your only salvation."

They stayed cowed and quiet until I was done. Then I felt Christ reaching down, beginning to touch them, particularly Tiny.

"Okay," Tiny ordered, "you guys take off."

They rose in phalanx and were out the door in seconds. Tiny moved me to a corner and asked me to sit down.

"You for real?"

"Real as Jesus."

"I'm interested in what you're saying."

Then Tiny unburdened himself. It was not a happy story.

He was only seventeen and the ringleader of a thirty-member gang, the most notorious teen-age gang in Anaconda. He lived with his mother and stepfather and had been in and out of trouble for four years. Somehow he'd escaped reform school, though he had appeared in court on charges of assault, robbery, drunkenness, and dealing dope.

"Hell they've got a file on me at Juvenile Hall high as the slag pile at the smelter," Tiny said. "Funny though, I don't need the money we steal. My mother'll give me anything I want. I turned wild at thirteen, wouldn't go to school, and began running the streets. That was about the time my mother remarried."

Tiny's gang rendezvoused at bars that violated the law by serving drinks to minors (all the members of his gang were below the legal drinking age). After several rounds of hard booze at the accommodating bars, the gang's idea of a big evening was to take off for the hills and have an all-night beer bust.

Now Tiny made a strange request.

"I want to be sure you're real. I want to see if you're some damn rich preacher on his way to a fat belly who's looking down your nose at me."

I took Tiny to my hotel room. I was thankful that a dollar a day didn't buy much ostentation. He was properly impressed at the modesty of my hole in the wall. Then we walked down the street to the church building. I didn't have enough money to eat in restaurants, so I'd installed a hot plate to warm the staples on which I lived all the time I was in Anaconda—mainly powdered milk, canned biscuits, and pork and beans. I whipped up a dish of canned spaghetti, and Tiny and I continued to talk. Tiny was beginning to learn of the spiritual nourishment offered by Christ.

In many ways Tiny was the stereotype juvenile delinquent. Everyone—his parents, schoolteachers, the courts, police, his probation officer—had given up on him. They felt it would be only a matter of time until Tiny was back in the hands of the authorities, eventually winding up in prison. He was smart enough to sense this, and I think it was the reason he confided in me. He was yet another searcher, and what I offered him—a new life through Jesus—had never been offered to him before.

Tiny did not make a quick, dramatic, emotional conversion. As he left, a thoughtful expression on his face, he said only, "I'd like to talk to you again."

Perhaps there was hope for Tiny.

Meantime, I was still the only official member of the First Southern Baptist Church of Anaconda. Roland Smathers, my lone parishioner, hadn't been baptized. So the Lord and I had a business meeting and together we voted to have a week of revival.

I put up a big sign outside the building and had some brochures printed. But I knew that wouldn't be enough to draw a crowd.

And there was no point in announcing the revival in the newspaper: My ad for my first service had drawn only Roland Smathers.

I decided once more to go out and knock on doors and share Christ with anyone who would listen.

In the next few weeks I don't think I missed one of the more than twelve thousand doors in Anaconda. It was a slow, grinding, discouraging task, but each time I received a promise from a householder that he would come to the revival, my spirit soared and was renewed.

The number of people that turned out for the seven days of revival didn't exactly strain the facilities of the building, but I was heartened by the several dozen who did come. And Owen Cooper came up from Mississippi for a visit. He was much too generous in his praise for what little had been accomplished. The church was yet an acorn, far from the strong, healthy oak I wanted it to be, but it warmed my soul to hear his words of encouragement.

During the revival, fourteen were saved and joined the church. At last we were on our way.

Among those who were saved was a big, redheaded teen-ager.

Tiny quietly came forward during one of the invitations and pledged his heart to Christ. Scratch one juvenile delinquent from the police blotter, I thought.

After giving his heart to the Lord, Tiny changed completely. Soon he was holding two part-time jobs, an early morning newspaper delivery route, and an afternoon job unloading trucks at a warehouse.

Tiny's newfound enthusiasm for Christ led him to disband his gang. One Sunday, Tiny shepherded all thirty of his pals and their girl friends to church to hear my message. Out of that crew, fifteen elected to go the way of Christ rather than Capone.

The building became the new meeting place of Tiny and his friends. We set up a Ping Pong table, and checkers and chess boards, and had hammer and tongs Bible study, where questions were flung at me by alert, thirsting, curious minds that challenged everything I knew about theology.

The conversions of these delinquents all took. Several were baptized, and today they are among Anaconda's best, most God-loving citizens.

Tiny became almost a full-time worker and my indispensable aide. But he did backslide once, a mistake that nearly sent him to prison before he rededicated his heart and made his final and irrevocable bargain with Christ.

A hard-scrabble town, Anaconda was infamous throughout that area of the West as a pocket of sin where everything was for sale. It was a magnet for roughhouse ranchers, cowboys, lumbermen, and construction workers who came in on weekends and vacations from all over southern Montana, northern Idaho, and Wyoming to whoop it up in a frantic search for pleasure.

There were more than forty bars in the city (outnumbering the churches, naturally). Though gambling was against the law, many bars had small backroom casinos where stud, blackjack, and dominoes were played with money openly on the tables. Most of the joints also had slot machines and were nesting grounds for prostitutes although both commodities were supposedly illegal. But the most upsetting abuse of decency practiced by the bars was their readiness to serve drinks to kids as young as thirteen and fourteen.

The crime rate in the town was high, law enforcement a scandal; this was accepted by the "respectable" people of Anaconda as "the nature of things."

The so-called respectable citizens, the churches, and the police were three pillars of indifference. A reform mayor, backed by an aroused citizenry, could have cleaned up the town simply by enforcing the laws already on the books.

Tiny's trouble occurred while I was in Denver for a week attending a Baptist convention. He went into a bar, had a couple of drinks, got into a fight, and was arrested.

When I returned to Anaconda, I found Tiny in a jail cell, deep in depression.

"Guess I've done it this time," he said. "They're going to put me away for sure, I know it."

Repentant and remorseful, Tiny prayed with me, and he came to the Lord a second time. I was certain of his sincerity and since I had seen so much good in Tiny I determined it would ill-serve the taxpayers of Montana to imprison him. Tiny belonged to Christ.

Not for a moment did I excuse his mistake. He admitted his guilt but I believed him when he said he wouldn't slip again. Given another chance, he could serve a long, useful, dedicated Christian life.

But there was another factor beyond Tiny's guilt. Why wasn't the bartender, who had knowingly served him illegal drinks, occupying the next cell? It was the height of hypocrisy for the law to be enforced against Tiny while the shoddy little profiteers who owned the bars got off scot-free.

I set myself the twin goals of preventing Tiny's sentencing to reform school and waging war against the honky-tonks that ignored the statute forbidding them to sell drinks to those who were underage.

Seething with indignation, I barged into the office of the chief of police.

"I want something done about the bars that are selling liquor to minors."

He feigned astonishment. "Now, that just isn't happening."

"I'll take you downtown this moment and show you."

"Sorry, I can't spare the time."

I drove to Helena, the state capital, and tried to see the Attorney General. He refused to meet with me. I talked with his aide who said, "Sorry, that's a local problem. There's nothing we can do."

Next I met with an official of the State Liquor Control Board, the agency that licensed the bars. An official told me vaguely, "When we get a chance we'll send someone by to check those places out. Sorry we can't do anything more right now."

Everyone was "sorry." It added up to a transparent runaround. The state was an obvious beehive of corruption. Each of the authorities to whom I brought my appeal had sworn an oath (on the Bible!) to uphold the law, yet they sanctioned the flouting of the law by Anaconda's taverns.

Tiny's mother was in court when I testified in his behalf.

"This boy shouldn't be sent to reform school," I pleaded with the judge. "He made an error, but otherwise he's been living right since he was saved. Check his record. You'll see nothing good ever happened to him before he came to Christ. Putting him away won't help him. I think you ought to crack down on the bars that serve Tiny and other kids. I'm begging for mercy for this young man, your Honor. If you show mercy, I'll be responsible for him."

The judge paroled Tiny into my custody.

Tiny never touched another drop and was never a problem again. He began to go with me on preaching missions and gave his testimony at revivals I helped organize in Great Falls, Missoula, and Three Forks. This once seemingly incorrigible boy headed for reform school helped inspire scores of people to embrace Christ.

Tiny subsequently joined the Army and went on to lead a zealous Christian life.

In my battle against the bars, meantime, I went, as a last resort, to the sheriff of Anaconda. I finally found a sympathetic ear.

"Why are you so concerned?" he asked.

I told him about Tiny and all the other Tinys running loose in town.

"You mean business, don't you?"

"Yes, sir."

"I haven't had any support in this city," the sheriff said. "I'm as opposed to what those bars are doing as you are. If you'll help, I'll try to straighten it out. But you've got to go into one of these places and see a minor being served with your own eyes. Then call *me*—don't talk to any of my deputies."

The sheriff gave me his private number. It wasn't an hour before I was calling him from a bar that was serving bourbon to a boy who couldn't have been more than fifteen.

The sheriff arrived, took the bartender downtown and filed charges. However, the district attorney refused to prosecute on grounds that there was no evidence—it had to be proven by chemical analysis that there actually was liquor in the glass.

But the sheriff was a courageous man. He called the juvenile authorities, and with his prestige they could do nothing but promise future cooperation.

Thus the sheriff now had the ammunition he needed. He visited every joint in Anaconda and told the bartenders and owners that if a minor was served, he would close them down, chemical analysis or no chemical analysis.

That scared the bar owners. From that moment on, they stationed a man at the door to check the I.D.s of all patrons. Minors no longer could be served in any bar in Anaconda.

But I wasn't through with the bars yet. Next I pushed the sheriff to do something about the illegal gambling. I'd seen men lose a week's pay, and wondered what their families would do for food until the next paycheck.

The sheriff sighed and flashed a grin. "All right, but it's the same situation. You'll have to see money being exchanged with your own eyes and be prepared to testify in court."

I reported dozens of violations in detail, branding the offending bars, describing the gambling, naming names of some particularly conspicuous losers, itemizing the amounts of money shuffled back and forth across the tables and into the slot machines.

The district attorney again refused to act. He said it would be impossible to build a case—there would be too many who would deny my charges. It would be the combined word of the bar barons against mine.

Accustomed to the D.A.'s don't-let's-rock-the-boat attitude, the sheriff took matters into his own hands and began a series of no-warning raids. He confiscated poker tables and slot machines, and stored them downtown as evidence. The owners were told they were "under suspicion." Though not a single case reached court, the sheriff's tactics dried up the public gambling.

Serving drinks to minors and gambling, unfortunately, were not completely wiped out. A teen-ager could still get a *sub rosa* shot and the gambling went underground, but at least the abuses were controlled, and undoubtedly many gamblers and underage drinkers found it not worth the effort to indulge their vices.

Incidentally, none of the newspapers throughout southern Montana printed a word about the efforts that were being made to clean up Anaconda. Freedom of the press evidently also meant the freedom to suppress news. One muckraking journalist, backed by an honest, crusading editor, could have started a fusillade that would have compelled the district attorney to really put Anaconda's house in order. But here, too, it seemed that apathy was king.

I continued to street-witness and bring sinners to Jesus. One night I was witnessing outside the bars, trying to reach the drink-sodden patrons as they emerged. From the corner of my eye, I noticed a tall, heavy-set man, about thirty years old, watching me.

One of the barflies was on her knees with me, accepting Christ. When the prayer ended and the girl promised to meet me the next day at church, the on-looker approached. "Can I buy you a cup of coffee?"

Astonishingly, he was an Episcopal priest. As we talked he told me that a crisis of faith had enveloped him—he was no longer certain of his belief in God or the efficaciousness of the church, though he was ordained and had been a minister for several years.

We talked for hours about the nature of Grace and the saving power of God, and in describing my own travails in building a church in Anaconda I emphasized how important faith was.

He said he'd like to hear me preach, and so he began coming to our Sunday services, always standing to the rear, not joining the congregation. Perhaps he was afraid of being seen in a church pastored by someone considered an apostate among most of Anaconda's citizens. He always left at the moment I gave the invitation.

One evening he came to my room and said he still didn't have the assurance of Christ in his heart. He asked me to pray with him.

The prayer we said together changed his life and gave him holy boldness. Now he was truly saved.

Several weeks later he told me, "I've transformed the whole focus and program of our church. I'm preaching like you, we're singing hymns, quoting Scripture, and I'm asking people to step forward and dedicate their lives to Christ so that they can be saved."

. He was, we both realized, departing in some measure from the tenets of Episcopal doctrine. "But," he said, "this is the way religion was meant to be."

Soon word of a stray lamb reached his superiors. A contingent of church investigators was sent to examine his ministerial conduct. Evidently, he didn't come off well.

He was transferred to Chicago where his "case" was under review. I tried to phone him several times, but no one would tell me where he was. I often wonder how he has fared. He was a good man of God and I trust time has dealt kindly with him, allowing him the opportunity of leading the lost to Christ.

The First Southern Baptist Church of Anaconda was now a congregation of more than fifty. We were formally constituted a church instead of a mission on September 28, 1962. Since I was now "legitimate," ministers from several of Anaconda's other churches began to visit me for the first time. They welcomed me into the official fraternity of the city's church community.

By early December, six eventful months had passed. The church was established, rock-solid, and I had led hundreds to the Lord through personal witnessing. It was time for me to return to school in Mississippi.

My replacement was Pastor Tommy Huskins, who carried on brilliantly. The church now has its own building, a new House of God, its cross emblazoned against the harsh Montana sky, a symbol of compassion, love, and honor to Christ.

Anaconda was a turning point in my life. "For verily I say unto you, If ye have faith as a grain of mustard seed, ye shall say unto this mountain, Move from here to yonder place; and it shall move; and nothing shall be impossible unto you." So said Jesus in Matthew 17:20, and so had it come to pass among the buttes and peaks of the Montana wilderness.

During many a long, sleepless night my faith and commitment to the ministry had reached their nadir in the face of so many disappointments, as had the faith and commitment of my Episcopal friend. But always the truth came back to me—I was being tested. Anaconda had been my proving ground. Come what may, I was going to stick with the ministry all my life. That and salvation through Christ became the two guiding certainties of the passing moment of my existence on this earth.

The snows of Montana fell in thick, twisting flakes the night I was preparing to leave Anaconda. I had preached my last sermon and had shared several wonderful hours of fellowship with my congregation at a small going-away party they gave me.

The temperature lurked at zero as I stepped into my car, which was still in abysmal shape—no heater, holes in the floor board, no muffler or tailpipe.

I fought the snow and ice, letting the car coast down the mountains and praying it up the steep inclines, without seeing a sign of civilization until I reached Billings. I drove straight through to Mississippi, eating once a day and sleeping at the side of the road. I arrived home in time to spend Christmas with the family.

"I don't know if you told us everything in your letters, Son," said Dad soon after I walked in to the house. "How was Anaconda, *really?*"

"Cold to the skin, warm to the spirit."

"Was it as tough as Mr. Cooper said it would be?"

"It *was* tough, but not too tough to crack."

6

In My Father's House Are Many Mansions

B YRON DE LA BECKWITH, charged with the rifle assassination of civil rights leader Medgar Evers, a slaying that had caused world-wide attention, was a southerner as southern as Peachtree Street, grits, and Jefferson Davis. (Beckwith's grandmother, the pride of his family tree, had been a personal friend of the Confederate president.)

I was back at school and back to devoting Thursday afternoons to witnessing at the Jackson jail. I had received permission to talk with Beckwith.

He was thin and ruddy-complected, five feet seven inches and 160 pounds of enigma. When I stepped into his cell the first time, I was surprised to find it so commodious. It was much larger than any of the other cells and was supplied with a television set, radio, and a raft of reading matter.

"Welcome, Preacher," Beckwith said smoothly after I introduced myself. I felt uncomfortable with the man. He was an avowed segregationist, a member of the notorious White Citizens Council, and, according to stories in the papers quoting his friends, capable of flying into a rage at the mere suggestion that Negroes deserved rights equal to those of white men.

"Did you do it, Mr. Beckwith? Did you murder Medgar Evers?" I asked him, not as a detective, but as an agent of the Lord concerned with the fate of his immortal soul if he had violated the commandment against killing, a commandment written by God's own finger.

Beckwith, shrewd and clever, had a quick, evasive answer. "I appreciate your being here. I'd like to talk to you about the Bible."

I wasn't certain if he was truly interested in the Scripture or was warding off ennui by amusing himself with a new visitor.

"It's a tragic thing to take the life of another man, Mr. Beckwith."

He looked at me noncommittally out of silent, piercing eyes.

"Are you saved?"

"I'm a Christian," he said.   Beckwith was an Episcopalian.

I witnessed to Beckwith for several months. He was, if anything, too friendly, given to frequent laughter. He didn't act like a man accused of murder. (He was later acquitted after two trials ended in jury deadlocks.)

I was interested primarily in his relationship with the Lord, and thought what a vaulting testimony it would be if Beckwith publicly committed his life to Christ.

I gave him a Bible and a number of tracts, but whenever I asked if he'd had a direct spiritual encounter with Christ, his answer was always the same, "I'm a Christian."

"But are you *really* saved?" I persisted.

"I've got Jesus in my heart, yes."

It was the right answer, but I still wondered about the strength of his commitment. He seemed typical of so many people in the South who've gone to church all their lives and have memorized just enough superficial religious jargon to get the preachers off their backs.

Beckwith's answer called to mind James 1:26, which poses the test of true belief: "If any man among you seem to be religious, and bridleth not his tongue, but deceiveth his own heart, this man's religion *is* vain."

I never had any peace about Beckwith's convictions. It didn't appear to me that he'd had a clear conversion experience.

"Don't worry about me, I'm okay," he said at our last meeting.

"Are you certain Jesus lives in your heart?"

"Sure, I've taken care of that. It's all right. You'd better get along and talk to some of these men who need more help than I do."

Aside from my uncertainty about Beckwith's kinship with God, I noted two obvious circumstances of his imprisonment: His jailors treated him like a hero, and the trustees, many of whom were Negroes, systematically avoided going near him.

Preaching and witnessing still came before my classroom work at school. Unbeknownst to me, the letters I had sent Mr. Cooper from Montana were edited by him and copies were sent to radio stations and newspapers all over the South. The Jackson *Clarion-Ledger*, the Atlanta *Journal*, the Memphis *Commercial Appeal*, and all the Baptist press printed stories about my stay in Anaconda. As a result I was asked to preach about Montana at two of the largest churches in the South, Jackson's First Baptist and Calvary Baptist. From February through mid-August, I preached eighty messages in forty-two churches throughout Mississippi and Louisiana. In addition to regular church services, I talked at youth revivals, retreats, rallies, and banquets. I felt like the Christian in Acts 4:20: "For we cannot but speak the things which we have seen and heard."

A rare, free evening coincided with an appearance of famed evangelist Eddy Martin at Calvary Baptist Church. I decided to attend with a friend, Bryan Knight.

During the singing Bryan pointed to two girls he knew sitting several pews in front of us. Thus I caught my first glimpse of lovely Sherry Simmons, her chiseled face smiling under a halo of dark brown hair.

When the sermon ended, Bryan introduced me to Sherry. She had the most electric brown eyes I'd ever seen. Standing in the church aisle, the crowd around us parting like the Red Sea, we talked for a few moments and I learned that she and her girl friend, Rebecca Skinner, were in training at Jackson's Baptist Hospital nursing school.

The four of us drove back to the girls' dorm and I jotted down Sherry's name and phone number on a card. I was attracted to her, but I was so busy preaching and attending class that it was two months before I had a chance to call her for a date.

We went to a drive-in movie, and never noticed the screen as we shared experiences about our lives—neither of us dreaming that in nineteen days we would be man and wife.

When I got back to the dorm I was in a daze. I woke Bill Mosley and announced excitedly, "I'm going to marry Sherry Simmons. She's the girl for me!"

Two nights later Sherry and I were parked outside town and I was telling her about an upcoming revival I was scheduled to preach. "Let's pray about it," I said. I prayed, but then I heard a prayer the like of which I'd never heard before. Sherry's prayer, calling for Divine guidance and aid for the success of the revival, was one of passion, glory, and beauty. I didn't know anyone could be that articulate and fervent in talking to God.

Sherry told me she planned to devote her life to full-time Christian service as a nurse.

Then I leaned over and kissed her for the first time.

"I feel numb," I said.

"So do I."

"If you loved me, do you think you could marry me?"

"Yes."

"Don't say another word, Sherry, because if you do, I *will* ask you to marry me."

Her eyes shone with surprise and she grinned deliciously.

It was all happening too fast, but I felt powerless to control the deep feeling I had so swiftly developed for her.

The next day we attended a party given by my Spanish teacher for his students. Except for Sherry's presence, it was a frustrating experience since we were all expected to speak Spanish. My ignorance of that language was still encyclopedic, so I barely said a word.

After the party, I drove Sherry home to Bogalusa. I was so broke that she had to buy the gas. We rolled over the hilly roads through 130 miles of southern Mississippi and Louisiana.

My mind was boiling and suddenly I swerved the car to the side of the road and parked on a small ridge. The only thing in sight was an unromantic oil well, but that didn't matter.

"Sherry, the Lord's given me a love for you."

"He's put love into my heart for you, too."

"I feel the Lord leading me. What would you say if I said I wanted to marry you?"

"I'd say yes."

The compact was sealed with our second kiss.

I don't recommend whirlwind courtship and marriage as a rule. I've seen far too many couples take their vows in haste only to repent soon afterward in leisure, turning to drugs and/or drink and/or promiscuity to drown their bitterness and disappointment. This is particularly true for teen-agers, whose divorce rate is the highest in the nation, now exceeding 50 percent and still climbing.

But Sherry and I agreed that in our marriage the Lord would always come first, and that is the reason why our union will last "until death do us part."

I was scheduled to graduate three weeks before Sherry did. I had decided to further my studies at Golden Gate Baptist Theological Seminary, near San Francisco, choosing California to broaden my experience outside the South. Sherry would fly out and join me as soon as she graduated.

The day I asked Sherry to marry me I had $3.08 in my pocket, but I preached at several revivals, and the offerings I received gave us $330 with which to start married life.

The wedding was scheduled for 2 P.M. at Superior Baptist Church in Bogalusa. I had made only two demands in connection with our ceremony: We were to have only one bouquet of flowers, the rest of the flower money to be contributed to the support of missionaries or the poor. I also insisted that Gladys Daniels, the good-natured Negro woman who had worked for Sherry's parents for fifteen years, attend the wedding. To my knowledge we had the first integrated wedding in Bogalusa, a hard-core segregationist town of twenty-five thousand, a stronghold of the Ku Klux Klan, which was to become nationally infamous when racial violence exploded there in 1965 and 1967.

An hour before the wedding I was in a drugstore looking for a wedding present for my best man, Paul Moody, who was loaning us his house in Clinton for our honeymoon.

As the lady clerk searched her stock for a suitable tie pin, I began witnessing to her. Seeing us in prolonged, animated conversation, the manager came over. I began witnessing to him, too. I found they both were churchgoers and saved, but weren't witnessing and serving the Lord the way they should. The three of us said a prayer together, and then I remembered I was due at the altar in fifteen minutes.

I hurried to the church, dressed in record time, and tried to ignore the questioning if not exasperated looks of Sherry's parents, my parents, the minister, Paul, and the guests, all of whom were no doubt wondering about the prospects of a marriage in which the bridegroom reaches the altar within seconds of the appointed time.

Sherry's pastor, the Reverend Sollie Smith, performed the ceremony, and after the reception we drove to Jackson. When we stopped for our wedding supper both of us began witnessing to our waitress. She got so under conviction she spilled water on the table, and in our zeal we almost forgot to order.

The first thing Sherry and I did on the first night we spent together was to pray and read from the Bible, a custom we have followed every day of our lives. We have continued to honor our pledge that in our house the Lord always comes first.

I naturally anticipated going to California with my diploma, but it was not to be. Because of my ingrained dislike of Spanish, I failed to graduate. I found out that I had flunked my last semester of Spanish only four hours before the commencement exercises. I came so close to graduating that my diploma was signed and ready, my name appeared in the list of graduates in the newspapers, and an embarrassed dean even called my name from the platform. ("He didn't make it," someone finally whispered to him frantically.)

I was urged to make up the course in summer school, but I didn't want to waste the time. I was primed for the seminary, and I was certain I had learned all I could at Mississippi College. The formal degree didn't mean a thing to me.

But the seminary was a disappointment. There were a number of things about it that irritated me. Friends from Mississippi and Louisiana had written about me to several churches in the San Francisco area, which resulted in a number of invitations for me to preach. But those invitations were kept secret from me.

When I finally learned about them, I marched into the president's office and asked for an explanation of why I couldn't preach.

"We heard that when you were at Mississippi College, you did so much preaching your grades were poor. We don't want you to preach that much around here. We want you to study for three years and prepare yourself. Then you can go out and preach all the time."

"Does that mean you're forbidding me to preach?"

"You're here to learn how to become a minister."

"I'm already a minister, and I've pastored two churches. There's no reason why I can't study *and* preach."

"It's your choice—you either study and make good grades or you preach."

I elected to do both. I preached at a number of nearby churches and maintained a straight B average except for a D in Greek. But I was beginning to chafe at many of my required classes. I had already completed a college course in Old Testament survey, and I didn't need further instruction on how to organize a song meeting and a mission station.

Denying me official permission to spread the Word was bad enough, but denying us permission to cook on a hot plate in our tiny basement apartment was a matter of some moment. Sherry and I were told that home cooking was strictly against the rules—we had to eat in the cafeteria. The only problem was that we couldn't afford to eat in the cafeteria.

There were some four hundred students studying to be preachers at Golden Gate. What a juggernaut for the Lord it would be, I thought, if we were all turned loose in shifts several days a week to witness in San Francisco. We could shake the city by the bay. Instead, what was shaking the city at this time were the first topless dancers. And Haight-Ashbury was beginning to fill up with what would become a legendary invasion of hippies. San Francisco led the nation in alcoholics, and the North Beach section was a stench in the nostrils of God.

What a mission field San Francisco was. It was a city that needed saving. But when I made the suggestion to several of my professors that every student in school be sent forth to witness throughout San Francisco, they looked at me strangely. I knew that they were thinking: I was either a lunatic or a religious fanatic, and I wasn't certain which they considered worse.

Only one or two of the professors were evangelical-minded and believed as I did that the Bible commanded men to spread the Gospel. As for my fellow students, the majority were arch-liberals in their interpretation of the Scriptures. They questioned, philosophized, and expressed doubt about much in the Holy Book instead of simply accepting it as the inspired Word of the Lord.

At Golden Gate, I didn't see any fires burning for God. Few professors or students believed that everybody had to be saved. They were cold in spirit. Nobody witnessed; there were no prayer meetings.

The courses were geared to training students to "adjust" to the communities in which they would eventually pastor, and it was made plain that it wouldn't hurt to ingratiate oneself with the best people in the congregation. "Best" translated into wealthiest. This emphasis infuriated me. Christ witnessed to all types of people, not just the "best" or the wealthiest. And Christ did not consider witnessing in public embarrassing, as did virtually all of the seminary's professors and students.

The school was trying to make the church fit the community instead of making the community fit the church. The focus was on making scholars out of the students. But I decided I would rather be ignorant and on fire than be a scholar and spiritually dead. I also decided that since the seminary offered no challenge, I was throwing away more precious time.

Then a wondeful thing happened on Christmas night while Sherry and I were driving down San Francisco's Market Street.

"I feel the Lord calling us to the desert, to Nevada," Sherry said.

It was a miraculous coincidence. I hadn't mentioned it to Sherry, but the same urge to bring the Gospel to the most sin-soaked state in America had been building in me for some time. Perhaps the call to go to Nevada was direct from God or perhaps it had formed in our minds when we heard from a friend that there was a large area in Nevada that didn't have a single evangelical church. We didn't stop to analyze the wellspring of our inspiration.

Instead we went home and packed.

On New Year's Day our car crossed the Nevada line.

I had no church.

We had no home.

Our assets were five dollars, a battered car . . . and all the faith in the world.

Also, Sherry was pregnant.

7

Circuit Rider,
Twentieth-Century Style

Sᴀᴅᴅʟᴇʙᴀɢ ᴘʀᴇᴀᴄʜᴇʀs, many of whom were as familiar with a six-shooter as with salvation, won all the enormous territory west of the Mississippi for God in the last half of the nineteenth century.

The vast majority of these circuit riders were lions for the Lord; a few were mutations. The bad ones reflected the violent era when plowshares were often beaten into pistols.

The Reverend Mr. McGilvary rode into Gun Sling, Arizona, on January 2, 1880, and headed straight for the saloon. Passing the tables jammed with miners and cowhands playing monte, faro, rondeau, chuck-a-luck, and keno, he laid his shooting iron on the bar and shouted, "Boys, let's pray." At the conclusion of the prayer—though it is unrecorded, it is unlikely that anyone was saved on that occasion—the Reverend Mr. McGilvary pulled up a chair and joined a game of draw poker.

Joseph Thompson Hare considered himself a preacher. But Joseph Thompson Hare was considered a bandit by lawmen of three midwestern states, since his sole means of livelihood was robbing stagecoaches. "Preacher" Hare read to members of his gang from the writings of John Wesley. He even converted several! He held prayer meetings before each holdup and between holdups he studied the Bible by the hour. His career as a connoisseur of the Scriptures and soul-saver came to an abrupt end when he was caught and hanged.

Kansas gunslinger Clay Allison was noted around Dodge City

for herding passers-by into a saloon whenever the spirit moved him to preach a sermon. They all listened. They had to. Clay had a Bible in one hand, a Colt .45 in the other.

The circuit riders experienced lighter moments, too, moments that illustrate the painful penetration of the Gospel in the early West.

Cheyenne, Wyoming, was part of the Reverend Cornelius Dowling's circuit. His small faith in the biblical knowledge of his flock was jusified when he asked a blacksmith, "Who killed Abel?" The man scratched his beard, thought a moment, and replied, "I didn't know he was dead. We just moved here last week."

The territory of the circuit riders extended over thousands of miles of harsh frontier. The riders preached against liquor and the Devil at camp meetings and revivals. They spread the Word, won millions to the faith, and built the churches.

They were tough, hardbitten, and dedicated men. They had to be to survive.

As I was to learn soon enough, the days of the circuit rider in the West were far from over.

The only preacher Sherry and I knew in Nevada was LaVern Inzer, founder and pastor of the First Baptist Church of Winnemucca, a small community of about 3,500. LaVern was a contemporary circuit rider who had established a string of twenty churches through the northeastern portion of the state. He had a grueling schedule, visiting each of his churches at least once a month. And he always responded immediately to an emergency call from anyone anywhere on his circuit.

The life of this wiry, tireless servant of the Lord is filled with fascinating incidents. For instance, while serving on a Pacific island during World War II, he arranged a Christmas truce between American and Japanese fighting men. The enemies spent the eve of the celebration of the Lord's birth in fellowship and singing carols!

When LaVern arrived in Winnemucca, he found the town harbored three thriving houses of prostitution. He also found that rarest of treasures in Nevada, an honest public official. With the aid of State Attorney General Roger D. Foley and several of his undercover agents, LaVern gathered enough evidence against the houses to force a trial. Prostitution was officially outlawed by the state, but it was a matter of local option as to whether the law should be enforced. On a complaint from a private citizen or organization the houses could be closed as public nuisances. LaVern had made such a complaint, but when the case came to trial, he lost for an understandable reason: The all-female jury was composed of three madams and nine prostitutes!

Unable to support his family on a pastor's salary, LaVern took a weekday job as a bookkeeper in a lumberyard. A local vice lord got him fired. After this latest intimidation, Foley wrote to LaVern from Carson City and released the letter to the press. It said:

It is a sad state of affairs indeed when a zealous minister of the Gospel jeopardizes the welfare of his family when he seeks only to have the law enforced. Or, stated otherwise, in Winnemucca a minister's family must suffer privation so that houses of prostitution can operate and public officials can flaunt the law.

Shortly after this episode, LaVern was having supper with his wife and five children when a bomb exploded in his basement. Flames licked quickly through the house and the seven Inzers barely escaped in time.

Despite these hardships, LaVern was still as tough and uncompromising as a hungry tiger. He greeted Sherry and me enthusiastically and invited me to preach at his church. His congregation held a food shower for us. The canned goods that Sherry and I gratefully received kept us eating for weeks.

"I can't cover the whole state," LaVern told me when we discussed my future in Nevada. "There's plenty of work to be done in and around Elko."

"Then that's where we'll go," I said.

Thus began my own baptism as a circuit rider.

In the eighteen months we spent in Nevada I managed to establish a network of five outposts for Christ within a fifty-mile radius.

1. Elko. Population, 6,300. After Las Vegas and Reno, Nevada's largest city. Cold, bare, and dead in spirit. Less than a dozen churches; fifty-four liquor stores; five houses of prostitution staffed by more than one hundred girls; three huge gambling casinos grossing between $3 million and $5 million a year.

With two blank checks given to us by LaVern we paid the first month's rent on a tiny furnished basement apartment and hired the Rebecca Lodge for five dollars an hour.

Sherry and I declared the Calvary Baptist Church of Elko as a new house of God.

I bought a half hour of Sunday morning time on KELK, the local radio station, on faith (the bill wasn't due until the end of the month), and announced our first service. I also placed an ad in the paper.

We set up seventy-five folding chairs for the anticipated crowd. Sherry played the piano, and we raised our voices to sing the hymns. Then I preached on "The Dedication of Our Lives to Him."

It was worse than my first service in Anaconda. This time not a single citizen of Elko turned out. Only Sherry heard my sermon. Yet it was just as important as any sermon I ever preached because it was heard by God, too. It didn't matter to me that all the chairs were empty. If your church is filled to overflowing with people eager to hear the tidings of Christ, that's wonderful, but if there's no one to hear you, that's wonderful, too. Our commitment to Christ wasn't based on whether people came to our church or not. Jesus said in Matthew 18:20, "For where two or three are gathered together in my name, there am I in the midst of them." Yet He also advocated spreading the Gospel, so Sherry and I set ourselves the task of rounding up a flock. The need in Elko was Grand Canyon–wide.

I buttressed my appeals on radio with a telephone survey (eight were led to the Lord over the phone) and knocked on every door in town.

The church grew, our membership seesawing between 50 and 120. Elko, like virtually all of Nevada, had a large floating population: in-and-outers, retirees who came for short stays in the dry sun, construction crews temporarily in residence for a one-shot building project, a sea of compulsive gamblers who went home slack-jawed when their finances were inevitably depleted, and a legion of hookers, barmaids, and cocktail waitresses, who eventually became disenchanted by life in the sin-splashed desert. We'd win people to the Lord, they would attend church for a while, and then move on, their places taken by fresh arrivals, each of whom we tried to reach as soon as possible.

Perseverance bore fruit as our congregation rose phoenixlike from the ashes of indifference. Among those who became loyal parishioners were three I brought to Christ, a trio who had been vegetating at the bottom rung of the sociological ladder: a convicted killer, once on the FBI's Ten Most Wanted list, who became my assistant pastor, a former prostitute who taught one of our Sunday school grades, and an ex-alcoholic who became Sunday school superintendent in charge of all our classes.

Our church expanded to the point where land was purchased for a building, which was constructed after my departure.

Sherry and I were named missionaries by the Home Missions Board of the Southern Baptist Convention, and $150 a month flowed in from this source. It was supplemented by another monthly check for $100 from the Linn Baptist Church in Mississippi, whose committed congregation had also helped me in Montana. This $250 wasn't our money; it was for the ministry. We made do with offerings and unsolicited and unexpected contributions from individuals and churches who became interested in our work. There were days when meals were missed, months when we were almost evicted from our apartment for nonpayment of rent. But somehow our personal expenses were always met. On one occasion a $100 check arrived when the power company was moments away from turning off our electricity, and we had no food or gas for the car. The Lord unfailingly bailed us out each time financial distress occurred. He did so, I am certain, because He wanted His work in Nevada carried forward.

2. Our second outpost for Christ was in Carlin: population, 1,023. A twenty-three-mile drive from Elko through a mountain pass. Three churches—Catholic, Community, and Mormon. And now a fourth! Sherry, myself, and Ralph Jackson, a member of our Elko congregation, were the only worshippers present during our initial service at the Oddfellows' hall, which I had rented for the day for ten dollars. The three of us voted unanimously to start the Carlin Baptist Church.

After distributing handbills throughout the town, our attendance the next Sunday was twenty-two.

Several weeks later we held a revival. Forty men, women, and children came. That may not seem like many to a minister of a large church in New York, Chicago, or Los Angeles, but it certainly impressed one six-year-old girl. Following the services she asked me, "Are all these people Christians?" "Yes," I said. Eyes aglow, she observed in wonder, "I didn't know there were this many Christians in the whole world."

Shortly after we arrived in Carlin, the town was hit by what the local paper described as "America's biggest gold strike in the 20th century."

Hundreds of people poured in. Trailer camps mushroomed. A ten-million-dollar gold-processing plant was built.

From the new arrivals came most of those who joined our church. Rootless and in need of God's comfort, ham-handed miners, masons, plasterers, and laborers with their wives and children came for worship. And soon our Sunday school had twenty young people.

Just before the gold boom, fortunately, we purchased a lot in town with a five-thousand-dollar loan from the Southern Baptist Convention. The Carlin Baptist Church building was completed shortly after I left Nevada. The new pastor: Bill Mosley, the college friend who had shared my outrage at the hands of the Jackson police for shaking hands with a Negro.

3. The Nevada Youth Training School, a euphemism for a tautly-run, old-fashioned reform school five minutes outside of Elko. Inmates: 150 boys under eighteen confined for everything from vagrancy to murder.

Only one boy came to our first service, but he received Christ as his Savior. He went back and told his buddies of the thrilling experience of his new birth. Soon more than half the boys in the school were attending our Wednesday evening service.

The toughest kid there was a seventeen-year-old who'd been stealing since he was six. Snotty, aggressive, mistrustful, he challenged me to prove my sincerity. I spent a great deal of time with him. I didn't put him down, fuss over him, or pamper him. I was firm and friendly and extended a fatherly discipline he'd never had. He finally won respect for himself, and learned to respect others and their property. He not only came to the Lord, but was one of two boys at the school who surrendered to preach!

In all, fifty boys were saved, each conversion changing each life in a meaningful way.

Escorted by guards, many of the boys attended Sunday morning services at our church in Elko. We didn't bunch them in a corner, segregating them from the rest of the congregation, or embarrass them by introducing "our visitors from the Nevada Youth Training School." They had suffered such unfeeling nonsense and needless humiliation at other churches in Elko, and they never made a second appearance at those churches, which apparently suited my fellow pastors and their congregations. They were afraid of the kids and had written them off as incorrigibles.

When there was time, the authorities let me check out a couple of the kids for a day's drive in the country, a picnic, or a home-cooked meal at our apartment. The boys would tag along, wide-eyed, as I witnessed at every opportunity.

After prayer and my sermon each week, the kids would gang around me for a bull session about the Bible. The questions exploded like flak, and I did my best to answer: "How do you know the Bible is true?" "If Jesus was God's son, who made God?" "You mean to tell me Jonah was swallowed by a whale?" "If they'd had social security then, how much would Methuselah have collected?"

4. Lamoille. A postage-stamp community of 230 set like an emerald in a green, grassy, beautiful valley twenty-five miles south of Elko. About 500 people, most of them ranchers, living in the surrounding hills. No one bothered to come to our first service in Community Hall. In fact, it was three weeks before anyone came. The trigger that activated the local population was our Vacation Bible School. Thirty youngsters enrolled; four of them were saved.

Lamoille was nearly as close-knit as Carlin. Since the children had not yet developed resentment against "outsiders," we drew our strength almost exclusively from the young people.

Lamoille is a children's mission that will one day mature into a fine church.

5. Wells—1,071 souls. Fifty miles east of Elko toward Utah. We made our breakthrough here by starting another Vacation Bible School at the $7.50-a-day Knights of Pythias hall. After visiting house to house, 25 adults also began attending.

The church was growing, until a scandal destroyed our work.

One day after Bible school, a seemingly pleasant, middle-aged couple volunteered to drive one family's two children home. I saw no reason to refuse their thoughtful gesture.

But the drive home was eventful.

I was shocked when I heard that the couple had sexually molested the children in their car.

It was the biggest crisis I had faced in Nevada up to that time. I called LaVern in Winnemucca, and he laughed bitterly. He knew the couple: They had been involved in a similar incident at his church.

I next called the district attorney, and he issued an All Points Bulletin.

When I went to visit the mother of the assaulted children, she cursed me for a solid five minutes before she thundered that she wouldn't permit her kids to attend our school again. Then, and no mistaking the finality, the door was slammed in my face. I hadn't had a chance to say a word.

The offending couple was finally traced to San Francisco, where they had joined a leading church. LaVern sent a note to their new pastor, warning him that he had a man-and-wife team of perverts in his congregation.

"You must have the wrong couple," the pastor wrote back, "they are two of the finest Christians I've ever known."

The pair successfully fought extradition, and were never brought to trial for their offense.

The incident clouded our work and credibility in Wells. The adult congregation dwindled to a dozen, and only twenty children remained in Sunday school.

The town has been slow to forgive a disgusting act perpetrated by a godless, emotionally sick pair of sex offenders, whose action I could not possibly have anticipated. Score a temporary victory in Wells for Satan.

The five-stop circuit made for a busy week. I navigated between the points of my network on an almost split-second schedule in a shambling Fiat I had traded for my Ford.

SUNDAY

    8 A.M. Radio broadcast, Elko.

    9 A.M. Sunday school, Elko.

  10 A.M. Morning worship, Elko.

    1 P.M. Sunday school, Carlin.

    2 P.M. Worship service, Carlin.

    4 P.M. Sunday school, Lamoille.

    5 P.M. Worship service, Lamoille.

    7 P.M. Evening worship, Elko.

MONDAY

    7 P.M. Sunday school, Wells.

    8 P.M. Worship service, Wells.

TUESDAY
Church witnessing, Elko, Carlin, Lamoille.
WEDNESDAY
6:30–7:30 P.M. Nevada Youth Training School, Elko.
8:15 P.M. Prayer meeting and Bible study, Carlin.
THURSDAY
7 P.M. Prayer meeting and Bible study, Elko.
FRIDAY
6 P.M. Youth Fellowship, Elko.

Saturdays Sherry and I devoted to street-witnessing, our own Bible study, preparing sermons, household chores and shopping, answering emergency calls from parishioners beset by sudden problems, and, occasionally, sneaking away to be by ourselves.

On a Wednesday night in August I was at the Training School when Sherry called, "The pains are coming every few minutes."

I rushed home and got Sherry to the hospital.

A few hours later the doctor showed me my beautiful, curly-haired eight-pound four-ounce daughter.

I ran to the phone and called Sherry's parents and my own folks with the joyful news.

A short time later the doctor came to see me again. He had a frighteningly sober look on his face.

"What's wrong?"

"We're having trouble with the afterbirth. Your wife's hemorrhaging. I don't know if we can stop the bleeding. She's under oxygen. We're doing all we can."

The tone of the doctor's voice was unmistakably pessimistic.

I went to the phone again and called everyone I could think of—our parents, members of our congregations, and friends.

We soon had a prayer chain extending from Nevada to Mississippi.

Two doctors and a nurse worked over Sherry for an hour and forty-five minutes. Then our doctor came out and said, "It's a miracle, a first-class, honest-to-God miracle. Your wife just made it by a few heartbeats. I thought we'd lost her."

The prayer chain had worked!

It is proper and natural that the beginning of a new life in some way mark the beginning of all life. Our first child was consecrated for the first book of the Bible.

From Genesis we derived the name Gina.

8

Trio

The Second Coming and the
Prostitutes of the Lucky Strike

Now A PEPPERY eighty-two, Eunice Slaughter had traveled with her husband from Missouri to a Montana homestead via wagon train. Construction of a government dam had forced them out, and they had moved to Elko.

Mrs. Slaughter was one of the first to join our church, and though she had never before in her long life witnessed for the Lord, she became imbued with the spirit and staked out as her special targets the girls who lived and worked at the Lucky Strike house of prostitution, located next door to her home.

One afternoon Mrs. Slaughter was sitting in the parlor of the Lucky Strike, surrounded by the madam and all her girls.

"I'm telling everyone of you to get right with the Lord. If you don't repent, you're all going to hell as soon as Jesus comes again."

"How'll we know when Jesus comes again?" one of the girls asked.

Mrs. Slaughter's wrinkled face was stern. "When Jesus returns," she said with a certitude that left no room for doubt, "the heavens are going to open up, the trumpets will sound, and you'll hear that good old gospel music!"

I didn't know about Mrs. Slaughter's witnessing session when I went down to witness myself the evening of the same day to the old, discarded prostitutes who lived in a cluster of squalid cabins directly behind the Lucky Strike.

As I approached, I heard a burst of raucous noise slash through the cold winter night from one of the cabins. The scene when I entered through the open door was straight out of the inferno. The small room was filled with perhaps twenty elderly men and women, all roaring drunk. One woman and two men were lying on the bed passed out.

A big fellow walked up to me. "I know you, you're the preacher."

"That's right."

"If you're a preacher, let me hear you preach." He called for quiet and in a moment all was stillness. "Now you preach."

I opened my Bible and read from John 3:16, " 'For God so loved the world, that he gave his only begotten Son, that whosoever believeth in him should not perish, but have everlasting life.' " Then I went on for about ten minutes, emphasizing the importance of embracing Christ.

"I want to be saved," one of the wizened whores pleaded.

I got on my knees and prayed, leading her to the Lord.

"That was a damn fine sermon and prayer," the big fellow said. "Now let's sing."

We formed a circle and joined hands. Soon the loud sound of "The Old Rugged Cross" filled the cabin and wafted out through the open door.

> On a hill far away stood an old rugged cross,
> The emblem of suffering and shame;
> And I love that old cross . . .

Above the music I suddenly heard piercing screams. I ran outside in time to see the powerful backyard floodlights of the Lucky Strike send shards of glare through the darkness. Less than twenty feet away, fifteen windows zipped up. The singing was still going on in the cabin, louder than ever. . . .

> So I'll cherish the old rugged cross . . .

At each open window was a prostitute. They were baying at the top of their lungs. I was thoroughly perplexed as I heard them shout:

"Jesus is here!"

"Just like Mrs. Slaughter said."

"Forgive me, Lord!"

The singing and shouting went on for a full fifteen minutes as I stood between the cabin and the Lucky Strike dumbstruck at the thought that everybody in sight had somehow come dramatically under conviction.

The next day as she was telling me about her witnessing session with the prostitutes, Mrs. Slaughter, who was partially deaf, said, "Preacher, I could swear I heard gospel singing last evening."

"You did," and I gave her the details of the impromptu revival in the cabin and the screams from the girls.

She looked at me out of wise old eyes. "Then that explains it," Mrs. Slaughter said.

"Explains what?"

"I stopped at the Lucky Strike on my way over here. That madam is as upset as a rooster without hens."

"Why?"

Mrs. Slaughter said, "She told me that for some reason last night her three best girls packed and hightailed it out of town."

"Killer Christian"

Louisiana-born Louis McDonald had brown hair, quick dark eyes, a firm handshake, an overwhelming personality, and perhaps the most amazing story of a restructured Christian life that I've ever heard.

I met him while Sherry was recovering from the birth of Gina and her near-miss with death at Elko General Hospital. After visiting Sherry, I'd go from floor to floor and door to door, looking in on patients.

Mac was in traction when I stepped into his room and introduced myself.

Truculent and bitter, he gave it to me straight from the gut.

"I don't want a thing to do with you. I've had it with every damn Baptist preacher in the world. You're all nothing but a gang of frauds and opportunists. I'm not interested in anything you have to say. Go somewhere else. I've got trouble enough. I'm paralyzed from the waist down and the doctor says I'll never walk again."

"Let me leave a tract with you."

"Keep it. I know it by heart. I know it backwards and forwards. I was a Baptist preacher myself!"

Here was a man desperate for help. Once a messenger of the Lord, he was living now outside God's will. I wasn't about to be discouraged, no matter how resoundingly he rejected me.

I visited him again the next day. He was still in high dudgeon. When I tried to talk about God he cut me off with a curse. After a week he softened and, maybe because he was bored lying helplessly in bed, he told me his incredible background.

At sixteen, using a shotgun, he had killed a man who was pistol-whipping his father. Sent to reform school, he escaped a number of times, but was always caught. At nineteen he enlisted in the Marine Corps and fought in Korea.

After his discharge, he killed another man in a barroom brawl in Texas. He claimed self-defense at his trial, but was convicted and sent to prison. He escaped soon afterward, taking with him two guards as hostages.

He then made the FBI's Ten Most Wanted list.

Cornered in a Sacramento, California, hotel, he was slapped into the local jail, and escaped again. He was caught once more. Then followed four more escapes from various prisons. He was hunted down after each breakout and taken back in custody.

After his fifth escape he was caught by the FBI. He went into deeplock at Kansas' Leavenworth prison. His sentence was ten to life.

By now Mac had tired of running and fighting the world. He determined to change. Through prison correspondence courses he earned his high school diploma and credits from the University of Kansas.

Then he was converted and brought to the Lord by a Mennonite minister. Completely rehabilitated, a model prisoner, he was paroled in seven years. Mac was licensed to preach and became an associate pastor at a Baptist church in Kansas.

The tale of the convict-turned-preacher attracted the attention of scores of churches in the Midwest. Requests by the dozens came in for him to give his testimony. Believing he was serving God, Mac accepted every invitation.

Whenever he was scheduled to speak in a city the local pastor, to drum up a crowd, sent a press release with the sensational details of Mac's life to the newspapers. He was heralded in print as the "Killer Christian." He was promoted as a former convict and murderer who had made the Who's Who of the FBI's most wanted list.

The crowds poured in, breathless to hear him, and Mac soon became something of a celebrity. But he realized he had become something else, too: a monkey on a string, a French poodle Christian, exhibited, combed dry, and then sent on his way. He was a showpiece being used to frighten children and sinners.

He began asking the pastors at the churches where he appeared to help him enroll in a Bible college. He wanted to grow as a Christian. But nobody was interested in helping him.

"I never had time to pray. I didn't have time to study. I didn't have time to get strong. I was just running from one place to another testifying."

He wasn't proud of his criminal past. He wished with all his heart he hadn't killed two men. Now he wanted only to preach, omitting most of his gory experiences. However, no one wanted to hear him talk about Jesus. The pastors told him to give his testimony and let them do the preaching.

"I got shook, not in my belief in God, but with the churches. They were exploiting me. Nobody wanted to hear me talk about the Bible. Nobody wanted me to give just a brief testimony about my life, tell how bad it had been and how happy I was since I'd been saved. Those preachers and congregations wanted every grotesque detail, every ounce of sin. The more horrible I made my testimony, the more thrilled they were. It was like a hanging or a bullfight."

In disgust Mac finally stopped testifying and disappeared into a small town in Tennessee. He met a pretty girl, married her, and they began raising a family.

He came to Elko, worked first in a construction gang, then as a truck driver. He earned as much as $7 an hour, working ten to twelve hours a day seven days a week. He had a beautiful trailer home, a luxury car, an expensive wardrobe, and more money than he could spend.

Then one day on the highway something went wrong with his steering wheel. His truck careened off the road and rolled over.

His world caved in. All he could look forward to now was a life as a hopelessly bedridden paralytic.

Week after week, I worked with Mac, trying to rebuild his faith.

"Mac, you got a taste of superficial Christianity and you rebelled. But God isn't through with you. He still wants to use you."

I finally made contact.

"You're my kind of preacher," he smiled.

He started reading his Bible again. We began praying together. I told him that if he had faith God would heal him. Mac then recommitted his life to the Lord.

From the day we said our first healing prayer to God, Mac began to improve. He felt a tingle in his legs. When the doctor pricked him with a pin, he felt pain. The doctor was amazed that he had come that far.

Mac was on the road back, all the way back, and the trip was punctuated by continuous prayer and faith and belief.

Sensation came coursing into his legs. Then a little movement. He got into a wheel chair for the first time to attend services at our church.

The doctor discharged him from the hospital but said there was only a feeble hope that he would walk again.

A few days after leaving the hospital Mac called. When I went to see him, he took a step toward me, then fell flat on his face.

Yet he had taken a step.

Soon he was managing two . . . three . . . a dozen steps. Sometimes his legs buckled under him, but he picked himself up and kept trying.

"God," he declared, "with your help I'll walk again."

From his wheel chair Mac went to braces. Finally, after a few months, he could walk again!

His legs were as good as new.

Mac joined our church, and I led his wife to the Lord and baptized her. Mac not only became my assistant pastor at no salary, but when I couldn't make a preaching service, he'd go in my place. At a church in Wendover, Utah, the congregation was so impressed with his fire that he was asked to become pastor.

He turned the offer down. "I'm not ready to pastor yet," he told me. "I need more training. I don't know if I'll ever pastor. I don't know if God is calling me as a pastor."

No one in Elko except myself knew of Mac's past. His days of lurid testimony were over. Now he preached about Christ, the Bible, and the thrilling life of dedication to God.

He led several people to Christ, and helped a number of kids stay out of trouble.

Now Mac lives in Chicago, earning a good living repairing automobile transmissions. He is a lay minister at midweek prayer meetings and he preaches on Sundays. He's living in serenity and peace, his days as the "Killer Christian" a memory long dead.

Him!

I don't expect anyone to believe this story, though I shared the luminescent experience with a friend who will testify to its authenticity. Because it goes beyond logic and rational explanation, I have never before mentioned it publicly, not in sermons, in witnessing, counseling, or in fellowship with those closest to me. This, however, seems the appropriate place to tell it for the first time. The agnostic will dismiss it as hallucination, the psychiatrist as autosuggestion, the lip-service Christian will perhaps question my sanity, even the most passionate, practicing churchgoer will raise a doubting eyebrow.

No matter.

I put it before you with pride and humility, unashamed and without apology. These few words of prelude are merely a recognition of the fact that in an age of nuclear weapons and space exploration whatever cannot be tested in a wind tunnel or a laboratory or formulated on an engineer's drawing board is generally treated with cynicism.

But the total knowledge of man doesn't bubble up from a test tube or flow from a slide rule. There are spiritual experiences that passeth understanding. This was one of them.

Consider:

I had been invited from Elko to preach at a two-week revival at the First Bijou Church in Lake Tahoe on the Nevada-California state line. Pastor of the church was Gordon Syler.

Gordon and I were both enormously gratified at the victories for Christ that were being achieved. Thirty-five were saved, and nearly one hundred decisions to live for Jesus had been made.

In the course of the meeting I met Ron Willis, who was leading the song services. Handsome, with dark, flashing eyes, Ron was one of those who had come to the Lord during the revival. Today he's the pastor of the Golden Gate Baptist Church at Oakland, California.

One evening, feeling the need for renewed inspiration, I asked Ron if he would like to have a prayer meeting with me along the lake shore. He agreed. I also invited Pastor Syler, who declined and thereby missed the most transcendent experience a Christian can have. "I don't think you should go out in the cold night air. You might lose your voice," he told me.

"The Lord will take care of my voice."

"Why don't you pray here at the church?"

"I feel the Lord wants me to go outside and pray."

It *was* cold when Ron and I arrived at the lake. We estimated the temperature at somewhere around zero. Snowdrifts like giant mounds of vanilla ice cream were piled high and we were both shivering.

Walking along the shore we fell into a conversation about Peter, the leading spokesman among the twelve disciples, one of Christ's earliest evangelists. We talked of Peter testing Christ's power in Matthew 14:28–31: "Lord, if it be thou, bid me come unto thee on the water," Peter said. "Come," Christ answered. But when Peter stepped into the water, a boisterous wind arose and he became fearful of sinking. "Lord, save me," Peter called. Jesus stretched forth His hand and caught him, saying, "O thou of little faith, why didst thou doubt?"

I criticized Peter for doubting, for taking his eyes from Christ and looking down at the water. Yet I admired Peter—the greatest triumph of his life was the courage and faith he showed by wading toward Christ.

Ron and I had reached an impassable snowbank. We could turn back or try walking on water ourselves. At that moment, however, I couldn't share Peter's faith.

We hadn't prayed yet. Perhaps I had made a hasty decision in suggesting we go to the lake. Besides the snow and cold, fog was beginning to drift in.

We decided to head back to the church. Teeth chattering, we were moving quickly along the beach, when something on our right caught my eye.

Him!

He was there!

Christ!

Standing on the water!

I shook my head in disbelief and turned away. Ron had his back to the lake. I didn't say a word to him. When he turned toward the water, he said, "Arthur, have you looked out over the lake?"

"Yes, I saw Him, too. Ron, what's happening?"

He stared at me blankly.

I looked again.

Him!

There still.

Unmistakably there.

And now He came walking toward us.

His garment was bright as a fluorescent lamp, glistening, shining and sparkling, so immaculate and pure that it looked more silver than white.

Ron and I slumped to our knees. I cried, "Lord, how vile and filthy and dirty and vulgar I am." I never felt so unwholesome and unworthy in my life. It seemed that I was nothing, that if I had never lived, that if I died at that instant, the world would be better, far better off.

Then, all of a sudden, I was suffused with peace, as if He were saying everything is all right.

He was coming closer, walking slowly toward us.

Closer and closer.

The nearer He came, the greater the joy and peace I felt welling inside me.

It seemed as if I were beginning to float out to Him, as Peter had.

Then He stopped.

He stood and looked at us.

If He had taken another step I think two bodies would have been found on the shore the next morning. Ron and I would have gone to be with Him. In that moment I understood what death is for a Christian. It is simply going to be with Christ, stepping out of the flesh into His arms and being with Him completely. And that is not death, but everlasting life, exactly as promised in the Bible. I also understood that if I remained a part of this life, I would never fear death again, no matter what the circumstances.

Now the fog thickened, enveloping Him.

Christ had not said a word.

Ron and I looked at each other. We rose and started to walk away.

After a few steps, I said to Ron, "I want to see Him again." I looked back at the water and shouted as loud as I could, "Lord, that we might see you once more. Bless us, bless us, bless us."

Him!

A second time.

The fog parted, He stood there, His arms uplifted.

I felt wave after wave of His power engulf me. He was passing to me, giving me as a gift more faith, more love, more belief. There is no vocabulary to describe the precious, tender moments of our union with Him.

The mist closed in again.

Slowly, Christ receded from our view.

And then He was gone.

Ron and I stood silent, gazing at the fog-shrouded water. We were cold no longer.

Finally, Ron said, "What should we do?"

"We can't mention it to anyone. You know what people would say."

"What about our wives?"

"Let's talk to them together. They won't believe it if we tell them separately."

I told Ron that Sherry and I would meet him and his wife at their house and we would try to describe what had happened.

I had forgotten the key to our motel room. When I knocked Sherry opened the door, took one look at me . . . and screamed! Then she backed away, her hands shielding her face.

Sherry said, "You've been with Jesus!"

"But . . . but . . . how could *you* know?"

"Your face, Arthur, it's glowing! It's radiant!"

On the ride to Ron's house, Sherry wouldn't sit next to me. She stayed in the back seat. I was incapable of comforting her while she sobbed.

The same reaction had come from Ron's wife, Barbara. Ron had found her in their bedroom when he got home and Barbara wouldn't touch or go near him. "There's a glowing light around your face," Barbara had said.

Ron and I looked at each other. I noticed nothing different about him, nor he about me.

Sherry and Barbara sat as far away from Ron and me as possible, huddling close together at the opposite side of the living room as we stayed up all night and told them in detail of our encounter. We all discussed and speculated on its meaning until early morning.

On the ride back to the motel, Sherry did sit next to me. "The glow, it's gone," she said. "I'm not afraid to be close to you any more."

9

Sinbuster in Sodom

FROM THE CAPITOL BUILDING in Carson City, Nevada, can be seen an establishment called the Moonlight Ranch.

The Moonlight Ranch is a house of prostitution that operates within sight of the governor, legislature, attorney general and other solons of the state.

Prostitution is wide open in fifteen of Nevada's seventeen counties (in the two counties where it is supposedly outlawed demand is met by call girls linked to the underworld and by an army of amateurs—secretaries, clerks, schoolteachers, etc.—who flock in from Los Angeles and San Francisco for the brisk Friday through Sunday trade).

Nevada is the only state that permits unchecked prostitution. Its highest officials rationalize the practice, torturously, as an institution serving the needs of the people, forgetting that leaders are charged with the duty and responsibility for setting moral standards, not justifying their breach.

A scheduled airline brings jam-packed flights of customers to the bawdy houses in the small towns of rural Nevada, where the house of prostitution is as familiar as the corner drugstore. These pockets of sin are a lingering reminder of the anything-goes American frontier of a century ago.

When I began my war against prostitution in Elko, I doubted that I could successfully fight the men and madams who profited mightily from the world's oldest profession, any more than La-Vern Inzer had in his battle against Winnemucca's brothels.

Yet the stand had to be made.

I couldn't anticipate that I was to reap a whirlwind of cruel and angry emotion, culminating in a Syndicate-called meeting whose sole agenda was a proposal to either find a way to stop me or to murder me.

There were nine houses in Elko County, five in Elko itself, two in Wells, two in Jackpot. Some of them were luxuriously furnished with deep red carpets, crimson curtains, paintings of nudes, huge mirrors and rooms.

The charge in Elko was ten dollars a trick, a dollar a minute. As soon as a customer entered a girl's crib, she set an alarm clock and, finished or not, she bolted from the bed when the ten-minute alarm sounded. A man could, of course, buy as much time as he wanted, and the per-minute price was shaved slightly to twenty-five dollars for a half hour of a girl's time.

Large profits were also made selling liquor. The minimum tab was $1.50 a shot on up to $20 for a bottle of inferior champagne.

The hundreds of girls who worked at the houses were floaters. They were switched at least every two months so that the quickly jaded men could enjoy the favors of a constant stream of new girls.

Many of the girls turned forty to fifty tricks a night. During rush hours every madam had a list of part-timers (Elko housewives and mothers) who could be called in to handle the overflow.

As an all-cash business, profits were easily hidden. The split ran 30 to 35 percent for the madams, 20 percent for the girls, and the rest to the Chicago Syndicate that maintained iron control over Elko's vice. From its take the Syndicate would parcel out the "juice," the payoffs to city, county, and state officials. The madams, too, contributed under-the-table money.

I began my attack by denouncing the houses on my radio program. I openly declared that all officials in the city and county were taking bribes to allow the houses to remain in operation. The sheriff alone was enriching himself by thousands of dollars a month.

I named names and challenged them to sue me (none did).

Then I went to the County Courthouse and stood at the end of a long table, rattling off my demands to the Elko grand jury.

My statement covered dozens of pages. Its three most important reforms, as quoted from the official record, were:

I charge that the nine houses of prostitution in Elko County are public nuisances and request that they be closed.

I further charge that the city of Elko is supporting these houses and condoning the vice of prostitution by granting them liquor licenses. I insist that their liquor licenses be revoked.

I extend these charges by asking that you order the responsible law enforcement officials to immediately close the houses and/or indict the district attorney, city attorney, county commissioner, city council, chief of police, and the sheriff.

When I finished only two men in the room were looking me straight in the eye. The others, heads down, avoided my gaze.

The grand jury took no action. The fact that several of its members derived their income in part or full from prostitution was unquestionably the major reason. One member of the jury owned the largest gambling casino in Elko and he steered many of his customers to the houses.

Next I drove three hundred miles to the offices of the Reno *Gazette* and talked to a reporter about my campaign. The banner headline next day read: "ELKO PASTOR CHARGES LAW WON'T FIGHT OPEN PROSTITUTION."

The story created a sensation in and out of Elko. Television and radio reporters and a correspondent from United Press International, which services almost every newspaper in America and thousands abroad, rushed to town to investigate my charges.

"ELKO OFFICIALS SNUB PASTOR'S WAR ON PROSTITUTION" was the headline under the UPI's follow-up story.

It quoted the district attorney as saying, "Our position is the less said the better. When the point comes that the majority of the people don't want it, I'm sure it will be eliminated."

This was the expectable cliché rationalization, but the attitude of my fellow pastors appalled me.

The story quoted a number of them:

"Prostitution presents no particular problem," said one minister.

Another so-called man of God: "We're not bothered by prostitution. I've been here five years and I'd say it's the lesser of two evils."

Another: "I can't afford to oppose gambling or prostitution. My church would run me off. I've got too many people involved in those businesses."

Another: *"It's none of my affair. I just preach the Gospel."* (Italics mine.)

The story got national coverage. The publicity put Elko's sin in the spotlight for several weeks and for a time income at the local houses dropped. Sides were quickly chosen and the pressure built. I received dozens of calls from private citizens, 80 percent in favor of my position. None, however, would declare openly.

The members of my congregation had voted to support my stand, and they suffered for it. Several lost their jobs, others were ordered to join another church or be fired. They were criticized and cursed on the streets. And because of our position, many prospective members avoided joining our church.

Then came the Tuesday night meeting between three Syndicate chieftains from Chicago and the nine madams of Elko County. The underworld fears nothing more than publicity, and the meeting was called to put the lid on it.

I later got the details from one of those who attended the meeting.

"Let's hit this damn Arthur Blessitt," one of the Syndicate men declared.

The vote narrowly went against my being killed only because it was pointed out that my death would cause a Niagara of unfavorable publicity.

Other tactics were devised:

Sherry received dozens of obscene and threatening phone calls, many warning us to leave town. Letters poured in from women who said they'd had sex with me. Other letters contained vile language mingled with more threats. I took the mail to the postmaster who told me, "There's nothing we can do about it. Just stuff from a bunch of weirdos."

The Elko police, too, were apparently afraid I would be killed, and they didn't want to handle the furor that would cause. They assigned me protection. At night a patrol car followed me everywhere. This went on for three weeks. We had moved to a small trailer, and one evening Sherry's grandparents, Mr. and Mrs. Frank Boyington, visiting us from Bogalusa, were startled to see two faces peering through the window while we were at dinner. "Who's that?" Grandfather Boyington asked. "The police," I said. He didn't believe me and went outside in time to see two Elko officers get into their car and drive off.

Sherry was verging on hysteria. Much of the time she was alone in the trailer with our baby. Hard thuds, probably caused by rifle butts, would sound against the door. When Sherry would gingerly peek out, the callers had disappeared.

One night Mac came to the trailer with a hunting rifle. "The next time they bang at the door, let loose with the hardnosed bullets in this gun."

"No, Mac. The Bible teaches us to love our enemies."

"I'm going to guard you twenty-four hours a day."

Afraid that Mac might revert to violence, I told him no, emphatically.

He left only when I agreed to take the rifle for protection. After he was gone, I hid it under the bed.

There were other means used to show Sherry and me that we were unwelcome in Elko.

When we went to a restaurant, it would take forty-five minutes to get a menu. When our order was finally taken, our food would be served burned or salted to the point of being inedible.

On one occasion I was walking down the street with Sherry when a man who knew us shouted, "There goes the pastor with one of the whores he's trying to run out of town."

In the meantime, once the publicity died down, the houses resumed normal business.

As a last resort I went to the Las Vegas office of the FBI. Three agents, cold as statues, heard me out.

"Some of the Elko madams," I said, "are violating the Mann Act. Congress made it a federal offense to aid or participate in the transportation of a woman from one state to another for immoral purposes. That, as you gentlemen know, is also called the White Slave Act.

"There's a federal stamp on liquor, so you can move against the houses on that basis, too. Otherwise the government is aiding, abetting, and condoning prostitution."

The answer I got from one of J. Edgar Hoover's men: "We know all about you and what you're doing and we know everything that's happening in Elko. But those houses afford us a good place to pick up people we're looking for. Those places draw them, and we also get a lot of information through these people."

"You mean you know what's going on; you know about the

prostitution and you're not going to do anything about it?" I asked.

"Our hands are tied, there's nothing we can do. You just don't understand."

So much for the FBI and justice.

There was one more solution, wild perhaps.

I considered running for sheriff to clean up the mess myself. I had good reason to believe that in the privacy of the polling booth there was an excellent chance I would be elected.

When I told Sherry, she said, "We're not going to be here much longer. You're going to be moving on."

Sherry had anticipated our move to Nevada from San Francisco. Was she now correct in anticipating another move? Seeking an answer, I left the trailer and drove my car up a steep, narrow, rugged road to a peak I had named Prayer Mountain. Formerly a lovers' lane, it had become a sacred place. We baptized members of our church in a pond at its base.

I stayed on Prayer Mountain all night, looking out over the lights of Elko, my heart burdened by its afflictions.

A new call from God came as dawn rose purple and gold over the city. The decision to leave Elko was a commanding order. God ordered me to Los Angeles, where I knew the need for Christ among those who knew Him not was vast. Though my work in Elko was far from finished, I didn't for a second question God's urging me to leave. I knew the Lord had a reason for telling me to move my ministry to Los Angeles.

On the drive back to California, Sherry and I reflected that in Nevada much work had been accomplished for the Lord, souls had been saved, five churches and missions had been kneaded into existence.

The campaign against prostitution, except for several girls who were led to the Lord and changed their lives, had failed.

But Moses, Elijah, John the Baptist, and Paul had also stood for right and fought wrong. And Paul had not cleansed Corinth of its famous Temple of Prostitution in which more than one thousand girls serviced the sailors of all nations who came to that biblical sin city.

As our car moved into the flow of traffic on the Sunset Strip, which we were seeing for the first time, I thought back to the hoods, the madams, the girls, the customers, and the law enforcement officials of Elko. I remembered again the reprieve Christ gave transgressors in Luke 23:24: "Father, forgive them; for they know not what they do."

10

Minister of the Sunset Strip

THE HISTORY of the Sunset Strip has been a bad trip, man, a bummer.

The California scene from the beginning was stained by the mark of Cain and the greed of money changers.

Starting in 1769, Franciscan Father Junípero Serra straggled along the California coast, and established his famous twenty-one missions. In the process he appropriated millions of acres of land from several local tribes of peaceful, docile Indians, becoming, in effect, the overseer of California's first land grab.

Today shiny-faced suburban kids are trundled off on weekends to visit the "picturesque" missions. But the missions weren't picturesque for the thousands of Indians, forced laborers all, who built them under conditions as heartless as those suffered by the Negroes who constructed the palaces of southern planters. For a dawn-to-sundown workday, the Indians were paid with a flacon of cheap wine to keep them drunkenly submissive. Thus, the Franciscans were California's first drug pushers.

Ignoring the true spiritual and material needs of the Indians they had come to "civilize," the Franciscan fathers turned the missions into vast income-producing enterprises. The San Gabriel Mission alone, a pioneer conglomerate, was a baronial complex of seventeen huge ranchos, stocked with gigantic herds of cattle, horses, sheep, and crop fields, worth almost $80 million. Of the three thousand Indians who worked at the mission, hundreds died of starvation and disease. Those who tried to escape were brought back—and it didn't matter if they were dead or alive.

The Franciscans eventually lost their lands to a series of buccaneer Mexican governments, who gave high-caste dons horizon-hurdling ranchos. Half the land was supposed to revert to the Indians, but when the dust settled the grandees had it all. They ruled as divine-right kings. One, brandishing an exquisite pearl-handled pistol, shot and killed malefactors while sitting astride his horse after impatiently enduring five-minute "trials."

When California became a state in 1850, the dons in turn lost virtually all their land. Whoring, gambling, and borrowing money at spectacular interest rates from rapacious American loan sharks finished them off. What few acres were left from their original grants were stolen from them by U.S. courts.

The don who owned the Rancho Rodeo de las Aguas was so poor he couldn't raise five hundred dollars in cash and eight hundred dollars in notes, the price for which it was sold—one of the most stunning bargains in real-estate history. Out of this rancho eventually was carved Beverly Hills and the Sunset Strip.

In 1900 the Strip was a tranquil lemon orchard. But with the invention of the automobile, paved roads began ringing the orchards and the growers were gradually forced out.

The area then went through a series of booms and busts, all masterminded by real-estate sharks. What should be very loosely termed the "golden age" of the Strip was ushered in during the 1920s following the establishment of the movie industry in Holly-wood. Speakeasies violating the prohibition law and illegal gambling spots sprang up. So did the mansions in Beverly Hills. Through the 1950s, fancy gin palaces like Ciro's, Trocadero, and Mocambo were playgrounds for Hollywood royalty who arrived in conspicuously chauffeured limousines. The newspapers and fan magazines chronicled in wearying detail the almost daily drunken brawls of movie stars fighting over the affections of a prostitute or tearing a club apart after a succession of losing spins on the roulette wheel.

The sensational stories turned the Strip into a tourist mecca, and a generation raised on the shallow verities of Hollywood celluloid came to gawk at their screen favorites. To accommodate them, the Strip blossomed with more gin mills, expensive restaurants, high-priced antique and specialty shops, and burlesque houses.

Such was the nature of the Strip's "golden age."

Next the Strip became home to multistoried apartment buildings with lofty rents, banks and savings and loan emporiums, and mini-skyscrapers that housed the West Coast headquarters of numerous large corporations and the flesh-peddlers who called themselves agents, public relations men, and talent scouts.

By 1964, according to the West Hollywood Chamber of Commerce, the Strip and adjacent arteries had become "targets in the land rush for business and apartment sites." The area was "pulsating with incomparable progress."

Property fronting the Strip (a mere twelve blocks within the 2.1-mile radius of West Hollywood, which, because of a zoning quirk, is an unincorporated city and technically independent of Los Angeles) was going for from twenty to twenty-five dollars a square foot.

But in 1965 the revolution hit.

From the far corners of the nation came an invasion of young people, lured to the Strip by easy access to drugs, the phony glamour image conjured by the movies, television, trash novels, and the West Hollywood Chamber itself. The kids, arriving by the thousands, made it a new ball game. They were "strange" kids, mini-skirted teeny-boppers and bearded young men, all anti-Establishment.

The chilling word was heard on the Strip: hippie!

The Strip suddenly was no longer "pulsating with incomparable progress." Big money paused and considered before making new investments. Which way would the Strip go? Was the hippie thing a fad? Would the straights keep power?

Nobody knew.

Some tycoons took a chance that the "golden age" would continue. A thirteen-story multi-million dollar house of childish, peek-a-boo sin called the Playboy Club was flung up in the heart of the Strip. Big-breasted girls were used as shills to lure suckers in for expensive drinks and meals and to hear comedians tell vulgar stories against a backdrop of titillating pictures of girls in various stages of undress.

Two giant luxury hotels were erected. One soon failed and was turned into a convalescent home for well-heeled senior citizens. The other, built by Gene Autry, was sold to a chain.

The kids, meantime, kept pouring in, tragically searching for meaning and excitement at the end of a needle or in a variety of pills, most of them eagerly manufactured and supplied by America's blue-chip pharmaceutical houses.

Now one thing became clear: The kids were on the Strip to stay, this was their scene, this was where it was happening.

Befuddled, angry businessmen, watching their profits drop at the alarming rate of $3 million a year, took their problems to Los Angeles County Supervisor Ernest E. Debs, a bland, talkative politician whose district included the Strip.

Debs blew his cool. "I'm pushing hard for more arrests," he said with a singular lack of imagination. "We will never surrender the area to a bunch of wild-eyed beatniks."

The supervisor's push for "more arrests" didn't discourage the kids; it only brought more of them out to defy authority. So the businessmen called on the law.

Helen Lawrenson, in a *Cosmopolitan* magazine article, wrote acutely:

> The resultant squawk has been less a result of moral disapproval than of pocketbook pain. Faced with the adolescent invasion, the solid citizens (or "property owners") who never turned a hair at the presence of gangsters, gamblers and stripteasers, panicked and called on the police to protect them. Help! Officer! Here come the teeny-boppers.
>
> Pressured by Strip merchants and restaurant owners to *do* something about the weekend traffic jam that was keeping away the older cash customers, the Los Angeles police began harassing the kids by means of a curfew law that says no one under eighteen can be on the street after 10 P.M.

The curfew was as a match to gunpowder. It forced confrontation and an explosion.

To protest the ordinance, more than a thousand kids gathered along the Strip on an electricity-charged day in November, 1966. They were defiant, determined young daredevils who would not be put down by threats or intimidation.

The police blew their cool, too. If they had spoken softly while carrying their big nightsticks, the ragged ranks of young people would have disbursed once their rage had been spent.

But The Man overreacted.

Helmeted and batoned, the law waded into the defenseless

ranks of young people. Gushers of blood stained the Strip as the Establishment collided head-on with the vocal but weaponless kids and lead-weighted batons crashed against the skulls of fourteen-year-old girls and sixteen-year-old boys.

·The kids had turned out solely to protest the curfew as discriminatory, humiliating, and unconstitutional. Their position might have been arguable, might even have been completely wrong, but the police didn't want to be bothered with the "technicality" of freedom of assembly, a part of the heritage that supposedly undergirds American democracy. The Man was under orders to sweep the streets clean of the kids. It was done efficiently. Forty-seven were busted in what proved to be a significant confrontation, significant enough to be reported in detail the next day on the front page of the Establishment's most influential voice, *The New York Times*.

A wave of sympathy for the kids gathered and broke. Moral and financial support flowed in from Woolworth-heir Lance Reventlow, Peter Fonda, and other celebrities. The American Civil Liberties Union, which since 1920 has fought impartially for Nazis, Communists, members of minority communities, and anyone else whose rights were in dispute, volunteered its services to defend the kids who'd been thrown into jail.

News of the senseless brutality of The Man spread through the high school and college campuses and the crash pads faster than booze at a corporation Christmas party.

The kids would not be cowed. The next weekend more than five thousand turned out for another confrontation. Again the law could have avoided mayhem by letting the crowd vent its anger via annoying but harmless shouting, a peaceful method of protest.

Instead, everything short of tanks and bazookas was marshaled to beat down the rebellious young. And beaten down they were. One hundred were busted and pushed, sobbing and screaming, into waiting police vans. Innocent bystanders were also hurt in the melee. Two ministers, observers only, were assaulted and clubbed to the ground. Another observer, an elderly college professor, asked a sheriff's deputy, "Where can I stand to watch the demonstration?" For an answer he was knocked to the sidewalk and kicked. Peter Fonda, on hand with a camera to film the action, was grabbed, handcuffed, and roughhoused into a squad car. The law was striking out blindly, without rhyme or rationality. Fonda later made a prophetic comment: "The police and the moneybag merchants may think they can win by force, but they never will."

The curfew didn't work, so the Establishment's next gambit was to impose a no-loitering law. It was so rigidly enforced that brothers meeting accidentally on the Strip for the first time after twenty years of separation could not stop and greet each other, much less spend time reminiscing. The late stripper-authoress Gypsy Rose Lee was one straight who was tuned in. She put it more colorfully: "We're not even allowed to stop to adjust our garters." She added cogently, "I love youth and I don't mind the kids at all. I rather like seeing them. I think they're interesting and gay. The streets out here have always had peculiar guys. We've always had crazy people out here. At least the hippies are young; they're fresh, and maybe something really good is going to come from this."

The Strip merchants and the law didn't see it that way. They had failed to note *the* most important factor of the youth rebellion: More than half the population of the world, according to a United Nations survey, is now under twenty-four! Not since the Creation have young people dominated the globe. By sheer force of numbers alone, the kids could not be denied.

Concluded Miss Lawrenson in her article: "Like it or not, they are going to set the style, call the tune and run the show. So the Sunset Strip scene is not just an isolated freaky community problem. It's not only what's happening, it's a guideline to what's coming."

And so, despite the curfew and the no-loitering restriction, the Strip had been captured by the young.

As I cruised the area, witnessing and talking to hundreds of kids, I saw a bottomless mission field. These young people, the majority of them, were of my own generation and, disastrously, were already turned on by synthetic thrills instead of the genuine thrill of knowing Christ.

The tons of publicity engendered by the riots backfired on the Strip merchants and the police. Thousands of other restless, disaffected youngsters came, all of them hungering for action. Almost none of these young people were from poverty-stricken or welfare families. They were the sons and daughters of the middle class. What had gone wrong in the Establishment's scheme of things?

Why couldn't the presumably desirable standards of the parents be grafted on to their children? Why were the kids disenchanted? Why were they dropping out? Why were they now turning the Strip into a teen-age skid row? Why was an army of young people giving up their chance for life before they had a real chance to live?

Parents from Los Angeles to Long Island, Dallas to the Dakotas, puzzled, pondered, and wrung their hands while patting themselves on the back for giving their kids everything ("They didn't have to struggle through the Depression like we did"). But had they given them everything? Had they given love, understanding, patience? Had they given them the immutable truths, morality, ethics, and values found in the abundant pages between Genesis and Revelation?

As the new lodestone for the nation's young, the Strip was a cruel hoax and an avaricious host. The versatile merchants, those who did not move out, set up new businesses to quickly part the kids from their money and meet any need they had, so long as a profit could be turned. Everybody was soon earning big bread except the barbers. Even straight-owned drugstores sold kids narcotics from doctors' prescription blanks that they knew were stolen and forged.

For most of the kids, the pain they found on the Strip was equal to or worse than anything they had endured at home. Caught in a vise, they easily succumbed to the drug culture, thereby compounding the tragedy of their lives.

When the kids came, the twenty-nine Protestant, Catholic, and Jewish churches of West Hollywood held back despite the claim of the Chamber of Commerce that "religious leaders of West Hollywood make a major contribution to the culture and character level of the area."

The ministers, priests, and rabbis did not want to ruffle the feathers of comfortable congregations. The churches said to the hippies, "Cut your hair; take a bath; drugs are bad for you."

Unfortunately, it wasn't that simple. Such sermonizing didn't even dent the minds of the kids. It was the same pap they'd heard at home. And so they ignored West Hollywood's twenty-nine churches.

It became obvious to me that since the kids wouldn't come to the churches, the church must come to the kids.

Sherry and I had a stake of $100 and, given the costly rents, finding a place to live near the Strip was a formidable three-day hunt. We finally located an apartment we could afford in that friendly kibbutz, the Jewish section of Los Angeles only a few minutes' drive from Sunset Boulevard. Fairfax Avenue, the main artery of the Jewish area, was out of sight. Bearded Talmudic scholars dressed in black mingled with the two-buttoned straights from nearby CBS Television City who came to Cantor's and other legendary delicatessans for bagels, bean soup, and thick pastrami sandwiches. The pungent smell of freshly baked bread spilled over into the streets, a doughy dream. The people of Moses were the first to give a Baptist family a warm welcome in the "City of the Angels." It would not be the only occasion when Jews would come to our aid.

To support us I preached at revivals in San Bernardino, San Diego, Phoenix, and elsewhere—but I always whipped back to the Strip as soon as possible.

I had already discovered that it was easier to win souls on the Strip than in Mississippi, Montana, or Nevada. Contrary to what I had heard, the young people of the Strip were not anti-God, they were simply against the rigidity and a lot of the nonsense of organized religion and the big churches. You couldn't capture these kids for Christ with taffy pulls, stringing popcorn balls, and choir practice. What they wanted was the essence of God, His relevance to their lives, His personal meaning to them.

Perhaps because I was under thirty, it was natural that the kids trusted me. I began to identify completely with them, except that I was dropping Matthew, Mark, Luke, and John instead of pills. I learned their language, and scores were brought to the Lord in conversations that began, "Hey, man, I know you're strung out. But there's a better way. Let me turn you on to a trip with an everlasting high. Jesus, man, He loves you. He won't hassle you. He'll put it all together."

I also let my hair grow longer and learned a quick lesson in dress. A collar or a business suit wouldn't get you anywhere. The first time I walked into a trip room I wore a tie and suit. The heads panicked. They thought I was a narc (narcotics agent) out to bust them. After that I switched to turtlenecks and psychedelically patterned shirts, slacks or bell bottoms, and sandals.

Then came the beads. About three months after hitting the

Strip, I met a teen-age girl on the street who was hung up on dope. I prayed with her and she came to Christ. Then I bought her a meal and we talked for hours.

"You've given me so much," she said, "I don't have a thing to give you except this." She took off her beads and put them around my neck. "Tell anybody who asks that I gave you these beads like you gave me a new life."

That episode was to be repeated countless times, and I was soon collecting anywhere from ten to fifty strings of beads a month. A tie no longer meant a thing to me, but each string of beads was a living testimony.

Street-witnessing was not enough. What the kids needed was a place to rap among themselves, a place where no one would hassle them. They needed a sandwich and a soft drink or coffee. They needed a place of their own where they could hear the word of Christ.

It was inconceivable to me that none of the churches were filling this need. The churches were meeting the rising tide of the youth rebellion by simply ignoring it, not only on the Strip, but throughout the country. The churches kept their eyes closed. Clergymen did not witness, but shuffled papers, kept a sharp eye on the budget, and planned ever-bigger buildings. I preached at a church in Mississippi with an $80,000 organ! And I saw a church in Texas protected by an intricate burglar alarm system.

Many of these cavernous, expensive buildings were open only a few hours on Sunday morning and a short time during the week for social functions.

To generate a spiritual rebirth in America and shepherd the lost to Christ, the churches should have a welcome mat out twenty-four hours a day with ministers working in three shifts. Churches, at the least, should keep bar hours. Where can the lonely, frightened, and troubled go when the gin mills and the nightclubs finally close? With an all-night open-door church operation thousands upon thousands could be converted.

Churches of all denominations have failed dramatically in reaching out to the kids. Tragically, most churches are run like profit-making corporations, when the only profit a House of God should be concerned with is the richness of winning souls, changing lives, and helping people.

Most rents were still high on the Strip, up to one thousand

dollars a month for a small building. (At that price, the eighty-thousand-dollar church organ in Mississippi would have kept a ministry on the Strip going for almost seven years!)

I finally found a rundown motel that had been converted into an office building at 8531⅛ Sunset Boulevard. I rented one room, barely twelve feet wide, but the rent was only sixty dollars a month.

I moved in a desk and an old couch. Friends donated a two-burner hot plate and a small refrigerator. Our altar was a beat-up coffee table covered by a white towel with an open Bible on it.

I passed out cards along the Strip, talked to kids and invited them to the modest headquarters of the Arthur Blessitt Evangelistic Association.

The kids came in numbers we couldn't handle. Some nights hundreds would crowd in and out. Most of the time Sherry and I managed to serve soup and crackers. All the time we served tracts and pocket-sized New Testaments designed with a psychedelic cover. And I preached at least twice a night.

Christ works constant miracles. His voice was now being heard on the Strip for the first time. I didn't meet a single kid who wouldn't listen. One of the positive things about the hippies was their total honesty and lack of pretense. They were open-minded. Not all were ready for Jesus, but the number who were finding answers for the first time in their young lives through Christ was amazing.

The kids on the Strip love nicknames and labels. Soon I was being called The Hip Preacher, The Night-Life Minister, The Hippie Chaplain, and The Turned-On Preacher.

But most of the kids called me The Minister of the Sunset Strip. That was the label that stuck, and it's become as precious as my certificate of ordination. Like the beads, the title the kids gave me meant something. It was their gift, their way of saying, "You're a groove, you're cool, don't split, make the scene."

I determined to keep making the scene as the Minister of Sunset Strip as long as there was need. The way things were going the Strip could have used a thousand ministers. Man, I thought, I'd like to pile-drive my way into every seminary classroom in Southern California and push those preachers hiding behind their concordances to do God's work where it counts, on the streets, to witness, to be an instrument of the saving power of Christ, to show the lost where it's at.

It was soon apparent that I needed a bigger, much bigger, location. And it had to be right on the firing line, at pointblank range in the center of the Strip where Jesus Christ could once again confront the money changers.

11

Bright Lights, Dark Corners

IN THE MONTHS it took to locate a suitable building, I continued to explore the complex world of the Strip. The Mother Lode—the Strip proper—runs from the edge of Hollywood to the tip of Beverly Hills. The major veins are LaCienega, Santa Monica and Beverly Boulevards, Melrose and Fairfax Avenues, and scores of small streets and cul-de-sacs that zigzag and crisscross the major arteries.

The Strip is a microcosm, unique, many-layered, and kaleidoscopic. Surprises lurk everywhere, most of them disappointing.

It is jungle and sophistication. Violent, rarely kind. Greedy, seldom generous. Razzle-dazzle and tomb-quiet. Above- and underground. Luxurious and indigent. Formless and highly structured.

Once the tourists came to worship their false movie-star gods. Now they come to see the hippies, clucking their disapproval as they drive by. Some of the tourists get out of their cars and make the scene, but their contact is superficial.

Few know the Strip's real character and its sewer society. The Strip habitués are all doing their own thing, and Christ is a stranger. Virtually no one considers Him part of his bag.

Some of the Strip's people and places, some of its bright lights and dark corners:

The weekend, after-five, and penthouse hippies arrive in Jags and Cads, wallets bulging, wearing forty-dollar hip-hugging slacks, thirty-dollar multicolored shirts, seventy-five dollar Indian leather jackets, and seven-dollar scarves. They live in affluent Westwood, Pacific Palisades, or the Hollywood hills. They're young, successful, long-haired—TV directors, writers, sons of politicians or movie stars. They have the bread to hit the plusher spots, the Factory discotheque, P.J.'s on Santa Monica, or Sneaky Pete's. They go slumming at The Experience and other places where the rock is acid-hard. They eat at Theodore's with the late night Hollywood crowd. They identify with liberal causes, say they feel empathy with the kids. They are cocktail hippies—three parts straight, one part hip. Part of the scene, they know, is turning on. They usually use pot, with an occasional trip on downers, though they may experiment with speed or acid. No matter how stoned or drunk, they are almost never hassled by the police. Their clothes and cars are too expensive.

At the corner of Doheny and Sunset two men cross against the light in full view of a motorcycle policeman. The dude in a business suit is ignored. The kid with the Harpo haircut is busted.

In souped-up Mustangs, Camaros, and Firebirds, rock music blaring from their car radios, the teeny-boppers swarm in from all the middle-class suburbs, including Anaheim, Pasadena, Granada Hills, and Burbank. Thirteen to eighteen years old, they stash their wheels several blocks from Sunset Boulevard because there's no parking on the Strip from 8 P.M. to 2 A.M. The big part of their trip is walking the Strip, ad libbing the night's action.

They're the wildest and in some ways the most dangerous of the Strip's inhabitants, because they're game for anything. Bread is of no concern; indulgent parents supply them with allowances of from ten to seventy dollars a week. Their scene is the psychedelic shops, then on to the clutch of clubs that cater to teen-agers, notably Gazzarri's and Whisky-A-Go-Go.

The typical teeny-bopper considers herself cool. If a guy pinches her rear, she's flattered rather than insulted. If she's offered downers or a cap of acid, she'll accept with a giggle. She won't chicken out of anything. Her thing is to conform, and conforming on the Strip frequently means taking part in a sex blast that would shock a madam or swallowing enough drugs to keep the girl in a psycho ward for life. Many wind up in sex orgies or freaked out at the UCLA Medical Center.

In almost every case, the parents of the teeny-bopper do not know she's on the Strip. She's supposed to be baby-sitting or spending the night with a girl friend and listening to Beatle records.

Then there are the cool cats who live off chicks. These male hustlers exist on the fringes of show business. "I'm cutting a record tomorrow." "I'm up for a part in a TV show." "I just need some bread to tide me over." The chicks they con think nothing of handing them fifty or a hundred dollars.

Sixteen to twenty-three years old, these chicks are practiced panhandlers. A good-looking chick with a winning personality can gull up to one hundred dollars a day. If she looks tender and innocent enough, a straight may hand her twenty dollars. She may remind him of his own daughter, but, man, she knows more about sin than the straight ever will. None of these panhandling chicks hauls in less than ten dollars a day. Some of them support two, three, or four guys. All these chicks are turned on to drugs. If she has a very expensive habit, she'll take up prostitution to support it.

Heads hawk underground newspapers along the Strip. You can buy narcotics with your news. The papers sell for twenty-five cents to twenty-five dollars, depending on what's between the pages.

She greets you at the door of the massage parlor with a smile, a vision in décolletage. You're led into a private room, where the girl, for an agreed price, will perform any sex act you request. The Strip is filling up with these brothels. The city licenses them freely; the vice squad ignores them.

Twelve dollars a week buys a crash pad in a once-famous Hollywood hotel for ten to fifteen heads who meet to turn on. Other heads, who won't waste a dime for a pad, sleep in deserted houses, apartment buildings, on the ground, in alleys or bushes. These kids get busted all the time for panhandling, vagrancy, jaywalking, trespassing. Pot, speed, and acid are passed around and consumed like Life Savers. They'll pop a pill as quickly as a straight will swallow an aspirin.

"Hi, man, how you doing?" My nightly greeting to Mescaline, a short, handsome Negro in a cowboy hat. He's been dealing on the same corner of the Strip for four years. His income some weeks is more than one thousand dollars. He's never been busted.

"I don't turn on myself," he says. "That's a scene for losers. I'm just a businessman."

"How about doing business with God?"

"When I do, Arthur, I'm counting on you to give me a personal introduction to that big cat."

I promise myself that someday I'll win Mescaline for the Lord.

The over-forty Lions, Rotarians, and Kiwanians—doctors, lawyers, Sunday school teachers, church deacons, Boy Scout leaders, supporters of the Y and the United Crusade—are out for a big night on the Strip. A couple of drinks and a dude of this stripe is heavy, man, heavy. He offers fifty dollars to an attractive teen-age girl who dances topless in one of the clubs. He fondles her breasts and runs his hand between her legs. Back in Toledo or Cheyenne or Evanston he's a pillar of respectability. He tithes to his church and agrees with his minister that today's young people do not have the moral fiber and character of their parents.

Big-name movie and television stars make the Strip scene every night, many scouting for new shack-ups. A surprising number are strung out on drugs. They don't buy their stuff from street dealers; it's prescribed by their M.D.'s and psychiatrists. They take uppers to get through their nerve-racking days, downers to lull them to sleep. There are dozens of famous faces destined to end their lives in drug comas, as did Marilyn Monroe and Judy Garland. Narcotics are dulling and heightening the senses of the Hollywood crowd in epidemic proportions. Pot parties in Beverly Hills and Bel-Air are common. Acid and speed are replacing the martini and mixed drink as the favored way of fighting off reality. Along the Strip a number of stars can be seen freaked out, but because they're celebrities they're never busted for taking the same stuff the kids do, nor are they ever searched on suspicion of possession.

She's smoking pot openly on the Strip, a nineteen-year-old girl who says she's a former model.

"Do you know Jesus in your heart?"

"I groove on Jesus, Satan, reincarnation, Taoism, astrology, Dr.

Timothy Leary. What turns me off is The Man, my folks in Cleveland, and a steady job."

Hopelessly confused, she looks at me through glazed and troubled eyes.

"I'm getting married next week. We're going to make the honeymoon scene hitchhiking across the country for two years."

"And then?"

"I hope I'll be dead."

"Let me tell you how Jesus can give you everlasting life."

She laughs from a mouth pitted with cavities. "Do you think Jesus would give me all the pot I want in Heaven? Man, that's a trip that would be the ultimate groove."

Before I can talk further with her, she turns and lopes off. I run after her, pressing a tract and a New Testament into her hand. Perhaps when she comes down, the message will touch her.

In the midsection of the Strip is a bar that looks like ten thousand others, only this one is filled with prostitutes and small-time underworld hoods, any one of whom would murder you in a minute. I move among the tables, distributing tracts. Not a soul shows a spark of interest.

"Mr. Blessitt, thank God I've found you." She's a matron of perhaps forty-two. She presses a picture of her teen-age son into my hands. "Have you seen Paul?"

"No, ma'am, but I'll keep my eyes open for him."

She says without hope, "He was released from Camarillo [one of California's state mental hospitals], and he ran away four nights ago. The psychiatrist said he couldn't do anything with him."

"What did the psychiatrist recommend?"

"A minister."

Dealing on the sidewalk is a sixteen-year-old girl I've been trying to win for Christ. Her post is in front of The Experience, a night-spot for teen-agers. She's selling reds three for $1, six for $1.75, and she tells me she's made $150 tonight. Her every move is watched by three men, the men for whom she's selling the stuff. Her cut is supposed to be 20 percent, but chances are she won't collect. They'll probably gang-rape her, toss her into the street, and pick up another chick from the plentiful supply always on the Strip to deal for them tomorrow night.

"Arthur, can I bum some bread?" she asks. "I haven't eaten in two days."

. The Blue Grotto is a bikers' hangout. The big room is filled with leather-jacketed, rough-hewn guys, some of them in their thirties. Their old ladies are all young, but already losing their looks to dissipation. I talk with a fourteen-year-old runaway who's on the scene for the first time. She won't go home; she won't accept Jesus; she's already a speed freak and proud of it.

The place is run by one of the most charming men on the Strip. His name is Foster and as I move into his cubbyhole office he's reading the New Testament. He's wearing a tribal shirt with a large glass ruby pinned to his Afro-styled headdress.

Foster keeps the place going as a refuge for the bikers. He does what he can to help them. The place barely shows a profit, but Foster is a religious man and this is his mission station.

The room is quiet tonight. The bikers are hunched over chess tables in drug stupors. Once the bikers turned on only with booze, but now they're also hung up on drugs.

The previous evening two bikers were shot to death on the sidewalk outside Foster's place.

At the Phone Booth, even the G-strings have come off. A transparent negligee hides nothing from the Christians sitting at the bar while two nude girls gyrate on tables.

A few blocks off the Strip on a lonely sidestreet three middle-aged men pull up to the curb in a green Volkswagen. Two, both bearded, stagger out. The other lies immobile in the car.

"What's he on?" I ask.

"Downers with a beer chaser."

I slap him for several minutes until he shows a sign of life. A tract and a Bible go into his pocket, too.

Thirty feet away a white Cad is parked. A couple in the back seat can clearly be seen having sex.

One of the most prosperous businesses on the Strip is the psychedelic shop. There are dozens of them. Some are owned by three or four hips who've pooled their money. Others are secretly owned by straight businessmen. A lot of dealers hang out in the shops, and the owners will shoo them off unless they pony up a commission on their sales.

The shops are popular with tourists as well as the hippies. Fifteen-cent posters bought wholesale are retailed at $2.00 and up. The posters are profane or mocking. One shows a group of five young naked men and women lying in a bed. Another bears a picture of Pope Paul under a caption: "THE PILL IS A NO-NO."

A book is on sale for $1.50: *One Hundred Ways to Prepare Pot.* Among the recipes are instructions for preparing "pot fudge" and "brownie pot." The book is not a joke; the ingredients, including the grass, are specified as meticulously as in a Fannie Farmer recipe.

Junk jewelry, rings and bracelets mostly, go for up to $50! Beads are a popular, less expensive item.

The biggest trade is in "roach" clips, which allow pot smokers to groove down to the last puff. Marijuana pipes, from $15 to $100, sell briskly.

Every night the psychedelic shops are jammed with patrons.

Most psychedelic shops once featured trip rooms at the rear, but they were busted so often they've given up this part of their business. Now the trip rooms are in small out-of-the-way places on Sunset and Fairfax.

They're dark except for strobe lights that cast a phosphorescent glow on the wild, fantastic designs of the posters tacked to the walls—concentric circles, jagged lines, zigzag patterns, twisted, misshapen faces. It's all part of the mind-bending trip. You can get stoned just from the fallout in the room. If you're dropping acid or mescaline or smoking grass, you're really on a trip. The rooms are packed with kids. They sit on the floor, their eyes open, just staring vacantly in front of them, completely out of their heads. The jukebox is turned up to its highest volume, but even at that pitch, I don't think the heads can hear the music.

It is a tough atmosphere in which to witness.

During the infrequent pauses in the music I am talking to a Jewish girl in one of the rooms on Fairfax. I'm trying to win her to the Lord.

A big guy in his twenties, over six feet and two hundred pounds, comes over, and he doesn't look or act friendly. He has an Old Testament beard, and his clothes are filthy.

"What the hell are you doing in here? You look like a narc."

"I'm a preacher, and I'd like to tell you about God."

"I don't need God. I need a place to crash and something to eat."

"I can help you."

He snorts a curse and walks away.

I continue talking to the girl. Now she's giving her heart to Christ. We bow our heads in prayer. When I look up, the guy is looming over us like Goliath.

"Did you say something about a place to crash?"

"You really need to know Christ and be saved."

"I'm not interested in that. All I want is sleep and food."

"You've got it."

We drive the three blocks to my apartment. It's two o'clock in the morning. I wake Sherry and ask her to fix bacon and eggs for an unexpected guest.

I still don't know anything about him except that he's a soul in torment.

Waiting for the food and sitting at the table he tells me his name is Danny and he's a member of a bikers' club in Michigan.

"Why aren't you wearing your jacket?"

"Can't fly my colors. I don't want trouble with The Man."

As he forks the food into his mouth Sherry and I both witness to him. He seems to have an instant, beautiful rapport with Sherry, and in less than half an hour he melts in her hands like snow in July. Gone is the rudeness, the outward, superficial toughness. He comes to the Lord like a lamb, the three of us kneeling in the kitchen praying for Jesus to accept a new follower.

Danny has received two meals, one for his stomach, the other for his spirit.

Bikers are extremely touchy about their clothes. It's part of their thing to wear them as dirty as possible. Only in Hollywood's know-nothing biker movies do you see chopper jockeys in starched blue jeans and freshly ironed shirts.

When Danny goes to bed, Sherry, holding her nose, picks up his foul-smelling clothes and puts them in the washing machine.

"Do you think you should?"

"I already have. You know what's next to Godliness."

Next morning Danny is confronted with the clean clothes.

"Hell," he shrugs, "I got saved, so I guess I'd better change altogether. Now that you've washed my clothes there's nothing I can do about it. I may as well have clean pants to go along with a clean heart. I guess I am starting a new life."

Part of Danny's new life is making a clean breast of his past. Now he tells us the most amazing part of his story.

Danny is under indictment for murder!

He'd gotten into an argument with a service station attendant over the price of gas for his bike. They began fighting, and Danny stabbed him to death. Frightened, he took off for the Strip, became enmeshed in the drug scene, hitting up on heroin.

Danny has been in touch by phone with his parents, who are influential in his home town. His uncle, a prominent lawyer who has been investigating the circumstances surrounding Danny's crime, has discovered that the attendant had a knife in his pocket.

It isn't difficult to convince Danny to return home and face trial.

Instead of first-degree murder, Danny was allowed to plead guilty to involuntary manslaughter and was paroled.

He came back to the Strip, his Army enlistment papers in hand, forever turned on by Jesus. I still receive an occasional letter from him. Danny is living his life completely for the Lord.

Hollywood is the homosexual capital of the world. At least sixty bars along Santa Monica cater solely to gay guys. One is owned by a famous singer who has had three highly publicized divorces.

There are some gays who act effeminate, but the lingering myth that you can spot a homosexual by dress or speech is not true. Doctors, attorneys, men in every walk of life, people these bars.

At one spot there are three stages and the music is loud, the lights hot. There is no air-conditioning. On most nights you can barely find standing room.

The entertainment consists of several go-go boys in skin-tight pants who dance harder than any topless girl I've ever seen. The dance invariably simulates a sex act.

When the show is over some of the gays dance with each other, but most seem to prefer dancing by themselves. The music is wild, paganlike, and the solo dancers on the floor appear to be having a climax.

The place grooves until six in the morning.

But most of the bars are quiet, soft music lolling in the background. Conversation is subdued. Some of the biggest dope transactions in town are consummated in these places. The gays are strung out, too. It's routine for a deal to be made at one of the bars for twenty thousand reds or dozens of kilos of marijuana.

Male hustlers are strung out like a necklace of tarnished pearls along Santa Monica. Cars stop and arrangements are made.

I'm allowed to preach and witness at most of the gay bars. My reception is always respectful and polite.

During a witnessing excursion one evening at a bar where female impersonators gather, a soldier walked in. He went to a table and sat down next to what he thought was a girl. Under-the-table sex play began, and the soldier was soon enflamed. When a certain point was reached, the soldier realized his companion was a man.

I walked over and talked to him, but he was already in Satan's coils. He was so ablaze with passion that he said he was going to the guy's apartment. I begged him not to.

"I'm not going to have a gay act," he answered. "I've never done anything like that. I'm straight. Just going over for a cup of coffee and some conversation."

"You don't know what you're getting into." I followed him to the sidewalk, continuing to plead. It didn't take. The soldier and the female impersonator strolled off hand in hand.

The Metropolitan Community Church, the first of its kind in the country, has a congregation made up primarily of homosexuals. The church holds services in a 385-seat theater every Sunday morning. It is pastored by Troy Perry, who was a minister in Florida and Santa Ana, California, before he admitted his homosexuality and was asked to resign.

His church, Pastor Perry believes, is providing an unmet need. He holds prayer meetings and Bible classes and "marries" homosexual couples who've been together for at least six months.

He says the biblical strictures against homosexuality have been too literally interpreted.

"Most churches in America don't openly invite homosexuals as homosexuals to come and worship God," he says. "They feel, if anything, they have to change the person and convert him from his homosexuality to make him a fit member for their church—and that's just impossible."

In my own experience I haven't found it impossible. I've prayed with dozens of homosexuals who've told God they would give up unclean sex. I've led seven to the Lord, notably a twenty-three-year-old gay named Carlos, who ran the largest ring of male prostitutes in Hollywood. He had a large pad, a big car and bank account, and had been on dope since he first tried opium while serving in Vietnam. I worked with Carlos for several days, and God granted him conviction, giving him a totally natural desire for women. He came to the Lord with his whole heart and soul, making a total commitment, finding the strength to overcome his deviation. He dates only girls now, and is as joyful a Christian as there is on this earth. He plans to marry and have a family.

After dinner Sherry and I are walking toward our car, parked on a back street off the Strip. We meet a doe-eyed teen-ager, looking disheveled and lost. Her leg is bleeding. It is one of the thousand random tragedies you can find on the Strip every night. The girl is a runaway turned prostitute. She says, "Four guys came up to me and said they were ready to go. They took me behind a building, threw me down in the bushes, and they all had sex with me." The girl is in tears, helpless. Sherry leads her to the Lord, and we arrange for her to return to her parents in Chicago.

Sheriff Peter Pitchess in a speech: "I'm not about to warn you that organized crime may move in [to Los Angeles]. They are already here. They have established a strong foothold, and if that doesn't shock, it should.

"We must recognize that a vehicle presently exists that is bringing big crime to our area and enabling these criminals to establish themselves. We must accept the fact that Los Angeles is the smut and pornography capital of the world."

The dirty-book stores, dozens of them, besmirch the Strip and its periphery, offering between covers and on film every known perversion. The most sickening are the picture books with twelve-, thirteen-, and fourteen-year-old naked, tumescent boys. The homosexuals groove on this filth.

Profits for the owners are high. A magazine produced for less than fifty cents sells for five dollars. The biggest customers are the legion of dirty-book freaks, all straights. One smut shop, next to a theater that features stag films, has a trade that is so brisk it is open twenty-four hours a day.

Most of the books and magazines feature fresh-faced young girls. How do the agents of the vast mail-order smut distributors recruit and convince the girls to pose?

Dozens of girls have told me similar stories. They are approached on the Strip and asked if they would like to work as models. Desperate, alone, broke, they are runaways to whom the offer of one hundred dollars is a fortune.

The girl is invited to a studio or a rented motel or hotel room. She's shy and won't remove her clothes. A couple of pictures of her are snapped while she's fully dressed. Then she's offered a glass of water. The water is spiked with downers. Soon she's so spaced out she isn't aware of what she's doing. Now in a sleeplike trance, she cooperatively removes her clothes and poses the way the pornography-makers want her to. If she begins to object as the downers wear off, she's given another glass of barbiturate-laden water. Soon she's committing sex acts before the cameras with lesbians and two, three, or four men.

When they're finished with her, the vultures toss her into a car and drop her off somewhere along the Strip. She's fortunate if she's given even twenty-five dollars.

A busty topless dancer and prostitute talks with me between numbers at a well-known Strip club.

"I'm a soul-winner, too," she says.

She's actually trying to hustle me into bed with her.

"After I sleep with these guys, I lead them to the Lord! We sit on the bed and pray. I like to read to them from the Book of John."

From memory she quotes more Scripture than could most preachers.

She's a doper, and in her confused mind, no matter how hard I witness to her, she doesn't see the twisted contradiction and sacrilege of preaching the Bible after renting her body.

"I'm saved, Arthur; I really believe in my heart that I am."

A new wrinkle in prostitution has been devised by the ever-ingenious purveyors of sin: brothels that mask themselves under the pseudonym of "model studios." They pepper Fairfax, LaBrea, and Santa Monica and have even spread to the stodgy straight bastions of Pasadena and Inglewood.

Large signs beckon you to photograph "professional models." You press a buzzer, a slot opens, you're given the once-over and if you're not from the vice squad (the managers know all the vice investigators, since they are never rotated) you are allowed inside.

The model studios operate under a legal city license, but they always fear a bust because all the girls working the places will go as far as a customer wants, provided he has the cash.

In the reception room there's a dim red light, so subdued you can barely see the tip of your nose. Suggestive pictures hang on the walls. The customer may choose from the half dozen girls in various stages of undress who are on hand.

The customers are well dressed, from forty to seventy-five years old. Some are regulars; some come in twice a week; some once or twice a month.

The mark is given a camera with a roll of film. The price for picture-taking is thirty dollars for thirty minutes. Once inside the private room, the lock is thrown, and the girl will pose in any acrobatic position desired.

The straight is soon roused to the point where he'll shell out another twenty-five or fifty dollars, whatever the girl can bleed him for, to have sex with her.

The girls are sixteen to nineteen, but the managers of the studios provide them with forged I.D. cards that say they're over twenty-one.

Business ebbs and flows. A hard-working girl can earn five hundred dollars a week when customers are plentiful. Her income plummets to under one hundred dollars when trade falls off. Her take ranges from thirty-five to fifty percent of her gross.

The model studios are wide open for me to witness. As far as sin dens are concerned, the studios are more receptive than any of the others.

Most of the time I wind up sitting in the middle of the floor with the girls gathered around me as I tell them about Jesus.

Several have been led to the Lord and led out of the business, but there is one girl named Linda that I despair of ever bringing to Christ.

Her personality depends on her mood. She can be sacred or profane, sweet or raunchy. One of the most beautiful young girls I've ever met, Linda, like most models who work the studios, is stoned every night. She has a wide following of regulars and is earning money hand over fist.

Her lantern-jawed, black-haired boss is named Al; he manages two other places of the same type. At one time he was a ministerial student at a California Bible college, studying to be a Baptist preacher!

On a night when business is lagging I find Linda in a bikini coiled in a lounge chair at Al's place.

"Things are going great," she volunteers. "No hangups. No hangups at all."

"You're lying and you know it," I say. "You're not happy. You're miserable. If you were really happy, you wouldn't have to take all that dope to rid yourself of guilt."

"Arthur Blessitt, I can handle anybody except you. You're right. I am miserable. Today I tried to jump out of Al's car on the freeway. He grabbed my arm and held me back."

I share Christ with Linda for more than an hour.

It takes! It is one of the most unexpected turnabouts I have ever encountered. Linda gets down on her knees with me and prays, her tears washing her mascara in streaks down her face. After we pray she looks up and her eyes sparkle.

"I'm saved!" she says joyously. "Jesus has found me and I'm going back to my baby."

Still on our knees, we hear the buzzer sound. I get up and go to the door.

"Are you open for business?" the customer, a fiftyish man with a crew cut and horn-rimmed glasses, asks.

"Yes, sir, come right in."

When he enters, I give him one of my Big Question tracts. He brings it close to his face and seems disturbed as he reads it. Then he looks at Linda, still on her knees. He starts backing off toward the door. "I must be in the wrong place."

"We're just having a little revival. You're welcome."

Linda jumps to her feet, runs to him, and points an accusing finger in his face. "I just got saved and you ought to give your heart to Jesus Christ, too. You're nothing but a dirty, perverted old man. You've been taking pictures of me for months. Now I'm clean, and I'm through with all that. You should do the same thing. Go back to your family."

The man is stunned and runs out like a fox being chased by a pack of beagles.

I tell Linda that I'll buy her a ticket home.

"No, I've got some pay coming. I'm staying at Al's place. All my clothes are there. I'll explain to him that I've given my heart to Christ. He'll understand why I'm quitting."

"No, don't, don't go back to him. Just leave. Come with me now. Get out while you can."

"It'll be all right, Arthur. Don't worry."

We arrange that I'll pick Linda up the next day at noon at Al's Fuller Avenue apartment.

When I come for Linda Al is there with three heavy-looking men. One moves behind me, stationing himself at the door, blocking any exit.

They have really worked Linda over. Her eyes are blackened, her lips swollen, bruises all over her. She sits petrified on a hassock. I can almost smell her fear.

"Al, Linda is going with me."

"No," Linda says. "Forget it, Arthur. I'm staying with Al."

"Did you tell Al what happened to you last night, that you became a born-again Christian?"

"Get out," Al orders. "You heard her, she's not going." Al's men move in closer to me.

"Al, you need to get right with God. You need to give your heart to Jesus Christ." The more I say the angrier he becomes. "You need to let this girl go and let her have a new life. You used to be a Christian. Man, you know what I'm talking about."

I turn to Linda and say, "Let's get out of here."

She doesn't even flick an eyelash.

"In the name of God, Al, let her go. God's got Linda. You can't take her away from Him."

There's a long minute's pause. Finally, Al nods his head and waves off his goons.

. Linda bolts from the hassock, two suitcases in hand, and leaves with me.

In the street we search for a taxi.

"Arthur, don't tell anybody where I'm going. Never. Not even the city I'm living in. I've got to leave all this behind forever."

I ask Linda if she wants me to take her home.

"No, I don't want you involved in this any more. I'm going back to my mother and daughter. I'll be okay."

A cab pulls up and Linda steps in after kissing me goodbye.

It was the last time I ever saw or heard from her.

I can never go back to Al's place. The one time I tried to, I was met at the door by a statuesque girl named Vivian. She had a letter opener in her hand.

"If you come in here, Preacher, I'll kill you."

One chilly, windy night as I make the rounds of the plushest spots on the Strip my mind is burdened. I'm flat broke, and the $60 for the rent on our little office is due tomorrow. There isn't a way in the world I can think of to raise the money.

Among my witnessing stops are Frascati's, Sneaky Pete's, the Playboy Club, and the tower restaurant atop the 9000 Sunset Boulevard building. My last call is at Dino's, about the fanciest gin mill on the Strip.

I sit at a stool at the bar. The bartender knows me. His eyes are friendly. He winks and says, "Preacher, how about a double?"

"Right."

He serves me a large glass of water.

At a table in back of me a loud-mouthed drunk has just ordered a bottle of champagne. In a voice that carries through the room the man announces, "I'm going to burn a one-hundred-dollar bill for kicks."

He removes the bill from his wallet, puts the flame of his cigarette lighter to it, and lets it burn until only a corner remains. The remnant of the bill is passed around the room. Everyone thinks it's funny.

But I'm appalled.

The man with money to burn has moved to the bar a few stools from me, talking to some people.

I can't resist walking over to him. "Sir, you're a rich fool, and the Hell that you are going to burn in is going to be much hotter than the fire that burned your hundred dollars. People on this street are hungry tonight and you're burning money. Ask Jesus into your soul! May God have mercy on you!"

He laughs, reaches into his pocket, and brings out a horse-choking roll of bills. He pushes back my coat and stuffs the money inside my shirt.

I fish the bills out and slap them all back into his jacket pocket. "Sir, you've met somebody you can't buy. You can't buy God's forgiveness, and you can't pay me off to soothe your conscience. I don't want your money."

I think about getting evicted from our little office the next day and know how easy it would be to accept this man's money and let it work for the Lord. But I just can't.

"If not money, what do you want?" he asks.

"I want you to be saved. To ask Jesus into your heart."

I begin praying for him. The crowd gathered around is taking in the whole scene.

As I pray the man suddenly falls backward. It flashes through my mind that God has struck him dead. Women are screaming. Waiters push toward him. I kneel and feel his pulse. After a minute or so he opens his eyes. He looks at me and says, "Don't you touch me. The power of God's on you. I believe in God. I'm a member of the South Baptist Church in Lubbock, Texas."

He raises himself under his own power and now seems sober.

"I don't care what you say. You're going to take at least a little of this money." He peels off a few bills. "God has told me to give this to you."

Not until I get back to my office do I look at the money he handed me.

Exactly sixty dollars!

12

His Place

"You mean you'd preach the Gospel like Billy Graham?"

"More like Arthur Blessitt."

I was talking with Bill Gazzarri, the proprietor of Hollywood-A-Go-Go, the flagship teen-age hangout on the Strip. In making my rounds, I had met and talked a dozen times with Bill, a rugged, gray-haired man who looked at the world through alert, dark eyes. In the name of Jesus, I had nagged Bill almost to death, pleading with him to take the unprecedented step of letting a minister tell the kids the good news of Christ from the stage of a Strip nightclub. At first he would unceremoniously throw me out, but I kept coming back and I was gradually wearing him down.

Bill was all straight, a businessman who'd been capitalizing on the teen-age invasion of the Strip for years, serving up hard rock, running dance contests for prize money, and featuring the kids in a dance-rock format on a widely watched local TV show. He also advertised his attractions heavily.

"Jesus at the Hollywood-A-Go-Go. I don't think it would mix," Bill said.

"Your midweek crowds are down. Give me a Tuesday evening, your slowest night, and I guarantee I'll pack the place for you. And no charge. You have nothing to lose."

"What if you bomb?"

I was proceeding on the assumption that God wouldn't let me wash out. He had always been at my side when I preached in church. Why would He desert me for spreading His message from a nightclub stage?

Perhaps too grandiloquently, I promised Bill, "You'll have more kids in here than you can handle."

"I've had every other type of attraction. Why not a minister? Okay, Arthur."

Once Bill agreed he did everything possible to ensure a crowd. He put my name on his marquee: "SEE AND HEAR ARTHUR BLESSITT TURN YOU ON WITH THE GOSPEL." He also advertised my appearance on Strip billboards, in several college newspapers, and on KHJ, the strident rock radio station most of the kids listen to in Los Angeles.

Bill had given me two hours to fill, from 10 P.M. to midnight. I arranged for several singing groups to perform, including the pretty Sunshine Sisters, who had sung gospel all over America and had made a tremendous impact in Brazil and the Middle East with their songs for the Lord. The other groups, specializing in psychedelic and soul gospel, were The New Creatures, The Disciples, and The Singing Stair Steps. I also arranged for two teenagers to give their testimonies, a former prostitute and a one-time junkie. I had led them both to Christ.

Tuesday night rolled around and I was quivering inside, wondering if the kids would come. I paced backstage and a moment before I was to go on I peeked out at the room.

It was jammed; standing room only!

Bill was in rapture. So was I.

Was any further evidence needed that kids could groove on the Gospel?

I preached on Life's Greatest Trip, urging the kids to let Jesus turn them on instead of drugs. Drop out of slavery to sin. Kick pot, acid, and speed. Be really free, be really happy.

The combination of singing, testimonies, and preaching scored solidly with the kids.

The entire evening was out of sight.

Bill was almost speechless. "Arthur, will you come back?"

I came back for six more rallies, and the kids came too.

Word that the Gospel had successfully invaded the Strip reached the news department at CBS television. Ralph Story, host of a popular West Coast program, devoted most of his half-hour show to the "swinging preacher" of Sunset Strip. Then a five-minute feature about my work was carried on a national newscast. As soon as it was aired, my phone began ringing off the wall. A bevy of

Hollywood agents—a breed I had never encountered before and would prefer to avoid in the future—came to me with fantastic offers.

A radio show.

A television show.

Las Vegas.

San Francisco.

A coast-to-coast nightclub tour.

$1,000 a night.

$1,500 a night.

$2,500 a night, plus a percentage of the gross.

The refrigerator in our apartment held little more than peanut butter and jelly, and that kind of money sounded incredible, until I discovered what I had to do to earn it.

Each of the agents had about the same idea. They wanted me to preach to whiskey-sodden straights in nightclubs, but they also wanted to make a freak and an entertainer out of me. They had no conception or understanding of my one abiding interest—winning souls for Christ. I didn't want to be bartered and sold like a dirty-mouthed comedian or a stripper. I didn't want to be exploited in that manner. That wasn't truly witnessing for Christ; that was selling Him out.

I went to dinner with one of the agents, and I talked about Jesus.

"Great, kid, you do your Jesus thing." Then he began talking money and percentages.

"I don't want to be paid for preaching in a nightclub."

"Sure, fine, okay. We'll call it a donation. You won't make a dime. It will all go into your Association." He winked at me as if we were conspirators in a con game with Christ as the sucker. The agent wouldn't care if I were selling dog food so long as I could make a profit for him. The agility of his scheming mind was incredible. He had a dozen ideas, each one more atrociously conniving than the last. I told him I'd starve to death before agreeing to anything he proposed. As I got up to leave he looked at me with startled eyes. "This Jesus thing of yours is Fort Knox, your own money-making machine."

Another agent, a lady in a wide-brimmed hat, read me her client list, some of Hollywood's most successful actors. She offered to represent me for six months without taking a commission. When I asked a musician friend how she could afford such an arrangement, he told me, "She'll get a kickback from the club owners every place you appear."

On that basis, God's message was not for sale. I swept the agents out of my life as Christ had the money changers from the temple.

The last time I talked to the lady agent, she said, "You're throwing away a million-dollar career."

She still wasn't tuned in on my wavelength.

My call, my obsession, was to continue my ministry to the kids on the Strip. Here there was need, here there was challenge, here there were great victories waiting to be won for Christ. Here there must be a church for the dispossessed young.

After months of hunting, I finally found a building on the Strip that rented for four hundred dollars a month. It was a series of small rooms, and I had really wanted a bigger main room in which I could preach to a large crowd. Though far from ideal, it was the best location available. I decided to rent it. The day before I was to sign the lease, I was driving down the Strip and saw a "For Rent" sign at 9109 Sunset. I slammed on my brakes and anxiously called the broker who had the listing.

The building was a two-story affair. Part of it had once been used as a recording studio. It was in abominable shape, with banged up walls and doors and old dirty curtains barely hiding the grime of unwashed windows. But I could see the upstairs as a prayer room, and the main room downstairs would be large enough to hold scores of kids.

This was it.

The owner wanted six hundred dollars a month and an unbreakable five-year lease.

The rent, to say nothing of a hard five-year commitment, was a heavy, chancy load. I had no idea if our church would catch on, and all the money Sherry and I could scrape together amounted to two hundred dollars.

The owner did agree to a one-year lease but in view of what was to come later I should have grabbed the opportunity to tie up the building for five years.

The only problem now was that I had to have the first and last month's rent—twelve hundred dollars—in twenty-four hours.

It seemed hopeless until I remembered the name of a man who

had sent word to me that he was interested in my work and that if I decided to start a church on the Strip, he would be glad to help. He was a fine Christian and a first vice-president of a leading Beverly Hills stock brokerage firm.

I phoned him the morning the money was due and told him about the building.

"How much is the rent?"

He nearly had a fit when I gave him the price. "I thought you'd get something for maybe a hundred fifty a month. I'll contribute seventy-five. How are you going to get the rest?"

"I have two hundred dollars. I'll have to pray for the other thousand."

"When do you need the money?"

"In an hour."

"What are you going to do?"

"I'm going to write a check for twelve hundred dollars."

"But it will bounce. A minister doesn't go round writing phony checks."

"It won't clear until tomorrow. I don't know how, but God will provide the money because He wants us on the Sunset Strip."

"You really believe that?"

"Yes, sir. Nothing can stand in our way."

I heard a deep breath on the phone. "All right, you have your thousand dollars. Go ahead and write the check."

Christ now was part of the Strip scene!

There wasn't a dime to pay salaries to anyone, not a penny for food. We couldn't afford to buy a lightbulb or a nail.

But He had put it all together, and He has provided for us ever since, meeting our needs for rent, Bibles, tracts, and other expenses, sometimes at the last moment, but always He has been there in time.

Christ has blessed our Strip ministry, and as our work has become known, unsolicited contributions have come in through the mail. A few churches consider us a mission, as do several individuals, and this support, Divinely generated, has allowed us not only to survive, but to grow.

From the beginning, I decided that I would not waste time chasing after money. Only God, not the dollar, is Almighty. Through prayer and faith we have been sustained.

Free of concern about money, we are at liberty to carry out the command of Christ to save souls and help people.

Four of us were on hand to whip the building into shape. Besides Sherry and myself there was Dale Larsen, whom I had met on the Strip. A graduate of the Detroit Bible College and a lay minister, Dale had also heard God's call to do His work on Sunset Boulevard. He had come from Michigan for that express purpose and he was a welcome, soon indispensable, member of our Team. Our other staff member was Mike, a speed freak I had led to the Lord. Mike's problems were primarily rooted in the bickering, short-tempered atmosphere created in his home by his parents. To escape he had turned on. After he accepted Christ and worked with us for a while, he met a lovely girl, married, settled down, and avoided seeing his impossibly argumentative parents. Ironically, Mike's mother was a Los Angeles County employee—a social counselor paid to advise the parents of young lawbreakers after they were released from Juvenile Hall!

We hammered, sawed, built, planned, and prayed nearly twenty-four hours a day, cleaning up the debris and getting our church ready. There weren't any frills. We hand-painted a couple of posters for the walls: "SMILE, GOD LOVES YOU"; "TURN ON TO JESUS"; "REAL PEACE IS JESUS"; "GOD IS LOVE." We painted the upstairs prayer room and placed a Bible on a battered old table. A few used cushions were the only other adornments. Downstairs we constructed a foot-high stage and strung some colored lights.

We improvised and scrounged for furniture. In a rented U-Haul, Dale and I went to the telephone company's warehouse in Santa Monica. We found a dozen giant discarded cable spools, and these, with a painted checkerboard on each, became our tables. We also found two weathered, abandoned telephone poles. We liked the wood. It had a rugged, used look. From those poles, we carved our cross. We sallied through the back alleys behind carpet stores and from garbage cans we rescued a number of rugs for our floor. (When the rugs got really dirty and stained we threw them away. There wasn't money to clean them. It was less expensive to go back to the alleys for a new supply.)

Opening day was suddenly upon us, and we were as ready as we would ever be, except for one thing.

We didn't have a name for our church.

To announce our opening we had ordered a supply of handbills which we were going to pass out up and down the Strip. The printer had come to the building and was waiting for us to decide on a name so he could complete the handbills.

The four of us brainstormed through dozens of names, including The Eternal Trip, The Lighthouse, The Door, The Temple.

None rang true.

The printer was tapping his foot impatiently. Perhaps we would have to open without a name.

"Arthur," I heard Sherry say, "we need a name that celebrates God. This isn't your place, my place, or even the kids' place. It's the Lord's, it's His place."

His Place!

That rang true and clear.

"His Place, His Place," I shouted. "We'll call it 'His Place.' "

Everyone agreed that the Lord had given Sherry the inspiration for the name of our church. Even the printer smiled when I told him to put "His Place" at the top of the handbills.

Our first night we expected perhaps fifteen to twenty-five kids. We had a sign in our window that promised free refreshments, but our only food was one loaf of bread and half a jar of peanut butter.

Nevertheless, we threw open the door at 7:30 P.M.

Into His Place, to our astonishment, streamed some 150 kids—hippies, dopers, bikers, teeny-boppers, drag queens, pushers, hoods, pimps, and prostitutes. A small army, all teen-agers, who needed God in their lives.

With the possible exception of three or four kids, every youngster who came through the door was stoned on downers, speed, acid, or H. It seemed as if we were hosting one tremendous freak-out.

A sort of controlled chaos reigned for a while. Then the kids settled down around the tables and started rapping. The four of us moved through the crowd, talking, witnessing, welcoming our flock.

Our food shortage was met when a number of Christian adults —I don't know how they heard of our opening or how they knew we needed food—arrived with armloads of peanut butter, jelly, and Kool-Aid. I had called a number of Jewish bakeries on Fairfax, and they came through with bags of bagels. The bagels have been a mainstay of the diet at His Place—the hard bread is a perfect snack for a doper whose trip is wearing off.

There were to be three confrontations during our first night. The manner in which they were met would determine whether His Place would earn a reputation as a church paying homage to God or a lunatic asylum in which various groups of kids would fight it out among themselves for control of our building. If that happened, not only would God be dishonored, but the sheriff would be certain to close us down.

The problem was, however, that the kids in His Place weren't exactly altar boys or a choir of angels. The room was bubbling with laughter and conversation when the first trouble erupted.

About twenty kids, sitting smack in the center of the floor, began a loud chant, drowning out everyone else. It was a cacophonous, eerie sound, all-engulfing.

I went over to them and shouted for quiet. "What's going on?"

"We're Buddhists," the spokesman said, "and we're praying."

"If you want to pray, you'll have to move upstairs to our prayer room."

They climbed the steps, but in a moment the renewed sound of their chanting caromed downstairs. Again no one could hear himself think.

I ran up and found they had all joined hands while they continued their high-pitched prayer.

I again shouted for quiet. "I'm not telling you that you can't pray to Buddha or anyone else. But in this room you have to pray in such a way that it doesn't disturb anyone else."

"It's a free country; we have freedom of religion," their spokesman said.

"This room is set aside for quiet prayer and silent meditation. I wouldn't allow any Christian group to pray aloud either if they were disturbing others. That's just the way things are going to be run around here."

They filed sullenly out with no further argument.

About an hour later Dale came over to me and said, "There's a gang of bikers in the prayer room smoking grass."

When I reached the prayer room, this time the door was locked from the inside.

"Open up."

When there was no response, I started pounding. I heard a hoarse voice cry, "Split, man, don't mess with us."

The odor of the grass, which has a distinct smell vaguely resembling incense, wafted through the door.

"You open up, or I'm going to pray my way in. I mean it."

I heard the lock turn, and as I stepped inside I saw at least twenty bikers and their old ladies. There was also a suffocating cloud of smoke. The bikers were all flying their colors, and they looked touchy and hard-jawed.

"You'll bust the whole place if you smoke grass in here. Put your joints out, and right now."

"Who's going to make us?" their hoarse-voiced leader said.

"God."

"Who makes the rules around here?"

"I do."

"You better split, Preacher, while you have the chance. Just let us alone, and when we're through, we'll go."

"No. You have to leave now."

"You going to throw us out?"

"Yes."

A couple of the bikers' old ladies giggled.

"How are you going to do it?"

"With God's help. This is His house. You're welcome as long as you behave. But pot smoking isn't allowed. Like it or not, you have to leave—now!"

Four of them came at me, and grabbed me by the shoulders and under my arms.

"You're going out that window," their angry leader declared.

The window of the prayer room led to a twenty-foot drop to the ground.

I knew the psychology of the bikers. Alone, no one of them was really tough, but in a pack they were like wolves. They wouldn't chicken out. They were perfectly capable of murder.

"Before I go out that window, I want to pray."

They loosened their grip on me as I sunk to my knees.

"In the name of Jesus Christ I ask that these young people be put under conviction. Stay their hands, Lord, strike them down if need be. Show them that Christ died on the cross for us and He rose again, that He is coming again, that you are Lord of lords, and this is Thy House which must be kept sacred in Thy name."

When I finished, you could have heard the flutter of an eyelash.

Then in a low, quiet voice, the bikers' leader said, "I can't stand any more of this damn preaching. I'm splitting."

One by one they left until I was alone.

I was still on my knees.

The threats of the Buddhists and the bikers to the integrity of His Place had been surmounted. Far more insidious and dangerous was the problem of handling the pushers.

The heads and freaks were bunched together, a school of hungry sharks waiting for their pilot fish. Potentially, a dealer had a ready-made market at His Place. I had to be certain to harpoon any dealer who came through the door. One report to the sheriff that junk was being dealt at His Place might close us down.

The most artful, devilish, clever dealer on the Strip was Richard, a short cat with matted, curly hair. As I feared, His Place proved to be the flame; Richard, the predictable moth.

He came in on our first night with his band of about fifteen assistants, some of them chicks. Richard was another dealer who kept his junk hidden in the bras of his chicks.

Shortly after he arrived, one of the kids whispered in my ear, "Richard's dealing."

I barreled over to him and laid the law down. "Man, you can't push in here."

Richard didn't bother to deny he was dealing. Instead he justified it. "I couldn't deal if the heads and freaks weren't buying."

"That doesn't wash with me. Unless you give me your word that you and your whole bunch will stop dealing in here, I'll call The Man."

"Sure, Arthur," he said with seeming sincerity, "you've got my word."

But half an hour later Dale told me that kids were making buys from one of Richard's chicks just outside our door.

I stepped out in time to see a bag of pills being exchanged for bread. I was furious.

Richard was rapping inside with some of the kids when I came storming up to him. "One of your chicks is pushing outside."

"I gave you my word we wouldn't deal in here, and we're not."

"Pushing a few feet from our door amounts to the same thing."

"What are you going to do about it?" Richard said truculently.

"All of you split or I bring the sheriff in."

"You can't afford to call The Man. You know how the kids hate the cops. You call them in and you'll alienate them all. You'll just be another fink."

"I'm not going to compete in a popularity contest with a pusher. Are you leaving or not?"

"No."

I went to the phone and called the sheriff.

Richard, completely unconcerned, walked to our stage, sat down, and rested his head against our cross.

"You still have time to split," I told Richard after hanging up the phone.

"This is a house of God, a sanctuary. They won't bust me in here."

"His Place isn't a sanctuary for a rotten pill pusher who doesn't have Jesus in his heart."

Richard had given me a cunning argument. If I had him arrested for dealing, I *would* lose the trust of the kids and any hope of reaching them. Yet I couldn't have him selling his junk in or near our premises.

I called for the attention of the kids. "I want everyone to know the police are coming and I'm going to ask them to arrest Richard. I'm giving him a chance to leave, but he refuses. I'm not turning him in for dealing. But if we allow Richard to push stuff in here, His Place won't be around much longer."

When I finished, there was no positive or negative reaction from the kids. Apparently they were content to wait and see the outcome.

When two sheriff's deputies arrived, I led them to Richard, who was still using our cross as a headrest.

"Officer, I want this fellow removed. He is disturbing the peace."

"Outside," one of the law men ordered. "We want to talk to you."

Richard didn't move a muscle.

"I'll say it one more time," the officer barked. "Are you going to step outside?"

When Richard still failed to stir, the officer reached for his handcuffs.

Now Richard nonchalantly stood up, brushing imaginary dirt from his buckskin jacket. Then ensued perhaps the most astonishing conversation I've ever heard. Richard, with a talent I never dreamed he possessed, turned in a dazzling performance. His act would have shamed Sir Laurence Olivier.

"Gentlemen," he said to the sheriff's men, "I guess this is the moment I have to surface. I'm a state narcotics bureau undercover man!"

It was pure poetry and the wide-eyed officers, incredibly, were buying every word.

"My assignment," continued Richard, "was to check out Arthur Blessitt. The bureau had to see how far this man would go. We had to determine if he would really honor his commitment to God and the law, if he would drive a pusher from his temple. I can report that this man is cool. He is a true man of God. Take my word for it, you can trust Arthur Blessitt. Now I have to move on to my next assignment. This is just one of a number of locations I'm investigating. We've got to put these pushers out of business."

With new respect in his voice, the officer who had barked at Richard asked, "Sir, do you have any official identification?"

Pure putty for Richard's agile brain. "As a state narc, you should realize I can't afford to carry any I.D."

Then Richard, in slow, measured steps, marched unmolested out the door and into the night.

Richard was wasting his time pushing junk. He could have made a fortune selling the Brooklyn Bridge.

"I guess that wraps it up," one of the lawmen said to his buddy. "Let's take off."

I watched them go, my mouth agape. I was awe-stricken and speechless.

Wave after wave of laughter rocked the room as the kids spread the story of how the biggest dope pusher on the Sunset Strip had outsmarted The Man.

I thought to myself that if Richard used his nimble mind for Christ, he'd be one of the greatest soul-winners in the history of the world.

Richard returned many times to His Place, but he never tried dealing again. He couldn't pull the same charade twice. We became good friends, and Richard later put up the bail money for me after one of my arrests.

That first night at least four hundred kids came through our door. Some carried weapons. Some had bottles of booze. We quickly separated couples who tried to pair off in a corner and we nipped a few fights before real trouble could break out.

I preached at midnight and fifteen young people stepped up to receive the Savior.

At 4 A.M. we swept everybody out. Several homeless kids asked if they could crash till morning. We had to refuse since sleeping in the building overnight was specifically forbidden in our lease.

The first night had taught us a great deal. We drew up a set of rules for the future and hammered it to the front door:

1. No dope.
2. No alcohol.
3. No hassling.
4. No crashing.
5. No making out.
6. No guns, knives, or chains.

Violators would be banned for thirty days.

Christ quickly won a special niche on the Strip. His Place caught on with the kids, caught on beyond my wildest hopes. It became *the* place to go. It was *in*. Hundreds trooped through our door each evening. On Friday and Saturday nights it was so jammed we had to empty the crowd into the street every few hours to permit a patiently waiting new bunch to enter.

Victory after victory was won for Him. Not a night passed without decisions being made for Jesus.

The "toilet service" became one of our His Place traditions. Whenever a doper gives his heart to Christ, we move him straight into the john. Once I counted eighteen bodies squeezed into our little bathroom.

"I don't need this any more, I'm high on the Lord," the typical convert declares. He pulls out his cache of grass, reds, speed, or acid and drops it into the bowl.

At each toilet service I read the soaring, life-changing verse from 2 Corinthians 5:17: "Therefore, if any man be in Christ, he is a new creation; old things are passed away; behold, all things are become new."

This is followed by prayer and by the ex-doper giving his testimony.

And finally, as the handle is pressed, as the junk swirls away, we sing:

> Down, down, down, down,
> All my dope is gone.
> Down, down, down, down,
> All my dope is gone.·

Among the junkies on the Strip, the word is still that His Place has the hottest head in town.

Our staff now was augmented by several new workers. Part of their job was to witness to people walking by on the street outside His Place.

So effective was their witnessing that our next-door neighbor, a topless club called The Session, one of the oldest clubs on the Strip, was forced to close. Too many straights just couldn't bring themselves to go inside and watch half-naked girls cavort after hearing the Word of God.

The owner of The Session told me, "Arthur, you've cost me seventy-five thousand dollars!" With its closing, I was a marked man.

13

A Night to Remember

THE SOUND is jackhammer-loud. A jackhammer for Jesus. It is the crashing gospel rock that slams and ricochets off the walls, searching for escape. But the sound is prisoner, captured for Christ.

Our flock grooves on it. It's all part of the His Place scene. Each time the door to His Place swings open the blast of music is a siren call to the kids. Tonight the leitmotif, played on and off throughout the evening, is "Tell It to Jesus." The Eternal Rush—our group of born-again Christians, all former alcoholics or dopers—is composed of O. J. on piano-organ and J. P. Allen and Jim McPheeters on the electric guitars. Over the galloping Christian rock, Jim's voice rings out:

> All you brothers and sisters,
> I want you to gather round
> For the good news about Jesus
> That's going all over town.

The refrain pounds the message home:

> You can tell it to Jesus,
> He understands everything.
> I'm talking about Jesus,
> The King of kings.

At the dozens of revivals I preach every year from Florida to Hawaii, the local kids have heard about His Place. "What's it like?" "What happens on a typical night at His Place?" they ask.

There is no typical night at His Place. Some evenings are relatively uneventful and quiet. Undramatic decisions are made for the Lord. In our counseling rooms the staff and I listen to the burdens of the kids and share Christ. Other evenings the action is more eventful. And then there are those evenings, too many of them, that are wild and woolly. His Place becomes a battlefield of life and death. And you are too busy to wonder how you manage to cope with it all.

A Saturday night and Sunday morning I'll never forget . . .

7:30 P.M. A crowd of some seventy-five kids has been waiting for us to open. The music is a thunderous welcome. This first group of kids is made up mostly of runaways and heavy dopers. They are all starving, and they head straight for the bagels, peanut butter and jelly sandwiches, the coffee and soft drinks. Some of the kids haven't eaten since they were in His Place the previous night. The runaways have no money and the dopers have spent their last dime on junk. To tide them over many secrete a sandwich or bagel into their jackets for their next meal.

> You can tell it to Jesus,
> He understands everything.
> I'm talking about Jesus,
> The King of kings.

"We've got an OD. He swallowed thirty pills," Dale tells me breathlessly.

The overdose has been taken by Roy, a nineteen-year-old I've witnessed to many times, thus far unsuccessfully. He is without Christ.

Lanky and sallow-faced, Roy is leaning against a wall, glassy-eyed. He speaks, slowly, understandably, but already some of his words are beginning to slur.

"Why, Roy, why did you do it?"

"The whole scene isn't what it's made out to be be. The hell with it."

"How long ago did you take the pills?"

"I don't know—maybe ten minutes."

Roy's eyes are closing now, and he has a sudden change of heart. "Help me, help me, man, I need help. I'm going to die."

I feel Roy's pulse. It's beating slowly. I slap his face a couple of times to rouse him from his torpor. It does no good.

Ten minutes since he swallowed the reds. A twelve-minute ride to the hospital at UCLA. Those thirty reds could kill him in half an hour. In forty-five minutes he'll be dead for sure.

With God's blessing I can make it to the emergency room with eight minutes to spare.

I carry Roy to my car, parked at the back of His Place, and speed to the hospital.

In the polished hospital corridor a doctor and nurse materialize. "He's OD'd on reds. Thirty, about twenty minutes ago."

Roy is moved to a stretcher. Safety belts are strapped over his chest and legs to keep him from thrashing.

It takes ten minutes to pump his stomach.

"He wants to see you," the nurse says.

I hold Roy's hand. He's crying. "Stay close to me, Arthur, stay close." In a few minutes he falls asleep.

I know that Roy is a runaway from Chicago. From his pocket, I fish out his address book and phone his home.

"My name is Arthur Blessitt. I'm a minister. I'm calling from Los Angeles about your son."

"Is this collect?" the angry voice of Roy's mother asks.

"No, ma'am."

"What do you want?"

"Your son's in the hospital. He just tried to kill himself. His condition is critical."

"Don't bother me with that damn boy. I'm tired of him. I don't want anything to do with him."

To my horror, she hangs up.

Before I leave the hospital, the doctor reassures me that Roy is going to make it. He's lucky. Another few minutes. . . .

8:30 P.M. As I arrive back at His Place, four sheriff's cars are parked outside, blinkers flashing.

I can hear the music and Jim's voice:

Seems that on a Saturday night
Everybody wants to go out and play.
But if you really want to get happy,
Fall on your knees and pray.

You can tell it to Jesus,
He understands everything.
I'm talking about Jesus,
The King of kings.

"You can't believe it," Ed Human says. "I asked the police what they wanted, and they just cursed me out."

This is the fourth sheriff's raid at His Place in two weeks. I'm seething with indignation as I storm up to the sergeant in charge. "What's going on? I didn't invite you in here."

"If you don't shut up, if you get in our way, I'll arrest you for interfering with police officers."

Two deputies are busting a pair of teen-age girls, moving them out the door and into a squad car. One girl protests: "My folks know I'm here." The other: "I haven't done anything wrong."

About 250 kids are in the room now. They're all uptight as the dozen policemen move around checking I.D.s.

"Pigs, pigs, pigs!" the kids scream.

I run to the stage and call for quiet. I've got to do some fast talking before a riot breaks out.

"I apologize for what's happening, but we can't answer hatred with hatred. I don't want to hear any of you calling the police pigs. Let's love them. I want every one of you to shake their hands and smile at them even if you despise what they're doing. You show them you're better than they are."

The sheriff's men, oblivious to what I'm saying, are still poking their flashlights into the faces of the kids. They have no intention of leaving.

The only thing to do is pray.

"Dear God, they treat us like filth and dirt, like pus-stained rags. They treat our ministry as if it was a criminal conspiracy when there are real criminals sitting at tables in every club on the Strip. Forgive them, and forgive the businessmen who've sent them here to defile your temple. Convict the hearts of these sheriff's men, who have no regard for the house of God or the work of God. Deal with their souls. Save them. Fill their hearts with love. Sanctify Your Place."

Then I issue an altar call, and the space in front of the stage is filled with young people ready to give their lives to Christ. The staff moves among them, passing out Bibles and tracts.

Welcoming those about to nestle into the bosom of Christ, I ask everyone in the room to bow in prayer.

There is total silence except for the police who are still clumping through the crowd. An officer taps a girl on the shoulder, "Let me see your I.D."

"Yes, sir, as soon as I finish praying."

Even the police can't cope with a roomful of praying kids. They finally trundle out.

> Well, I'd rather go to church on Sunday,
> To sing about my Lord.
> I'd rather go to worship on Sunday
> Than hang around and get bored.
> You can tell it to Jesus,
> He understands everything.
> I'm talking about Jesus,
> The King of kings.

10:15 P.M. His Place has simmered down. The two girls who were busted are back. The sheriff's men drove them around the block, found their I.D.s in order and released them. Their action was nothing but a roust, a humiliating and frightening intimidation of two guests in our church. Imagine the outcry if police tried similar tactics at St. Patrick's Cathedral in New York or First Baptist in Dallas or New Orleans. The hue and cry would cause a sensation, sending shock waves of indignation throughout the country. Yet our church, admittedly unorthodox because it feeds Christ to an unorthodox congregation, is as sacred and inviolate as any temple of God anywhere in the world. This was a concept beyond the understanding of the Strip's police-businessman alliance.

"Jesus loves you," I say, picking up the ringing phone in my office.

"Arthur?"

"Yes. Who's this?"

"I can't go on any more. I've had all I can take. I've tried and tried and tried and nothing works. Some people just aren't meant to make it. It's destiny. I'm a born loser. I thought everything would work out. I love him, I really love him, but it just isn't turning out the way I expected. Arthur, I want you to go to him because he's going to need you and my children are going to need you."

"Who is this?"

"You met me once and you tried to save me, but you didn't."

"I can't save you, only Jesus can save you, and He will. He'll give you another life, a new birth. Let Christ come into your heart. He'll take the clouds away and show you the sunshine. He'll pull back the veil and show you that life's worth living. He'll show you what it's really all about. Give your heart to Him right now; trust Him."

"It's too late, it's too late." Her voice is getting progressively slower, the red flag of suicide by drugs.

"What did you take?"

"Not . . . going . . . to . . . tell . . . you."

"Downers! How many?"

"Couple . . . of . . . bottles. . . . It's . . . all . . . over."

"Where are you?"

"No . . . too . . . late." Her voice is fading fast.

"Can you hear me? Talk to me. Kick a little bit. You don't have to fall down and die. Give your heart to God. Please! He can help you."

"That's . . . a . . . cop . . . out . . . not . . . for . . . me. . . . Promise . . . you'll . . . help . . . Fred."

Fred! The caller is Connie, a straight who until recently worked as a salesclerk at a department store on Wilshire Boulevard. Her husband is a bartender at a nearby Strip joint.

Poor Connie. I remember clearly now our one conversation. She had never been accepted by anyone, not from the start. She was an unplanned child. "When they got mad, my folks would tell me I was a broken rubber," I recall Connie saying. Her marriage to Fred hadn't gone well. He cheated on her repeatedly. Even her two children give her no satisfaction. Connie had carried the albatross of rejection all her life.

Fred, when I find him, is, to my astonishment, stoically unconcerned about his wife. "She tries this every two or three months. Don't worry, she'll sleep for three days and then she'll be all right."

I plead with him to come with me to his apartment. "Man, this is your wife."

He reluctantly agrees.

It's a nerve-tossing fifteen-minute ride. When we enter the apartment, the living room is in disarray and the dining table is piled with dirty dishes, signs that Connie has lost pride in herself and her household.

She's sprawled across the bed, her hand still on the phone. Two bottles of yellow jackets are on the floor.

I bend close to hear Connie's heartbeat.

Not a murmur.

Unlike Roy, Connie hasn't made it.

Fred's heart is cold. He greets his wife's death with a shrug. I fall on my knees at the bedside and say a prayer.

If only she had heeded Jim's refrain:

> You can tell it to Jesus,
> He understands everything.
> I'm talking about Jesus,
> The King of kings.

Midnight. Still terribly hurt that a life that could have been spared has been tragically ended, I shamble toward His Place.

Dale and Ed are standing at the door. Confronting them are four of my friends, Gene, Corey, Willard, and George, wearing black leather jackets and berets. They're Black Panthers who've been frequent visitors at His Place.

Gene is the leader and he's very stoned and uptight. "I want to go inside and get that s.o.b., Hank."

"No, Gene, you know you can't go in."

A week before I had barred Gene for a month after we found three hundred reds he had hidden on the roof of His Place. I'd flushed them down the toilet. Gene had been upset—the pills represented an investment of several hundred dollars. But in the end his temper had cooled because I didn't have him busted.

Dale tells me that Hank is inside fingering a knife. Hank and Gene had been in a fight at a nearby pool hall and Hank had taken refuge in His Place.

"I'm going in, Arthur, don't try to stop me."

"No, Gene."

Gene's first approach is wily.

"I want a glass of water."

"I'll have Dale bring it out for you."

"I want to use the john."

"There's one across the street at the gas station."

Gene turns angry, insanely angry.

"I'm going in to cut Hank. If you don't let me by, I'll kill you."

"Gene, you know I can't let you get at Hank. I've taken you home when you've been drunk. I've taken you home when you've been stoned. I took you to the doctor when you had that attack of hemorrhoids so bad you couldn't stand. I've tried to be your friend. Man, I love you."

Gene moves his left hand from behind his back. He has a Coke bottle filled with gasoline, a rag wick stuffed into the mouth.

A Molotov cocktail.

Gene produces a cigarette lighter in his other hand, which he moves toward the rag.

"You don't let me in and I'll burn the place down."

Through my mind flashes the terrible headline: SUNSET STRIP CHURCH SET ABLAZE; 250 BURNED TO DEATH.

If Gene lights and tosses the Molotov cocktail through our window, no one inside has a chance. Our back door is always kept locked to discourage couples from having sex or taking or hiding dope in the alley.

"It's cool, man, cool. You don't want to throw that thing." Bible in hand, I move closer to Gene. "You can kill me where I'm standing. But you can't incinerate 250 innocent people. I won't let you do that."

"I'm going to burn them all if you don't let me through that door."

He flicks the lighter. The flame comes to life. Gene's right hand carries the flame toward the wick.

"In the name of Jesus Christ, Gene, don't do it."

Though I abhor violence, even striking a man, if Gene moves the lighter another inch I plan to throw my body against his with force enough to knock him to the ground. With all those lives at stake, I have no other choice.

Behind Gene a sheriff's car cruises by. The officers do not notice the drama being played out on the sidewalk.

"If you light that bomb and throw it, there are many lost people inside who'll die and go to Hell because they aren't saved."

"This is your last chance to let me in."

Since there's no apparent way of getting through to Gene, I talk to his pals, who up to now have given tacit approval of the unthinkable act Gene is about to commit, perhaps because they are as stoned as he is, perhaps because they agree with what he is threatening to do, perhaps because they are frightened of him.

"Corey, you remember the night I picked you up on the street when you were spaced out and brought you to His Place until your trip was over. Willard, you spent two days with Sherry and me at our apartment when you were hungry. George, I testified as a character witness at your trial when you were busted. Are all of you going to stand there and let Gene slaughter all those people inside?"

Gene's pals retreat a step or two. But they aren't planning to do anything to stop him.

"Lord," I pray, holding my Bible aloft, "don't let it happen. Don't let it happen, Lord."

I move closer to Gene. "Before you throw it, man, touch the Bible."

"What for?"

"Touching the Bible is touching God."

"No Bible's going to change my mind." But Gene says it with a shade less anger.

"Are you afraid to touch the Bible?"

"I'm afraid of nothing."

"Then hold it, hold the word of God and see if you have the heart to throw that thing. Man, you don't want to kill all those kids."

The psychedelic colors on the cover of the small Bible grip Gene's stare. Involuntarily, he reaches for it. As he does, the Molotov cocktail falls from his hand and shatters harmlessly on the ground.

Gene pockets the Bible, looks at me out of calmer eyes. His face has softened. A hand has touched him; the merciful, gentle hand of the Lord. Gene's anger has spilled from him like water out of a glass.

He and the other Panthers turn and move down the Strip. They are soon swallowed up by the throng.

Gratefully, thankfully, humbly, I go inside, step up on to the stage and tell the kids, "I've never doubted the saving power of

Jesus, but it has just been confirmed. I'm not going to give you the details, but as honestly as I believe in the Lord, I want to tell you that the Bible is more powerful than a Molotov cocktail, more powerful than bullets or an atomic bomb. I hope every one of you here tonight comes to that realization."

The jackhammer beat drowns the room again in a rush of sound:

> The kids today are taking pot
> Cause it seems like the way to fly.
> But if you're tired of the same old trip,
> Tell you what you can try.
> You can tell it to Jesus,
> He understands everything.
> I'm talking about Jesus,
> The King of kings.

1:45 A.M. "Arthur, I've got to talk to you." She's an attractive brunette, about twenty-three.

"I'm planning to preach. I want to give another invitation. There are so many here tonight who need to be saved."

"I need saving, too," she says. She tells me her name is Cora, and there's a tone in her voice that says the girl needs help.

I call Dale over and ask him to give the sermon while I talk to the girl.

Cora and I go into my office.

"What's on your heart?"

"I've got a lot of problems and there are a lot of questions I want to ask you. This may take some time."

Her voice is suddenly submerged under a gut-splitting chorus of laughter from the kids outside.

"Just a minute, Cora." I fling the door open, and I'm appalled. I thought I had seen it all at His Place, but this is new. Standing directly in front of Dale is a doper named Chester. He is twenty-eight or twenty-nine years old, with an emaciated body, tooth-pick legs, and hair down to his shoulders.

Dale is rapping the word of God passionately. He's quoting from Matthew and John, and though he must know that all isn't as it should be, he keeps preaching with dignity.

Chester is drinking in every word of Dale's sermon. But Chester is also standing in front of Dale and in front of 250 people buck naked!

The crowd has quieted, curiosity and anticipation replacing laughter. Everyone is waiting for Dale to react, but he continues preaching, totally unflustered.

For perhaps two minutes I'm transfixed. I'm almost ready to laugh myself, but more important, of course, is to get Chester into his clothes.

Thank the Lord none of the straight Christians who often come from local churches to help us witness are on hand at this moment. I could offer them no word of explanation. Even the thought of their reaction makes me shudder.

As I finally rouse myself and reach Chester, Dale's sermon runs down at last. The crowd is again in an uproar. I raise my hand for quiet.

"Chester, don't you think we should step into the rest room so you can put on your clothes?"

"Preacher, don't you believe in the Bible?" Chester asks with extreme grace under pressure.

"Certainly."

"Well, they were naked in Genesis. Adam and Eve were naked, weren't they?"

"This isn't the Garden of Eden. I wish it were."

"I thought you could do anything you wanted in His Place."

"I allow a certain amount of freedom. But, Chester, I think you're pushing things."

"I'd like to hear Dale preach some more."

"Fine. As soon as you get dressed. What kind of a trip are you on?"

"Acid."

I put my arm around Chester's shoulders and lead him out of sight, the crowd's laughter trailing after us.

In a few minutes Chester is back and Dale is preaching again. Unflappable Dale. He hasn't shown even a glimmer of reaction. As I return to continue my talk with Cora, Chester, hand against chin and one foot on the stage, is paying rapt attention as Dale raps on about Christ. Chester is now fully dressed.

"I'm going to blow your mind," Cora says. "You've probably never met anyone like me."

"What makes you special?"

"All I like to do is have sex." (She used the far more explicit four-letter word.) "I'm really screwed up."

"Tell me about it."

"No one's ever understood or tried to help me. I was married and my husband didn't love me. He just wanted my body. He just wanted sex, and when he got through, he'd roll over and go to sleep. We had no love, no communication, nothing. I started on pills and things got worse. I became pregnant, but before the baby was born my husband and I broke up. I gave the baby up for adoption.

"After we were divorced, I worked as a secretary and started living with a girl friend. She'd gone through some of the same experiences in her life.

"One thing led to another. We would lay down on the bed and start talking. Our bodies craved for something. It seemed like every guy we went out with only wanted to go to bed. I found love in her, and we fell in love with one another. We wanted to be together more than we wanted to be with anybody else. Before long, we were sleeping together.

"But it wore off after a while, and I was still filled with anxiety and frustration. I started hitting up on heroin, and to support my habit, I dealt junk and prostituted."

She shows me the needle marks on her arm, some of the punctures still fresh.

"I'd have a guy sometimes, but I never met one that really turned me on. Then my girl friend and I met these two other girls. They were lesbians. The four of us decided to live together, and we rented a house.

"We have a guy or two in occasionally, and every night we have an orgy of some kind."

She describes the sex play in grotesque detail.

I believe every word she tells me. There is no reason not to. Can this girl be leading up to a decision for Christ?

The answer is no.

She slips to the edge of the chair and opens the first two buttons of her blouse. She is not wearing a bra.

Her mood now has changed. She's Delilah in a mini-skirt.

"Hey, you're cute. What would be wrong with a little sex right here? I think you could make me a real woman again."

"There's nothing wrong with sex within the bonds of marriage. God created man for woman and woman for man, but the Scriptures speak against adultery and fornication."

"But God gives you the desire for sex, doesn't He? So what's wrong with expressing your sexual need?"

"It's true He gave us the need, but He also gave us a set of morals. Sex can be used as an instrument of good or evil."

"Do you like sex?"

"I'm happily married."

"But do you dig sex?"

"A normal person who has nothing wrong with his body and mind and is in love with his wife is going to enjoy being with his wife. I only dig my wife."

"Do other girls turn you on?"

"My wife satisfies me in my soul. We have much more than bed in our life. We have love, and love is in the heart, not the flesh."

"Don't you think you could enjoy having sex with me?"

"No. It's wrong, and I want no part of it. I visit these topless clubs and talk with near-naked women, and I see the mixed-up souls they have. It doesn't make me want to join them in Hell. They can have the most beautiful bodies in the world, yet most of them are crying for love and happiness. Someone like you with a life filled with anxiety and frustration asks me to give up the peace in my heart, the satisfaction of my home and wife. You want to drag me down. That's not much of an invitation. What have you got to offer me? To become a junkie like you or go out and pimp for you? Get confused, disturbed, nervous, and obsessed with sin? I can offer you Jesus Christ, love, joy, happiness, and a life worth living. You offer me nothing. My life belongs to God. God makes my life what it is. Why don't you trust Him and give your heart to Him? Accept Him as Lord, I'll help you. Let's have prayer."

She moves in closer. "I'm just burning up for you. I don't care what you say. I know you want me."

She opens the last two buttons of her blouse and unzips her skirt. Then her hand reaches for me.

I grab a New Testament from my desk and slap it into her palm.

She stares down at it as if the words of Matthew through Revelation are hot coals searing her hand. She tosses the book back on the desk. "You mean you really don't want me?"

"I want you to get saved. Jesus can change your life. He actually can."

She utters the foulest of curses.

Now she opens the door and calls, "You can come in."

Three more girls—a redhead and two blondes, all good-looking, all braless and wearing low-cut dresses—enter.

"He's as cute as you said he was, Cora. He's out of sight," the redhead says.

I introduce myself, and before I can blink, the four girls are in a circle around me, brazenly rubbing their breasts and bodies against me.

Man, I think, Satan is working overtime tonight.

"If you'll have a seat, we can talk."

Two move into chairs, one hovers at the end of my desk, and the other sits cross-legged on the floor.

"Are you all gay?"

"We dig it every way. Are you coming to our pad tonight?" one of the blondes asks.

"If you want to have revival."

"We don't care why you come, just so you get there."

"I'd come only for a preaching session and Bible study."

"You can preach and bring your Bible," says the redhead. "That might make the evening more interesting."

"All right. When we close tonight, I'll be over with my staff and we'll have a real service."

"No, come alone. We'll love you to death."

"Are all of you alike?"

"It's just that we all want you. How would you like it right here?"

"The only thing I would like right here is a prayer meeting."

"If you want to pray, go ahead."

I kneel. All the girls move in close and kneel around me. I plan a long prayer, perhaps ten minutes. Whenever I have a group of people who are not sincere, I pray them near to death, working in a sermon while I address the Lord. During prayer, the unsaved sometimes get under conviction.

"Dear God, I ask you now——"

Cora takes my right hand and puts it on her naked bosom. The redhead places my left hand on her leg.

Freeing my hands, I conclude quickly: "Dear God, save them, save these sisters joined in sin."

Cora curses the name of the Lord.

"Okay, this is Satanic. Satan has sent you here to destroy me, and I'm not going to stand for it. If you want to get right and pray, I'll help you. But not one of you is remotely close to God. If you were, you would at least have respected me while I was praying a moment ago. I've listened to you befoul the name of the Lord and cast cheap temptation before me instead of your souls. Right now, in Jesus' name, get on your knees, start praying and beg Him to save you. If you don't want to do that I think it's best that we end our meeting."

"You're getting uptight, Preacher," Cora says smirkingly. "You're not as holy as you pretend. You hate us."

"I don't hate you. I only hate Satan for filling your hearts with yearnings for perverse and twisted sex."

I walk to the door and call for Dale. As he enters, I say to the girls, "I want you to meet a real Christian."

"He's not real, either," Cora says.

"He is, Cora, he is."

"Are you coming to our place or not?" the redhead asks.

"Only if I can bring my staff and we come for revival."

Cora scribbles their address on a piece of paper and leaves it on my desk. "See you tonight," she laughs.

"I pray I'll see all of you entering Heaven with me. But if you walk away from Jesus, you are going to be consumed in the fire that burns forever."

The girls walk out giggling. The episode apparently has been a lark for them. But perhaps, just perhaps, a seed has been planted that one day will blossom into a victory for God.

I tell Dale what has just taken place.

We lower our heads, close our eyes, and pray for four of the most troubled souls I have ever met.

> You've heard the false rumor that God is dead,
> But I'll tell you right now it's not true.
> I just talked to Jesus a while ago,
> And His love it a'shinin' on through.
> You can tell it to Jesus,
> He understands everything.

I'm talking about Jesus,
The King of kings.

4:15 A.M. STP is the dreadnought in the psychedelic ocean of
the Strip, little known, rarely discussed, so dangerous and reared
that even hard-core addicts will swallow it as the last of last resorts
and only on those rare occasions when a police crackdown has
dried up the supply of routine junk.

There are no STP addicts. One trip so savages the mind that the
user either swears off drugs or ends up a mumbling, brain-damaged
vegetable for the rest of his life. It is so potent and mind-bending
that it hurls the unsuspecting off on a stark, chaotic trip from
which there is often no return. Psychiatric wards throughout the
nation are filled with young people who've never made it back
from the bottomless darkness of STP.

A devil's brew, one of the most horrific concoctions conceived
by the mind of man, it is homemade or mixed by the most un-
scrupulous pushers in the underground drug factories that ring the
Strip.

STP is a dynamite-laden conglomeration:

Acid.

Speed.

Usually rat poison.

Arsenic.

Uppers.

Downers.

And no one knows what else.

Each ingredient triggers a separate reaction. It is a trip within a
trip within a trip. The acid may hit the system first, only to be
overpowered by the speed. The rat poison and arsenic set up
another chain reaction of sensation. The barbiturates and am-
phetamines cause yet another conflicting rush of emotional shock
inside the delicate apparatus of the mind. It may be compared to
an out-of-control machine gun, each STP "bullet" firing wildly in
a different direction. The drug roars through the mind like an
encapsulated hydra-headed monster screaming to free itself.

Bringing a kid down from an STP trip is as delicate a procedure
as brain surgery except that for tools you have only your voice,
your imagination, and Divine guidance. It is a task I view with

almost the same enthusiasm as spending eternity in Hell, yet it is a task I have performed more times than I like to recall.

His Place has ushered out its last gaggle of dopers. I'm bone-tired and eager for sleep. The night already has been too much. I'm about to snap off the last light when I hear a moan. A slim, tall boy is standing near the stage in the shadow of the His Place cross. Except for the lights above the stage, the big room is dark, eerie.

In his early twenties, the young man may or may not be a hippie. He's wearing nondescript clothes. His hair is fairly long. His piquant face is wedged between sentinels of rectangular sideburns.

I have never seen him before, and as I step over to him on cat's paws it takes only a glance to realize he's on STP. He's lost control of his nervous system. His body is jerking like a fitful puppet. His blue eyes burn with a fear that has no name. His breathing is heavy and he prances a few feet forward then several feet backward.

He is eons and a universe away from rationality. Whether or not I can bring him back is solely in the hands of God.

One shout or a wrong word could irrevocably snap his mind. He is at a point in time and space that is uncharted, perhaps forever marooned on his trip beyond a trip. He is so freaked out it would be dangerous to take him to the hospital. A stranger, a policeman, the sound of traffic, the scuffle of doctors and nurses could completely blow his mind.

I know he can't see me as a human being. From the pit of his mind I probably appear to him as a monster, perhaps a fleshy blob, perhaps something indefinable, a shape, a form, an apparition that is indescribable.

The job is to relate somehow to him, to find a point of contact and communication. First he must become accustomed to my voice. The pitch has to be soft, friendly, understanding.

I rap for twenty minutes—quoting Scripture, the Lord's Prayer, the Twenty-Third Psalm. I could be reading the phone book. Nothing penetrates. He is still moaning, prancing, jerking.

Another thirty minutes of rapping.

Now it may be safe to approach him. "Hey, man, let me say a word about Jesus. Man, He's out of sight. He really is. You think you've got a high? Man, Christ can take you higher, all the way to Heaven. You ever think of getting spaced-out on Jesus?"

His eyes, still fear-filled, lope around the room like a mountain lion searching for prey.

It's going to take an hour, maybe two, to bring him down, if indeed he can be brought down. There's an endless amount of rapping to be done.

I plunge on, hoping something I say will strike a chord of recognition inside the tangled ganglia of his brain. The planet Mars, I figure, is as good a place as any to seek the beginning of comprehension.

"It's groovy on Mars, isn't it? Peaceful, man. Quiet. Filled with love. Nothing but love. And the colors. They're a groove, too. Lots of yellow, orange, pink. It's great, man, to be floating out there. It's all love now. Everything's a groove. No hate, no fighting, no hassling, no problems. It's all together. There's some really groovy stuff happening up there. Man, it's a great scene."

A frown crosses his face. Have I guessed wrong? Mars may be a bummer for him. If he isn't on Mars, where is he? Please, Lord, don't let me lose him.

I start rapping again, avoiding Mars, or any mention of hate or violence or trouble.

"Let's groove on the ocean, man. Look at those waves, rolling in gently. And the beach, white as love, man. Over there is a tree. The bluest spruce you've ever seen. Be great for Christmas."

Should I talk about his mother or father? Can't take the chance. The mere mention of his parents might freak him out even more.

From somewhere inside that involuted mind comes, after another half hour or so of talk, a flicker of sanity. Some of the fear has left his eyes. He still can't talk; the best he can manage is a hoarse groan. He hasn't jerked for some time. It's probably safe to touch him. With an arm around his shoulder I move him to the big silver coffee pot and scoop up two chairs. I'm going to risk taking him into space again. Sitting side by side, I point to the coffee pot.

"Man, look at that wild instrument panel. Buttons, dials, knobs, lights. Check the throttle, man, and glance out the window. We're moving, man. Dig those cotton-picking stars. Ever see anything so beautiful?"

You can't bring him down too fast, you have to tool along at a pace he can absorb. We tour the solar system, stepping out of our rocket to wander around. We hit:

Jupiter.

Venus.

The Milky Way.

The sun.

The moon.

He's no longer groaning. He's transfixed by the instrument board. He's grooving on the trip.

I shape my fingers into binoculars. "Man, take a look." I move my thumbs and index fingers over his eyes.

"It's the earth, man."

These are the most crucial moments. We're coming in for a landing. Earth represents reality and he probably hit up on STP to escape reality.

Mercifully, he's smiling. His hands shift and weave over the instrument panel. He's helping me land the rocket.

Now there's the terrible suspense of choosing where to land. If you bring him to the wrong place you've blown it.

I know nothing about his past, whether he digs mountains or grooves on the forest or the ocean. Purely on instinct I bring our rocket to a halt on the hilly timberline above Malibu. We coast to a smooth stop.

"Man, doesn't this scene blow your mind? Look how perfect everything is, the rolling hills, the trees, the water. Nothing like this back on Jupiter or Venus."

Without warning he jumps up and begins screaming.

He isn't ready to land.

We soar back into space for another thirty minutes after I coax him into sitting down again. We revisit the planets. Finally, I think we're set to try another landing.

This time we're coming down on Sunset Boulevard. I know he can relate to the Strip. We step out of our craft.

"Dig the scene, man. Look at the action. All the cats are cool. There's love everywhere."

I stop to talk to people I know on the Strip and I introduce him to several friends I meet as we walk along.

"Man, let's get over to His Place. It's out of sight there."

His face is wooden. His Place may or may not be a wise destination. But I think he's at the point where he may recognize his surroundings.

It seems to work. He hasn't freaked out again. The jerkiness is gone. We're still sitting in front of the coffee pot.

"Hey, man, my name's Arthur Blessitt, and I'm the minister here on the Strip. We've got groovy chicks in here. Out-of-sight music. We rap a lot about the Lord—how He loves everybody, how He can save, put you on a trip you'll never forget."

For the first time there's a real connection between us. His face and attitude seem almost normal. But the acid or speed or something else in the STP capsule could send him spinning out of reach again any second.

More than three hours have gone by.

It's nearly seven-thirty in the morning. I'm so dingy and dull-witted myself that it takes every ounce of effort to keep rapping with him. I'm too tired to think, and so nonsense spills out.

"Hey, man, what would you like for breakfast? Chicken, baloney, spinach, oysters?"

He digs breakfast. He smiles a broad grin. He looks around at His Place and seems enthralled and enraptured.

I hand him an imaginary drink of pineapple and tomato juice. He gulps it down gratefully.

His first word: "Cool."

"Want me to add a little prune juice?"

He nods and drinks once more.

"Let me put in half a glass of buttermilk."

He bolts from the chair. Buttermilk. Bad association. He begins to vomit. He claws his way along the walls, and he's moaning again. Another thirty minutes until his energy is completely spent.

Slumped against the wall, he looks at me at last with intelligent, comprehending eyes. He is down, all the way down.

He tells me his name. He tells me he's a graduate student in math at UCLA!

We barely speak to each other as I drive him to the dorm. Both of us are too exhausted.

Hands in his pockets, head bent down, he walks away from my car. There are no eloquent words of parting, no thanks expressed.

I'm not certain if he knows where he's been.

I catch a last glimpse of him as he disappears into a huge red brick building on campus.

It's almost nine-thirty when I stagger home.

"Hi, Daddy," says five-year-old Gina. "Can we go to the park today and have a picnic?"

"Daddy loves you, but he's going to have to go to sleep. Daddy's been down on the Strip working with all those boys and girls that are not living right. They needed a lot of help last night."

"When I get big," says Gina, angel-voiced, "I'm going to pass out tracts to all those hippies and go in the topless clubs and witness to those girls and tell them about Jesus."

"Fine, darling. I'm too tired to tell a Bible story. So let's have prayer for all those people who are in bad shape and those who gave their hearts to Jesus tonight."

"Daddy, can I say the prayer?"

"Yes, Gina."

"Dear God, I pray for you to save all the hippies on Sunset Strip. I pray for everybody in the whole world to get saved. Amen."

"Amen."

"Breakfast, Arthur?" Sherry asks.

"When I wake up."

It takes excruciating effort to navigate the few feet to bed. I don't bother to undress.

Soft arms carry me into unconsciousness. The last awareness I have is the tattoo of Jim McPheeters's voice. Now it isn't the sound of a jackhammer, but a muted guitar strumming gently . . . gently . . . gently . . . begging mankind . . .

> You can tell it to Jesus,
> He understands everything.
> I'm talking about Jesus,
> The King of kings.

14

The Night They Put the Acid in the Kool-Aid

A FEW MINUTES after I finished preaching my customary midnight sermon one memorable evening, some 150 kids at His Place were busy doing their thing: rapping, playing checkers, grooving on the music, queuing up for bagels, sandwiches, coffee, and our favorite soft drink, Kool-Aid. Because of its modest price and the fact that a small quantity can be mixed with a large amount of water, Kool-Aid is always on hand in plentiful supply.

As usual there were a number of heads completely freaked out, those on downers spread supine on the floor like toppled bowling pins and those on uppers moving around wild-eyed. Many, however, weren't stoned, either because they didn't have the bread for a buy, hadn't made a connection, or weren't in the mood for a trip.

The scene was no worse nor better than any other average night, except that it had been a particularly lucrative evening for Christ. After my preaching service almost thirty kids had come forward to accept Jesus.

My staff and I were busy in the counseling rooms working with the new converts, witnessing, praying, charting Bible study courses, trying to tidy up some of the loose ends of mangled lives.

I was with an unmarried sixteen-year-old girl who had run away from her home in Kansas City after discovering she was pregnant. In accepting Christ, she had also accepted the inevitability and wisdom of returning and working her problem out with her parents. After making a phone call to her grateful mother and father (they hadn't heard from their daughter in a week), I accompanied the girl to the curb and flagged a taxi. Clutching her New Testament, she stepped in for the ride to the airport and a late night flight back to Kansas City. She was that rarest of runaways, one who had the fare home.

I walked back into the club and looked around. Everyone on the His Place staff is trained to be Argus-eyed, to scout the room in free moments and keep his eye open for trouble and anything, down to the smallest detail, out of the ordinary.

Walking through the crowd, the only not-as-it-should-be detail I noticed was that our ten-gallon Kool-Aid container wasn't in its accustomed place near the back door. That was no cause for alarm. Dale was probably whipping up a new batch.

A few moments later, however, a Mayday alarm sounded inside me. I suddenly realized something drastic was amiss. There was more excitement than usual coursing through the building and all at once there seemed to be more kids freaked out, far more than when I had preached only thirty minutes before.

Then I heard a burst of noise upstairs and I could see that all the big heads (the heavy dopers, the real addicts) were pushing and shoving their way into the prayer room side by side with the kids who were part-time heads.

I raced up the steps and had to muscle my way through the throng.

Everybody was shoving everybody else. It was a formidable hassle.

I heard cries of "Man, let me have the cup." "It's my turn." "You've already had your share."

Churning through the crowd, I managed to reach the center of the packed prayer room.

A dozen feet away, sitting on the table we used as our prayer altar, was the Kool-Aid container. The Bible had been shoved aside to make room for it.

"What in the world is going on?"

"Hey, Arthur," someone shouted, "the Kool-Aid's hot!"

I had prayed it would never come to pass. The staff and I had discussed bolting down the top of the coffee pot and the Kool-Aid container as a precaution against exactly what was now taking place.

A nightmare had become reality. Someone had dumped a load of acid into the Kool-Aid.

It was bedlam around the container, but like a halfback threading his way through the opposition's line, I finally reached it.

There was only about an inch of liquid left at the bottom.

"Who did it?" I called out.

One girl, obvious admiration in her voice, snickered, "Couple of groovy dudes."

No one, of course, would tell me the names of the offenders.

I lifted the container, holding it over my head, and moved through the mob of protesting kids down the stairs. I was roundly booed as I trooped through the club to the sink and poured out the remainder of the contents.

The wallop of LSD hits some users in fifteen minutes. In others it may be delayed for an hour or more. The average reaction time is forty-five minutes.

When an hour had ticked by virtually everyone in the church was turned on. Between 100 and 125 kids were spaced out. Some sat staring vacantly ahead with glazed eyes, some had passed into unconsciousness, some were giggling, evidently having a good trip.

The only ones who weren't stoned were the staff members and those who'd been saved. The staff and I fanned our way through the crowd on the alert for anyone having a bad trip who might need help.

Apparently everybody's ride was smooth.

I was thankful The Man didn't show up. The whole club would have been busted, including me, and I couldn't logically picture myself before a judge attempting to explain how more than 100 kids had been freaked out in a church.

There were no fights. The last thing a kid on acid wants is to become belligerent. That spoils the trip.

Scratching his head, Dale asked, "What are we going to do?"

There was nothing funny about it, yet I couldn't help but laugh. "It's a lot happier crowd than you'll find in most churches," I said jokingly.

We decided the only sane course was to proceed as if nothing untoward had occurred. Actually, the bizarre evening wasn't far removed from many nights at His Place when the overwhelming majority of kids who come through the door are already stoned.

I thought of closing early, but that would have sent a small army of freaked-out bodies into the street, an unthinkable course of action.

As the night wore on it got wilder, some of the heads reaching the peak of their trips, but by our 4 A.M. closing time most of the kids were down or on their way down.

We checked each one as he passed through the door, trying to be certain he could make it home.

A generous Providence saw to it that every kid in His Place that evening survived the experience. Nobody's mind had been blown. As far as I know, not one youngster had any negative aftereffects.

There was no backlash from the sheriff's men. I was never questioned about the episode.

If anything, when word of the weird incident ran through the Strip, our attendance increased!

But from that evening hence some member of the staff was always specifically assigned to keep an eagle-eye on the coffee pot and soft-drink container.

After the last kid had gone through the door on the night they put the acid in the Kool-Aid, Dale wondered, "How could it happen?"

"Either the Lord was napping," I answered, "or we didn't pray hard enough."

15

Joel's Candy

AFTER CLOSING TIME at His Place we are often too tired to clean up until the next day. Any doper on the Strip would gladly volunteer for the job. Among each day's debris there is always a batch of junk. Everything from pot to STP is forgotten, lost, misplaced, or accidentally dropped by heads too stoned to realize they're being parted from what they consider their most precious possessions.

We don't run a lost-and-found department for the junk that's left behind. The daily haul is flushed down the toilet.

Sherry and Gina had joined me for clean-up one afternoon about three o'clock. Also with us was our two-year-old son, Joel, named for the biblical prophet.

Joel (the name means "Jehovah is God") was a blue-eyed, curious-as-a-kitten oval-faced youngster, his blond hair styled in a John-John Kennedy haircut. Both Gina and Joel, who come to His Place often, were adored by the kids on the Strip. There were hippies, bikers, dopers, and pushers who would have given their lives for our children.

Sherry was vacuuming, I was clearing my desk, and Gina and Joel were scampering about picking up papers from the floor. Everything seemed peaceful.

I heard the hum of the vacuum cleaner die and in a moment Sherry was at the door of my office. She was clutching Joel. I had never seen such fright in Sherry's eyes.

"Candy, Mama, candy, Daddy, I find candy," Joel said.

I rushed to my son. From his open hand I grabbed the "candy" he was showing us. I stuffed the pill in my pocket, then pried

Joel's mouth open. On his tongue were half-chewed remnants of another pill.

Panic seized me.

I turned Joel upside down and Sherry held him by his legs while I pushed my finger into his throat, trying to make him vomit. With my free hand I wiped the remains of the pill from Joel's tongue with his shirt tail.

Joel gagged a bit, but didn't vomit. His rosy cheeks were beginning to turn white.

I decided to race him to the hospital on Santa Monica Boulevard. As I twisted and hurled my car through traffic with one hand I punched Joel in the side, slapped his cheeks, and shook his shoulders with the other. "Hurt, Daddy, don't." He was already so groggy he couldn't keep his eyes open.

At the hospital's receiving desk sat a middle-aged man in a white coat.

"My son's swallowed a drug, something powerful. He needs treatment—now!"

The man had the compassion of a jackal. "Sorry, we don't take children."

"This is an emergency!"

"Try Children's Hospital on Sunset."

If I wasn't a preacher, I would have slugged that dense medical bureaucrat to pulp. It was one of the few times in my life when God allowed my reason to be overwhelmed by emotion.

Precious minutes lost. . . .

Back in the car I pinched and spanked Joel and opened the windows hoping the air might help revive him. "Please cry, son, get mad at your daddy, scream, howl in pain, react in some way. Joel! Joel! Show me you're alive!"

He couldn't hear my frenzied shouting. He had lapsed into unconsciousness. I felt his pulse; it was so faint it was hardly beating.

I fought back the thought that Joel could die at any moment. Only God knew what he had swallowed. Pills cut with rat poison, both uppers and downers, were at that time big on the Strip. It triggered a faster trip. From his reaction, I was certain Joel had taken a downer. But in what strength? Any downer was dangerous enough for a two-year-old, but if it was mixed with rat poison, he didn't have a chance.

After I hurriedly explained Joel's condition, the nurse at the emergency desk of Children's Hospital handed me a card and said, "Fill this out."

By God, I was going to tear that hospital apart if someone didn't help my son. I could be filling in an idiotic form while his life ebbed away.

"I want a doctor, I want a doctor this minute." Even in my anguish I could recognize the unaccustomed ferocity in my voice.

The nurse got the message. She bolted from the chair and in a few moments was back with an obviously capable take-charge doctor. Apparently he had already been briefed by the nurse and he swept Joel from my arms and carried him into the emergency room to pump his stomach.

Ten minutes later I was at Joel's bedside when he opened his eyes.

At least he was alive.

"I don't know what else to do until we find out what he swallowed," the doctor said.

I took the pill from my pocket and showed it to him.

"Come on."

We raced to the pharmacist's counter and the three of us began tearing through books and folders trying to find a drawing or description of the pill.

"No use," the pharmacist said when our search was completed. "It must be a homemade job."

"Do you have any way at all of identifying the contents of the pill?" the doctor asked me.

I ran to the phone and in quick succession called four pushers I knew. To each I described the pill. The clues, however, were scant. All I could tell them was that it had a curlicue marking on the outside and was shaped irregularly. None of the pushers could tell me offhand what it was, but all promised to hurriedly ask around and see what they could find out.

Did Joel's life now hinge on the detective work of four pushers, all of whom were so habitually tripped out they barely knew what they were doing?

Sherry and I went back to Joel. He was still groggy, and as we watched he shut his eyes and slipped into unconsciousness again.

I held Sherry's hand. We looked at each other helplessly and silently. There just wasn't anything to say.

Through my mind now blazed questions I had never before considered:

Was it worth it?

Was the Strip worth the life of my son?

Was my ministry worth the death of my bone and flesh, the matchstick flame of a life that had been alive for only a few seconds of eternity?

While I pondered, the doctor came to our side again. "I don't want to mislead you. We don't know what to do. It will take days to get a report on that pill from the lab. Your son is in very critical condition. He may die."

"Is there anything you can try?" Sherry pleaded.

"The only hope is to give him a stimulant, something to perk up his heartbeat and respiration."

I heard myself being paged to the phone. One of the pushers was returning my call. "Arthur, I can't be one hundred percent sure, but I just talked to a guy who's dealt the junk you described. Most of the time it's a downer mixed with speed."

Speed!

Speed kills, man. If it doesn't kill, it can cause paranoid psychoses and brain damage.

I ran to the doctor and told him what I'd learned.

"If it is speed," he said, "I don't think a child his age can live through it."

But the pusher's call had come in time to at least give Joel a chance. Speed is a stimulant and if the doctor had given Joel another stimulant on top of what was already in him, it surely would have killed him.

Now as Sherry and I prayed there was nothing to do but commit Joel to the hands of God.

"He's yours, Lord, and whatever is Thy will is ours as well."

Understanding came flooding back to me. I felt ashamed for my thoughts while confronting the indifferent clerk at the first hospital. He was only a front-man, a cog in the tragically un-Christian and often barbaric policy of too many American hospitals, which will not admit emergency patients on a help-now, ask-questions-later basis.

As for His Place, the Strip, my ministry—yes, they were all worth the life of my son if God so ordained. If necessary, I would sacrifice Joel for even the opportunity of leading the most seemingly hopeless hippie on the Strip to the Lord. If Joel died, he would be with God. If the sinners on the Strip died, they would suffer everlasting punishment and torment.

An hour later it seemed that the Lord had decided to spare Joel!

He'd been moved to another room for observation and was lying peacefully in a baby bed, his eyes bright. He appeared normal, as if he had never been sick.

Our elation, however, was premature.

Without warning Joel jumped to his feet and began pounding his tiny fists against the slats. He tried to climb out of the bed. He hollered, then wailed like a lonely, frightened animal. His eyes were popping out of his head. I felt his heart and it was racing.

He had slipped into high gear.

Joel Blessitt, barely twenty-four months of age, was freaking out.

Now I was fearful that the pill Joel swallowed might contain LSD. His reactions were similar to those of hundreds of acid heads I'd seen on bad trips.

The fit lasted about fifteen minutes. After it was over, the doctor said, "I'm sorry, but there's nothing more we can do. You can take him home. I'm afraid you might have problems, assuming he lives, with his mind. His emotional stability may have been destroyed. There's also physical danger, perhaps to his heart, body cells, nervous tissue, genes, and biochemical functions."

We prayed all the way home and by the time we arrived Joel had become rambunctious again. It was impossible to hold him in check.

He leaped on the bed, jumped off, and ran around like a weaving, senseless drunk.

The phone jangled.

It was Dale, terribly worried about Joel. The pushers I had called had spread the word. I told Dale that at the moment Joel's condition was not promising.

"I know this isn't the time to bring it up, Arthur, but it's very important that we open tonight."

"Dale, I haven't even thought about opening tonight. I want to stay close to Joel."

"If we don't open," said Dale, "there may be a riot or a killing.

The kids are uptight. They think someone purposely turned Joel on! Arthur, we need you here, the sooner the better."

When I got to His Place a short time later, Dale rushed over. "The kids have narrowed it down to three heads who they think might be responsible for what happened to Joel. I've got one of them locked in your office. He's too afraid to come out."

I went to the stage and called for silence. There were more than one hundred angry kids scattered through the building.

Softly, I said, "Joel right now is freaked out. But I want everybody to cool it. What happened to my son was a terrible accident. Nobody turned him on."

One kid shouted, "The junk was left on the floor intentionally. Whoever did it knew Joel would pick the stuff up."

"No," I said, "it was impossible for anyone to know that Joel was coming to His Place today. I didn't know it myself until Sherry decided on impulse to come down with the kids."

It took me more than half an hour to calm the crowd, squash all the rumors, and convince them that it was only a horrible mischance.

After a good deal of coaxing, I was able to reassure the head locked in my office, a dark-haired, twenty-one-year-old kid with tattoos on his arms, that it was safe for him to come out.

"You sure?" "Yeah, man, it's all cool." He moved quickly to the door and started running down the Strip.

When I got home, Joel was still spaced out. He was lurching from one room to another. Then, suddenly, he keeled over. We put him to bed and I called the doctor.

"He's burned out all his energy," the doctor told me. "He'll probably sleep for several days."

Would he wake up a vegetable? Would he have to be committed to an institution? Would he be retarded?

Joel slept for three days.

When he finally flared to life he was weak and wan. We took him to the hospital again.

Diagnosis: a mild case of pneumonia.

But with medication, tender loving care, and prayer Joel recovered. He was home in five days.

And now, praise God, he seemed normal, the effects of the drug no longer apparent.

And Joel has been normal ever since. There has been no recurrence, no reversion, no flashback, no sign of emotional or physical damage.

When the report arrived from the hospital's lab, it merely confirmed the pusher's information. Joel had swallowed a pill that contained methamphetamine and Nembutal—speed and downers.

Often when I look at my son, I think of the terror he suffered and how close he came to death. Tears well in my eyes when Joel bounces into my arms and says, "Tell me a story about Jesus" or "Let's play, Daddy, let's play."

I returned to my work without rancor toward anyone.

God had put it all together in my mind. If Joel had died, he would have gone into the arms of Christ. My son's death would have been His plan.

The son of David and Bathsheba had died an infant. In 2 Samuel 12:23, David said: "I shall go to him, but he shall not return to me." The meaning of the passage was clear. Joel would only have preceded me to Heaven by a little while. Father and son would be reunited before God.

There was also a passage from Joshua 1:9 that sustained us after the first careening shock of Joel's ingestion of "candy."

"Have I not commanded thee? Be strong and of good courage; be not afraid, neither be thou dismayed: for the Lord thy God is with thee wherever thou goest."

16

Two Angry Disciples

IN THIS CORNER at 140 pounds and five feet seven inches, filled with hatred for the world and everything in it, particularly white men, was Jesse Wise, a nineteen-year-old hot-tempered black, suspicious of kindness, cynical, defiant, his heritage chockablock with liquor and violence.

His 195-pound, six-foot-seven opponent was a "nigger"-hating soldier in the Chicago wing of the Cosa Nostra who at twenty-five had already killed seven people. His name isn't really Dominick Rizzo, but when a man says he's honored seven contracts for murder, and you believe him, it would be violating a trust to reveal his true identity.

The battleground for Jesse and Dominick was the House of Disciples, the Halfway House I had founded as a companion facility to His Place. The Halfway House on South Oxford is about nine miles from the Strip, far enough removed in geography and atmosphere to afford an isolated Christian environment for new converts still struggling to remake their lives.

The facility was organized for saved dopers and emotionally scarred dropouts from straight society who needed critical follow-up work. More than five hundred converts have passed through the reorientation program at the House. They are free of drugs, no longer uptight or hung up in any major way. Now they are scattered to the four corners of America, integrated as useful members of their communities, God-loving citizens who once were disowned by every segment of the Establishment—organized religion, the schools, their parents, relatives, friends, and employers.

The work accomplished at the Halfway House has been and

continues to be one of the most satisfying aspects of my ministry.

The rules are strict and enforced with a loving but firm hand. The operative word is discipline—discipline for chaotic individualists who must be taught a sense of orderliness and appreciation of routine. Forbidden are drinking, cigarette smoking except in the backyard, dope, and dating girls during the required month of quarantine. In some hard-core cases the new disciples of Christ are allowed to stay on longer, until their problems can be more effectively treated.

The freshly minted Christians pass through the House in groups of twenty. Wake-up time is 7 A.M.; lights out at eleven. Each is assigned a task: cooking, scrubbing floors, cleaning rooms, making beds, landscaping. While we try to find jobs for these in-transition Christians or strengthen them to return to high school, college, or their hometowns without fear, there are daily Bible studies, prayer meetings, and fellowship and Christian-centered group-therapy sessions where Scripture may be challenged and where everyone is permitted to criticize, rip apart, and tear into anyone else.

After the first two weeks of isolation, each disciple has two nights off. One evening he goes out by himself as a test, the other is spent in street-witnessing on the Strip or working at His Place.

Jesse Wise came to the House through the aid of two of my friends, a tall, handsome young Negro known all over the Strip as "Solo," a nickname he had taken as a symbol of the loneliness he felt in his soul before finding the companionship of God, and O. J., who doubles indispensably as a soul-winner and one of our His Place musicians.

Solo and O. J., on their way back to Los Angeles from a witnessing mission in Indianapolis, met Jesse at a Denver crash pad housing a large number of kids. They held a preaching service, and Jesse at first ignored the word of God. But when he started to listen to Solo and O. J. with his heart, he began to realize he needed Christ and that Jesus was the answer to his life. So Jesse came forward and committed himself. Solo and O. J. then told Jesse about the Halfway House, and Jesse hitchhiked to Los Angeles to go through our training program.

A child in Christ when I first met him, Jesse had a keen, intelligent mind. He'd spent one semester studying psychology at the University of Colorado before dropping out. He wasn't a head or an alcoholic. His hang-up was his volcanic wrath against whites

—he felt his people had been persecuted and given the short end of the American dream for four hundred years.

At the House Jesse dug through the pages of the Bible. He was entranced with the Scriptures, reading, digesting, accumulating the backbone of Christianity.

As he poured through the Book, Jesse caught fire, and he learned compassion and forgiveness and developed a devout love for the Lord. So passionate was his conviction and progress that I made him director of the House.

Jesse had finally lost his hatred and mistrust of whites—until Dominick arrived.

Dominick was a human spike; there was nothing on his long frame but bone and muscle.

I spotted him at His Place after he became a regular. Night after night he came in, but he said nothing, did nothing, just kept measuring the scene through clever brown eyes. When we closed, he would leave with the last stragglers and crash, as I learned subsequently, in a deserted motel or house, a culvert or on a side street.

I tried to witness to Dominick, but he would have no part of it. He'd barely acknowledge my presence, much less speak to me.

No one could figure Dominick's bag—he had no apparent vices. He wasn't a doper or a boozer. He didn't even date, and he had no friends.

Since I surrendered to preach, I have never gone to bed without leading at least one lost soul to Christ. After two weeks of indifference from Dominick, I set my cap for him. I sensed he needed Christ, was ready to be led to the Savior.

He was sitting quietly at one of our tables when I approached.

"Dominick, wouldn't you like to get saved?"

I was astonished when he said simply, "Yes!"

"Do you mean it?"

"If you think I'm worth saving, I'm for it."

From my New Testament I read several passages from the Book of John. Then I said, "Dominick, I'd like you to read a few verses aloud. I want to hear Scripture from your lips."

"No!"

"I thought you wanted to be saved. You have to know His words if you want to become a new man."

Dominick hung his head in shame like a scolded child.

"Man, what is it?"

"I can't . . . I can't read. I just never learned," he said in a whisper.

"No problem, man. I'll teach you. Right now let's go up to the prayer room."

Dominick kneeled beside me and I said a prayer, a supplication to the Lord to accept yet another sinner.

When the prayer was over Dominick was smiling, the first time I had ever seen him smile.

"Would you like to give your testimony to the crowd in here tonight?"

"All right."

Dominick went centerstage and he told the kids, "I've just been saved. I don't understand much about what's happening to me. But I feel good. I'm going to try to behave myself a little bit. At least I'm going to do the best I can."

It wasn't much of a testimony. Christ deserved a more fervent commitment than Dominick had volunteered.

Dominick stayed until closing time and as I started to lock up I happened to mention to him that His Place had been burglarized the night before. A tape recorder and a few other items we used to do the Lord's work had been stolen.

"I'll take care of it," he said.

"What do you mean?"

"Just leave me here overnight. Lock me in. The guy might come back."

"What if he does?"

"I'll kill him, man, I'll kill him! Nobody's going to steal any more of your stuff."

"Dominick, are you saved? What about Jesus?"

"And nobody's going to steal any of His stuff, either!"

He was dead serious, and it took me a long while to convince him that the last thing I wanted at His Place was a murder.

"I've killed before, seven times," Dominick said matter-of-factly.

I froze in disbelief.

Dominick proceeded to tell me the bone-chilling, despairing sequence of events that had brought him to His Place and Christ. If he had given his real testimony to the crowd, no one would have come within a mile of him.

Dominick's father had been a bitter man who traveled throughout the Midwest earning a precarious living drilling water wells for farmers, sometimes tucking his equipment as deep as three hundred feet into the earth before hitting a strike. Often there were long and agonizing weeks when his father bored sixteen hours a day and his search for water ended in failure. On such occasions, he was paid nothing.

Dominick helped his father, and the nomadic life kept him out of the classroom. His father became a defeated, self-pitying man, drowning himself in drink and malice. In his frustration, he frequently used a gun butt and a whip to beat Dominick. So was the angry twig bent.

When Dominick was seventeen, a train ran into his father's car. He pulled his father's unrecognizable remains from the wreckage.

Broke, unschooled (he could neither read nor write), he went to his only relative, an uncle high in the ranks of the Cosa Nostra. Dominick became a soldier in the Chicago Family, a strong-arm man and killer. Seven contracts for murder were given to him. Seven times he killed as ordered.

The eighth contract changed his life. He was supposed to hit a man whose business had been taken over by the Cosa Nostra. But the man now was ready to testify in court. If he did, some famous, notorious heads would roll.

On the day of the hit Dominick was secreted in a tall building overlooking the hotel where Chicago police were holding their star witness. With Dominick was another Cosa Nostra soldier and a young girl who was more vicious and lethal than most men.

When the witness arrived at the hotel and stepped out of the police car, he stood on the sidewalk talking to his bodyguards. Dominick had a clear shot at him.

The high-powered lens on his rifle magnified the fleshy face of the man who would be dead in another second. Dominick had only to pull the trigger.

But something stayed his hand. He couldn't go through with it. "I just panicked," he recalled. The other soldier grabbed the rifle and took aim. But Dominick didn't want the man killed. He lurched at his confederate, knocking the gun to the floor. While they battled, the girl picked up the gun, went to the window, took aim and fired.

She missed.

The shot brought the police, drawn guns blazing. Dominick and the girl managed to escape. The other soldier was mowed down by police bullets.

Knowing his superiors brooked no failure, Dominick split for Los Angeles, though he realized there was no real point in running. He would be found.

Dominick's knowledge of the inside workings of the Cosa Nostra was voluminous. He mentioned the names and crimes of the top bosses in the country and told me the names of the Los Angeles Cosa Nostra leaders who owned nightclubs on the Strip and controlled most of the Strip's prostitution and dope traffic. His information squared with what I had learned from other sources about the Cosa Nostra's infiltration of the Strip.

"I'm sure they're looking for me," Dominick concluded, "and I'm scared."

I invited him to the Halfway House for temporary refuge.

Dominick accepted gratefully, but he was appalled when he saw that whites and Negroes mingled together freely in the House.

"I can't stand niggers," he said. He flat-out hated them. When he learned that black-skinned Jesse Wise was the director of the House, he was almost ready to walk out and take his chances with the Cosa Nostra. A clash between Jesse and Dominick was inevitable.

Jesse was saved and serving, but I knew if he was pushed by someone as prejudiced as Dominick, he might explode. It would not be enough to preach the Ten Commandments and the Sermon on the Mount to Jesse and Dominick.

The first few days they merely stalked each other. Except for a few random insults, there was an unspoken truce between them. But the truce could be broken at any time, so I determined to head off any possible clash by letting Jesse and Dominick go at one another in one of our group encounters.

There were ten in the group when we gathered together, but the other eight were only spear-carriers. Jesse and Dominick dominated the session.

"I've hated niggers since my sister was raped by one of you black bastards," Dominick said.

"I didn't rape her. Man, we got brown brothers, tan brothers, yellow brothers, every shade of brother you can imagine. How do you think they got that way? Talk about rape! There's white blood flowing inside most of my brothers, and that's the blood that makes them hate. Man, if I had a sister, I wouldn't trust you with her."

Dominick popped from his seat like a jack-in-the-box. His hands were around Jesse's throat when I pulled him off.

I told them, "We can fight and go on spouting hatred all night, but it won't get us anywhere. Jesse, I want you to say something good about Dominick. Dominick, I want you to say something positive about Jesse."

Sullen, stubborn silence.

Jesse finally volunteered, "If he's saved, truly saved, then I suppose there's some good in him."

"There's only one black man I ever admired, Martin Luther King," said Dominick. "He had guts. I could never figure out how he came so far without using muscle. I guess Jesse's got the same kind of guts."

The session went on for several hours. Jesse and Dominick would flare at one another, but the remarks grew less personal. The exchange became a discussion of the historical wrongs that whites had committed against blacks since the days of slavery. Dominick conceded that Jesse was telling it like it was.

Afterward they didn't volunteer to become roommates. But often a slow coming together is more binding than an instant, unexamined friendship. Jesse began helping me teach Dominick to read and write. Once Dominick mastered the alphabet, he could manage simple books and then Bible verses. Dominick, a whiz at electronics, fixed Jesse's broken radio. They began spending hours together, candidly exchanging the stories of their lives.

They both grew as Christians and in Christian brotherhood. They came to the point where they not only liked each other, but were militantly protective of one another's welfare.

I was out of town one night preaching a revival when Jesse went up to His Place to help the staff. Three Black Panthers came in and started hassling some of the kids. When Jesse asked them to cool it, the Panthers cursed him and called him an Uncle Tom.

Before he was saved, Jesse, who was so proud of his race, would have pulverized anyone who hurled that insult at him. Now he let it go by, but the trio of Panthers, doped- and boozed-up, continued hassling the kids and ragging Jesse. Jesse politely asked them to leave.

The Panthers tore into Jesse, belting his head and face with their fists and kicking him with their boots. Through it all, Jesse stood firm. He didn't raise a finger to defend himself. He finally crumbled to the floor. One last kick in the groin, and the Panthers took off.

When Dominick heard about the beating, he was ready to hunt down the offending Panthers and kill them all. Only Jesse's protestations that such revenge was not Christian restrained Dominick.

"Man, why do you think I took it? Because I'm saved!"

Dominick was wide-eyed with admiration for Jesse.

I learned about the fight and the interaction between Jesse and Dominick when I got back to town.

A few nights later Dominick called me aside and said without melodrama, "I've been visiting some guys I know on the Strip. There's a contract out for me."

The Cosa Nostra had not forgotten.

"Let me talk to some people. Maybe they can help," I said.

"I'll work it out in my own way. You can't find anybody bigger in the setup than my uncle. He's the only one who can shake me loose."

Dominick called Chicago.

A meeting was arranged in an alley behind a Strip building. Three heavy hoods in a black car pulled up. One of them said to Dominick, "Well, you live, but you get one hell of a beating."

Dominick didn't choose to follow Jesse's nonviolent example. He chose rather to defend himself. He could lick twice his weight in wildcats, and he proved it by slapping the tar out of the Cosa Nostra men.

He told Jesse and me about it when he got back to the House. The skin on his knuckles was raw, and there was a cut on his cheek. He was otherwise unharmed.

And Dominick was smiling.

"That's it," he said with relief. "I'm out now—for good."

"Won't they be after you again for what you did to those three men?" Jesse asked.

"No, that's considered a draw. A soldier has the right to protect himself when he's being worked over. If you can handle it, there's no hard feelings."

It was Jesse's turn to be wide-eyed with admiration for Dominick.

Jesse went on to Bible school, then became a member of my Team. He plans to become a minister.

Dominick met a girl at His Place, married her, and now is working on a farm in the Midwest.

Jesse Wise and Dominick Rizzo, the Lord's two angry disciples, are angry no more.

17

Hard Riders

A BACKFIRE heard round the world was ignited in 1950 at Fontana, California, home of the state's largest steel mill.

The backfire was from a Harley Davidson motorcycle, and it kicked into gear a new breed of outlaw, a new anti-Establishment subculture, aptly christened the Hell's Angels.

By the 1960s the mother club had become parent to dozens of other biker gangs, curiously many with names derived from religious sources. The Hell's Angels spawned the Jokers Out of Hell, Satan's Slaves, The Straight Satans, The Chosen Ones, and The Chosen Few, among others.

Perhaps there is some backhanded logic for the defiant religious names adopted by the clubs. Roaring down the road at speeds up to 115 miles an hour, the bikers experience feelings of euphoria, exhilaration, and freedom. It is a twisted and dangerous high, but in intensity it matches the vaulting joy experienced every day by those who honestly live for Christ.

Among the bikers, worship of God is replaced by adoration for their machines. The Harley Davidson manual becomes their Bible. In some clubs when members "marry" their old ladies, they take their vows with hands placed on the manufacturer's manual.

Contrary to popular opinion, the bikers do not come from poverty pockets. Virtually all of them have middle-class backgrounds. Also contrary to popular opinion, most bikers keep one foot in middle-class society. The majority hold down straight jobs during the week: It takes bread, up to three thousand dollars, to buy and maintain a noisy, zooming, chrome-encrusted chopper. It is on the weekends that they band together to fly.

In their rebellion the bikers have gone to outrageous, disgusting, law-defying extremes, and by the 1960's California had set up a special police intelligence network to monitor the activities of several thousand bikers organized into dozens of clubs. Similar surveillance of bikers was undertaken in a number of other states.

Bikers' crimes run from murder to rape, assault, and robbery. The bikers' *modus operandi* is to thunder en masse into small communities, sometimes treeing the town, or attacking bars and roadhouses a good distance from the nearest police station.

My ministry among the bikers has convinced me that they are as hungry for Christ as anyone else. But they have to be reached with the Gospel in terms they understand. They, like everyone else, long for identity and importance. The gangs serve these needs. Their Nazi insignia, patches with the letter M signifying use of marijuana, their filthy bodies, scruffy beards, nauseating sexual initiation rites, and criminal conduct are surface manifestations of their deep need for help.

These thousands of chopper fanatics seem, by the chances they take in challenging the Establishment and riding their machines at death-defying speed, to be unconsciously bent on suicide. Perhaps this is because the environments from which they stem give them little reason to cherish life, particularly in its most meaningful form, as an adventure in Christian commitment.

Still the bikers are not hopelessly godless. Some two hundred of them, once consumed by dope, booze, violence, and severe emotional problems, have been led to the Lord at His Place and in cities throughout the nation where I have preached at revivals and crusades. "Better is the end of a thing than the beginning thereof," says Ecclesiastes 7:8.

My first contact with the bikers came while I was preaching at a revival in San Bernardino. I had read the newspaper stories about their frequent arrests and I was concerned. If anyone needed the Lord, the bikers did.

I learned that there was a biker camp near Cucamonga. I piled into my car and drove over a blacktop highway until I reached a sign that said, "DO NOT ENTER."

I slowed down, prayed some, and made my way over a winding road until I sighted a ten-foot watchtower, a vantage point used undoubtedly to guard against intruders like me and from which an oncoming police raid could be spotted.

The camp was closed off by a barbed-wire fence. On it was another sign: "TRESPASSERS WILL BE SHOT. BLOW YOUR HORN."

I tried the horn on my car but it wouldn't work. I couldn't rouse anyone when I let go with a few shouts. I was terribly disappointed. I felt God had called on me to make this excursion and I was anxious to fulfill His will.

As I turned around and drove back I thought of a friend of mine, Steve Mayhill, the son of a preacher, who lived in nearby Upland.

I went to his house and got straight to the nitty-gritty. "Steve, are you saved?"

"I sure am."

"Steve, are you really saved?"

"Absolutely!" he declared with conviction.

"So if you died this moment, or in the next hour, where would you go?"

"Heaven, naturally."

"Right. Does your car horn work?"

"Sure, but what's that got to do with my being saved?"

"I want you to go to the Hell's Angels' camp with me and blow your horn. Mine's out of whack."

Steve looked at me as if I were inviting him to shake hands with the Devil.

"No!" he said after thinking it over for a moment. "I'm saved and ready for Heaven, but I don't want to go in the next load."

It took a great deal of convincing before Steve agreed to accompany me, and even then he did so reluctantly.

Back at Hell's Angels' headquarters, Steve (I'm sure he said a silent prayer first) blew the horn on his Fiat—a timid beep. We sounded the horn several more times before we saw a sign of life.

From behind a tree emerged a big, bearded, unfriendly looking biker in his twenties wearing a blue denim shirt and jeans. In his hands and aimed directly at us was a .30-caliber rifle.

"Can't you read? What the hell are you doing here?"

"I'm a preacher," I said uneasily. "I want to be the chaplain of the Hell's Angels."

That shook him up.

"If you'll point that gun down I won't have to fight to keep from stuttering."

He dropped the rifle a few inches.

"I've been reading about your problems in the papers," I continued. "I'm here to help any way I can and to talk to you about the Lord."

He let loose a stream of invective that fouled the air like soiled linen. "We don't need a preacher," he concluded. "What we need is a lawyer."

"That's why you need the Lord. Christ can work on the judge and jury. You can really get the heat off your back when you've got Him."

"Are you for real?"

"I'm a real preacher, if that's what you mean. I'm not a narc or a plainclothesman."

"You've got more guts than brains coming here," he said, opening the gate and allowing me in.

We rapped together for several minutes. Soon we were joined by a group of six or seven other bikers, fearsome-looking but not disturbed by their unexpected visitor. In the distance I saw a couple of their old ladies. Without a specific invitation from their old men to join us they hung back.

We all sat on the ground and they listened to everything I had to say. It was a tremendous opportunity to witness. I suggested they change the name of their club to "God's Angels" and live for Christ. I explained the saving power of the Lord, told them not to rebel against God but to accept Him and by accepting Him to lose their hangups.

They heard me out for about an hour. They didn't interrupt except to ask a respectful question or two.

I wasn't able to lead any of them to the Lord, but as the rap session ended, one of them said, "You're cool, man." The bikers admire boldness and anyone who has conviction.

I gave each of them one of my cards and said, "If there's anything I can do, let me know."

Some rapport had been established. At least they had paid polite attention, which is more courtesy than I get from many unsaved dudes when I talk about the urgency of coming to Christ.

As I walked out, the biker who'd been at the gate let me examine his rifle, which in his mind was a gesture of friendship.

Steve was waiting when I reached the car. His hands hadn't

moved from the steering wheel and he had kept the motor running since I'd entered the camp.

Shortly after this visit, the police closed that biker camp, but that experience with them showed me that given time and effort the bikers could be convinced to exchange worship of the Harley Davidson manual for the Bible.

My next encounter with a biker came at an unlikely place. I was in one of the mangy model studios on Santa Monica Boulevard, witnessing to Carol, who had once ridden with the Hell's Angels. She was a young girl, madonna-faced, so beautiful that she had appeared on the covers of several straight high-circulation magazines. Carol worked at the studio because there she could earn twice the bread of a legitimate model.

She told me a great deal about her boy friend, a biker named "Buddha." As we talked, Buddha walked in. His name derived from his Japanese ancestry; his father had a highly successful business in Hawaii. Buddha's hair was shoulder length; his beard had seen the growth of a thousand days. An expert in karate and foot-fighting, no one in his right mind would tangle with him despite his diminutive size. Buddha rode with the Jokers Out of Hell. From his expression it was clear he thought I was flirting with his old lady. It took quite a while to assure him that I was a preacher interested only in Carol's soul.

"I'm in charge of her soul," he said, signaling Carol to leave with him.

I saw Buddha a few nights later at The Blue Grotto and began witnessing to him. Seemingly, I made no impact. The next evening I ran into him again at the model studio, and on this occasion God provided a golden witnessing opportunity.

Buddha had laryngitis!

He had no choice but to hear me out as I rapped about God. Finally, I said, "Buddha, let me pray for your laryngitis; let me pray that God will heal you."

He looked at me out of skeptical eyes, but nodded his agreement. Buddha went down on his knees with much hesitation. He had never before bowed to God or man.

I prayed for Buddha's soul and as usual worked in a sermon during the prayer. Then I asked God to cure his laryngitis.

"Now, Buddha, you pray."

In a perfectly clear voice, its clarity surprising even him, Buddha said his prayer aloud. God accomplished more than the trifle of healing his laryngitis: He moved Buddha's heart. In Buddha's prayer he invited Christ into his life!

On the wine-colored rug of the model studio, Buddha was saved. After giving his heart to the Lord, Buddha declared wryly, "Now I'm really a Joker *out* of Hell."

I began spending a great deal of time with Buddha, and I accompanied him often to a bikers' hangout, The Omnibus, on Hollywood and Cahuenga. Buddha introduced me to dozens of bikers from his own and other clubs.

Six weeks after his conversion, his reverence for God soaring, Buddha quit the Jokers Out of Hell. And Carol left the model studio.

Buddha and Carol had been living together for more than a year, but now that he was saved Buddha wanted to get married. He and Carol asked me to perform the ceremony.

The wedding took place on a Sunday afternoon at the First Baptist Church in Beverly Hills. The last time I saw him before the wedding Buddha hadn't cut his hair and beard, and so it came as something of a shock when he turned up for the exchanging of vows in a neat black suit, white shirt, bow tie . . . clean-shaven and short-haired.

"The Lord has really ruined you," I said, smiling.

Carol was a dream in a white wedding gown.

Buddha is now managing a gas station, and Carol is working as an instructor in a legitimate modeling school. And both are living for Christ.

Working with the bikers is akin to a seismologist measuring the intensity of an earthquake on the Richter Scale, the sensitive instrument that records the magnitude of a given tremor on a scale of one to nine, the larger the number the more severe the up-heaval.

One evening around nine I walked into The Omnibus and found some seventy-five uptight bikers and their old ladies in the midst of a shouting, angry strategy session. That crowd of Satan's Slaves was a human Saint Andreas Fault, already rumbling and about to crack. The only thing keeping the pressure in check was that no one knew who was responsible for gunning down one of their members and his old lady.

At Biff's restaurant around the corner an unknown dude had stepped to the table where Cliff and Ginger were eating and had unceremoniously pumped three bullets into each of them. Then he had split, not to be seen again to this day.

"They're in bad shape," said Stoney, as rugged a biker as ever mounted a chopper.

Another slave of Satan, named Moose, hirsute and jackbooted, said, "Preacher, maybe you can say a prayer for them."

In a moment when death hovers, bikers like anyone else call instinctively on God.

Every biker and his old lady in that huge beer bar got down on their knees while I asked the Lord to be merciful to Cliff and Ginger.

The prayer brought the Richter reading down to a less dangerous two or three, but the needle could zoom to nine again if the circumstances warranted.

The room now spontaneously emptied into the street, and the frustrated bikers headed for their choppers. Like zinging bees around a hive, a cluster of forty or so bikers and their old ladies formed behind my car as I led the way to the Los Angeles County Hospital on North State Street.

Arriving amid a cannonade of noise, the bikers swept inside and swarmed onto the elevators to the fifth floor after a terrified nurse told us where Cliff and Ginger were being treated.

The Satan's Slaves, their jackets bedecked with swastikas and Iron Crosses, fanned out along the floor, taking up their stations and holding it captive as if they were a Nazi raiding party canvassing a block for hidden Jews.

A bespectacled elderly doctor emerged from an operating room and took in the scene with a horrified expression.

Stoney stormed up to him. "We want to go inside and see how they're doing."

"That's impossible," the doctor declared. "They're in critical condition. Besides, we never allow anyone in the operating room."

The bikers' insistence on entering the operating room became a fixation. They simply didn't trust the doctors. I thought of the needle on the Richter Scale.

"Hold off a minute, Stoney," I said, and took the doctor aside. I told him I was a minister and added, "If you want to protect the other patients on the floor, your own safety, and the nurses, and probably prevent a killing, I suggest you compromise. Give your consent for two of them to go into the operating room."

"I'd need permission from the director. The only possible exception would be members of the immediate family, and even that would be stretching the rules."

"These guys are tense. Let two of them in and when they see the blood and gore they probably won't stay more than a few seconds."

"All right, but just members of the family," the doctor insisted. I couldn't help but admire his courage. He called out, "Which of you is related to the patients?"

Every biker's hand shot up.

The perplexed doctor went down the line, asking biker after biker, "How are you related to the man in the operating room?"

Answered Stoney: "Brother."

Answered Moose: "Brother."

Answered all the others: "Brother."

"Very well," the doctor sighed. "Two of you can come in." He let me enter as well.

Cliff was lying on a table, blood pouring from his open stomach as a doctor worked feverishly to remove the bullets. Ginger was prone on another table, unattended for the moment.

As I suspected, Stoney and Moose, tough as they were supposed to be, couldn't take it. One look and they lurched outside.

Everything was cool now. There was nothing to do but sweat it out.

Not a single biker left the hospital through the night. When the blood bank opened at 8 A.M. they were all in line. Cliff and Ginger had received massive transfusions from the hospital's emergency blood supply, and the bikers were volunteering to replenish it.

However, they didn't prove to be ideal donors. The careful technicians tested each biker before taking his blood. Only one in ten qualified as a donor. The rest had venereal disease or too much dope in their systems.

Learning this, I felt there was still an obligation the bikers had to the hospital. I took off in my car and went to every biker hangout I knew. As I passed the word the bikers descended on the hospital, over a hundred of them. Finally there was enough acceptable blood to restock the hospital's supply.

About noon, as I sat with Stoney, Moose, and the others, a doctor came out and said, "They're both going to make it."

To the enormous relief of the hospital staff, the bikers filed quietly out and took off.

Cliff and Ginger were patched up, and recovered from their wounds. In about two months they were riding again with the Satan's Slaves.

The rise, fall, and rise of a biker called "Beast" is the stuff of novels, not real life.

At twenty-five, living and working on the eastern seaboard, he was a promising young man with a boundless future. For the biker who came to be known as "Beast" was a Baptist preacher!

What happened?

"Everybody in my church was a hypocrite," Beast recalled bitterly. "They were thieves, too. You had to check the Sunday offering three times to make sure none of the deacons, ushers, or parishioners had dipped a hand in. Several times the entire offering was stolen.

"The leaders in the church fussed and argued endlessly.

"Several were worse drunkards than winos on Skid Row.

"Wife swapping and adultery were epidemic.

"The parishioners gossiped viciously and lied habitually.

"I was visiting the wife of a deacon one night and he came home and accused me of sleeping with her.

"The allegation of the pastor sleeping with a deacon's wife spread like smallpox through the town. Rumor convicted me. I was powerless to put it down.

"I finally reached the conclusion that it was a hopeless, thankless job. I quit, walked away from the church, dumped it all.

"If this was religion, I wanted no part of it."

Like Gauguin leaving behind everything for exile in the South Seas, he dropped out and disappeared. Unlike Gauguin, he created nothing except a reputation so loathsome he soon earned, and deserved, the name of "Beast."

His personality had turned 180 degrees. He joined one of the Hell's Angels' West Coast chapters, let his appearance become so raunchy and foul that even fellow bikers were offended. He was so mean and ill-tempered that he would fight over anything. He became a doper. The miracle was that he hadn't killed anybody.

Conversion material?

Certainly. Christ can rescue anyone, no matter how depraved he's become.

Converting Beast fell on the slight shoulders of a born-again runaway, Estelle, whom I had led to the Lord. She was a quietly militant Christian who would do anything I asked except return to her parents, so polluted with hate and hassling was her home in the Midwest.

Estelle talked to Beast endlessly, and finally struck a chord. A flashback came to him of what God offered the believer. It had been senseless to judge and dismiss God from his life because of one congregation of pseudo-Christians.

Through Estelle, Beast recommitted his soul to the Lord. Then Estelle brought him to me. Beast and I prayed together, talked over where he'd been, where he could be. "I've got to get out of the Hell's Angels," he concluded. He soon gave away his chopper, jacket, and colors.

A few days later he no longer looked like a beast. He'd shaved, had a haircut, and bought a suit. He phoned his parents and told them he was returning.

The biker once called Beast is back at a Bible college for refresher courses. He plans to preach again. And when this once Devil-consumed ex-biker takes to the pulpit in the future and talks of sin he'll know whereof he speaks. He's a fortunate man; he raged through a hell on earth for three years before re-embracing Christ. Now he has one foot in Heaven.

Beast was one of two bikers I've met who through Christ ended up serving God in the pulpit. The other was named "Preacher." Born, raised, and educated in Florida, he'd left his home state at the age of nineteen. He migrated to the Southwest and took up with a bikers' gang called The Bandidos. He was against everything, the Lord, the Bible, all that the Establishment represented. He would run off at the mouth for hours and so, naturally, they called him "Preacher."

I ran into Preacher for the first time when I was at a revival at Castle Hills Baptist Church in San Antonio, Texas, which is pastored by hard-working Jack Taylor, a friend for years, an easy-

going man on the surface who has a will of iron when it comes
to the things of the Lord.

When I arrived in San Antonio, I wanted to conduct an un-
scheduled Sunday afternoon service.

"There's no singing group available," Jack said.

"Then let's go out and save a group and have them sing and
play at the service."

It seemed the logical way to meet God's need, and Jack accompanied me on a tour of San Antonio's nightclubs. We reached one
joint that was featuring an all-female, five-member group called
The Pink Panthers. Except for their black boots everything about
them was pink—miniskirts, hats, blouses; even their guitars and
drums were painted pink.

We talked to them after their show and led three to the Lord.

When Jack and I asked if they would play at our service, they
said they didn't know any church music. "You can learn, you can
come up with something," I said.

Next day, after they had practiced through the night, they
played at our service, which was jam-packed with a crowd of more
than seven hundred. The Pink Panthers played "Amazing Grace"
with a sound I'm certain no one had heard before. It was in rock
tempo and it was out of sight. The kids cheered and applauded
lustily. The three converted girls each gave their testimony, then I
preached.

I was ten minutes into my sermon when a gang of bikers,
unmistakable in their colors, clanked in noisily. Spotting them I
began telling stories of converted bikers.

About seventy-five people were saved at that service.

After I finished counseling with those who'd been led to Christ,
Preacher introduced himself and told me, "Man, I need something more in my life than I have now."

"Do you want to be saved?"

"Yes."

Not only Preacher, but several of his fellow bikers came forward
to embrace Christ. Jack subsequently baptized all of them.

A few weeks later I was back on the Strip when Preacher walked
into His Place. He was low.

"Man, I've backslid," he said. "I've been hitting up. But every
time I take junk it's awful. It's better the way I am when I'm right
with God."

I worked hard with Preacher and when he finally rededicated his life he really meant it.

Today he's an assistant pastor at a church in Atlanta, Georgia. Preacher is a real preacher now.

18

The Runaway Generation

Age: 17.
Height: Five feet four inches.
Weight: 105 pounds.
Eyes: Gray-green.
Complexion: Fair.
Hair: Light brown with auburn tint.
Identifying marks: Dimple right cheek.
Characteristics: Always neatly dressed, wears eye makeup.
Favorite foods: Pizza, hamburger, French fries, apple pie, and cake.

That could be a capsule portrait of Miss America.

And the girl on the poster is pretty enough to be Miss America.

The poster, one of scores that come to my desk every week from frantic parents, pleads: "A reward of $2,000 will be paid for information leading to the definite location and safe return of our runaway girl."

Poignantly, the poster adds:

We are a churchgoing family, and our daughter was always in morning and evening worship services and in youth fellowship. She seemed well adjusted. She is quick to smile and has a very charming personality.

She is extremely afraid of lightning and becomes very nervous during a thunderstorm.

Her leaving left us in shock as well as grief, for we had no reason to suspect she would abandon us.

The girl has been missing for more than two months. The parents can only wait and wonder where the daughter is who's afraid of lightning and thunder, but wasn't afraid to strike out on her own.

She might be anywhere. Haight-Ashbury. Chicago. New Orleans. Greenwich Village. More than likely the Sunset Strip.

It's certain she's in one of those concrete jungles, and may God help her.

J. Edgar Hoover, responding to a letter I wrote him about the runaway problem, said that according to his estimate "based upon reports submitted by law enforcement agencies, there were over 170,000 persons under eighteen years of age taken into protective custody as runaways" in 1968.

But the FBI's figures only skim the surface. An Associated Press story that polled police officials, juvenile authorities, and clergymen around the nation declared: "An estimated half-million youths between twelve and eighteen run away from home every year. The exact figure is unknown because police believe thousands of runaways, particularly boys and older teen-agers, are never reported missing."

The AP estimate of 500,000 annual runaways, plus who knows how many more, leads to thought-provoking statistical conclusions: At least one in every hundred American kids is chucking home and hearth. Together their number is larger than the population of Alaska, Nevada, Vermont, or Wyoming. And the disappearance of the runaways leaves another million people in trauma—their mothers and fathers.

The runaway is yet another middle-class phenomenon, the middle class that is the alleged guardian of bedrock American values.

"Favorite foods: Pizza, hamburger, French fries, apple pie, and cake," the poster said. "We are a churchgoing family, and our daughter was always in morning and evening worship services and in youth fellowship."

It's apparent that apple pie and church attendance are no longer sufficient "values" to hold many young people.

"She seemed well adjusted."

It appears she wasn't at all well adjusted.

So young, so inexperienced, what drives them from home so soon?

They leave for a constellation of reasons, everything from bad grades to a vague search for something better. But the experience of ministering to thousands of runaways—more than six hundred of whom we have sent back—highlights several inescapable facts.

The overwhelming reason most kids take off is because of their parents. Middle-class mothers and fathers busy getting and spending must shoulder the blame for the lack of meaningful communication. They are too preoccupied, indifferent, uncaring, and insensitive to handle the needs and problems of their children. Parents will tear to shreds a psychedelic poster a young boy hangs on his wall and smash a daughter's Beatles' record. Then, instead of leading them to solid values, they'll lambast the "damn long-haired hippie Communists."

The clash of cultures and polarization between generations is at least bearable for most kids. They don't skip because of that in most cases. What does turn them off is the constant arguments, hassling, recriminations, and tensions between their parents. The atmosphere in the home is poisoned, and so as soon as they are able to they split. Who needs the hassle?

Significantly, I have never met a single runaway from a home that was truly Christ-centered. In Ephesians 6:1 Paul commanded children nearly two thousand years ago to "obey your parents." But he said "obey your parents *in the Lord; for this is right.*"

How can a kid obey his parents in the Lord when the Lord is a stranger in his home?

Paul added in Ephesians 6:4, "And, ye fathers, provoke not your children to wrath, but bring them up in the nurture and admonition of the Lord."

There lies the solution to splintered homes. That's where it's really at.

Perfunctory church attendance on Sunday mornings isn't enough. I've had dozens of kids tell me their folks fought bitterly during the drive to church. The parents arrive at their pew, they're properly humble and attentive while the minister raps out his sermon, they are generous when the offering is taken, then on the ride home they're at it again hammer and tongs.

The kids see the phoniness and insincerity. They reject not only their parents but what passes for religion. I don't blame them for wanting something better.

The terrible problem, however, is that when they run away what they encounter is infinitely more wretched than what they've left behind.

These kids are trapped. They're virtually in the position of a convicted murderer in Utah who is given the choice of death by hanging or a firing squad.

The Sunset Strip probably—and tragically—gets the lion's share of the nation's runaways.

But the Strip is a bummer from beginning to end.

It's a bad trip.

There's nothing groovy or cool about it.

Don't come.

Skip the scene!

No matter how tough it is at home, the Strip is worse.

It's almost impossible for a teen-age boy to support himself on the Strip. Drugs, despair, and often death are what he's running to. For a runaway girl, the scene is totally impossible. Not only drugs, but hunger, panhandling, and white slavery are waiting for her.

Runaway girls are the cheapest commodity on the Strip. They are treated with less concern and dignity than cattle on the way to a slaughterhouse. A runaway girl is fortunate if she's busted and sent home because if she stays loose the barracudas are lying in wait.

"You look like a cool chick. Need a place to crash?"

"Yeah."

The crash pad, swarming with bodies, is her first taste of the hippie life. She's immediately turned on to sex and drugs. Virginity and a clear mind are soon only memories.

The hippie trip sounds bad but it's better than some of the other possibilities. The really tragic runaway girl is the one who is scooped up and enticed to a room where a dude mainlines her with heroin for a couple of days. When she finally comes off her trip, she's hooked. "You sleep with the next guy I bring in or you don't get another fix." This practice perpetuates the Strip's reputation as the largest white slavery recruiting ground in America. The runaway girl now becomes another Strip prostitute. In time she's moved to a brothel in the Fillmore section of San Francisco or to a house in Nevada. But as an addict her looks fade fast and she's cast aside quickly.

No matter. The Greyhound busses bring in a fresh supply of young, eager newcomers every day.

At His Place I can spot runaways as easily as an Indiana farmer locates his red barn. They are usually the last to leave—timid, frightened, uncertain, no place to crash.

It is absolutely crucial to get runaways to return home no later than three weeks after they hit the Strip. After that time they usually become hooked to sin like a trout to a baitline.

Karen, a doe-eyed teen-ager, was hovering around the coffee pot one night while we were closing.

She burst into tears when I asked where her parents lived.

I drove her home. Home was a three-bedroom house adjoining one of Southern California's best-known churches. Home was where her father lived, one of the most prominent ministers on the West Coast.

Karen had her first decent meal since leaving two weeks before. She then was ushered to bed by her still uncomprehending mother. "Karen, whatever possessed you . . . ?"

I sat in the minister's cozy study while he unburdened himself.

"Do you know what we told our congregation and friends? We said Karen was on a little vacation out of town, visiting friends.

"I was so ashamed.

"I'm a minister, a servant of God. I've tried to be a good man, a good father.

"But I realize now that while I was trying to save the world, I spent none of my time with my own daughter. I gave her nothing of myself.

"I would sit in this room by the hour writing my sermons, telling others how to live.

"And all the while I didn't know how to live myself and function as a parent.

"Can you believe that I can't count the times I've counseled other parents about *their* runaway sons and daughters?

"God has sent us a warning. I intend to heed it.

"I'm going to have the time of my life with Karen. She's seventeen years old and I know practically nothing about her.

"I never thought," he concluded as do all parents of runaways, "it could happen to us."

That's what it was like in a minister's home.

What is it like in homes where the name of God is never uttered except as a prefix to a curse?

Unbelievable.

Brown foothills climb and weave above Burbank, California, a city of some one hundred thousand inhabitants. Lockheed guns the local economy, and Frank's mother and father both worked at the sprawling, ugly plant of the aircraft company.

Frank was down from an LSD trip one evening at His Place when he confided that he was a runaway.

"Let me take you home."

"No, it's hell in that house."

"Man, there's no other way. Come on, let's surprise your folks."

In thirty minutes we were at the front door of Frank's neat stucco house. The time was four-thirty in the morning.

The printable part of the tirade Frank's mother spewed at me after barely taking note of her son, who'd been gone four days, was, "Don't you realize we have to get up early? What are you doing here this time of night? Couldn't you bring him back in the morning? We're hard-working people; we don't have time to sit around like all you rich, lazy preachers. We work for our money."

She cuffed her son across the side of his head. He staggered back. She went after him and dragged him by his hair into the house.

Then she slammed the door in my face.

I had led Frank to the Lord an hour before and convinced him over his strenuous objections to return home. "I'll talk with your folks. I'm sure we can work things out. I know your mother is worried about you."

I've never seen Frank again. I would barely have the heart to face him. What could I say after encouraging him to go back to that demon mother?

It occurred to me as I left Burbank that even the fiercest animals in the jungle show affection for and protect their young.

At thirteen Evelyn found life unbearable with her parents. She was crouching in a corner at His Place when I came over. At first she denied she was a runaway, then in tears admitted it.

I witnessed to her for several hours and she came to the Lord.

"My mother hates me," she said afterward, "she's told me a hundred times she wishes I'd never been born."

"What about your dad?"

"He's my stepfather. He never says anything."

She finally agreed to let me call her home.

When her parents walked into my office, the mother looked at her daughter. "You little bastard," Evelyn's mother said.

I called Dale and asked him to hold Evelyn outside while I talked privately with her parents.

"How could you say that to your daughter?"

"That girl is driving me crazy. I'm a nervous wreck. I hate her."

"Please shut up or leave," I told her. "No wonder the girl ran away. You've told her so often you hate her she believes it."

"I want her to believe it because I hate her with all my soul."

"We could spend hours discussing the condition of your soul."

The woman looked at me with contempt.

"I've advised your daughter to go home."

"I don't want her back."

"Do you want me to call the authorities and have the state assume custody?"

The stepfather spoke for the first time. "Let's take her," he said without enthusiasm.

"Oh, all right, but nobody knows how much that girl has hurt me. I don't know how I'm going to put up with her."

"Ma'am, I would like to share Christ with you before you take your daughter home."

She got up from her chair and let the venom out. "What kind of a lousy minister are you? What do you know about Christ? If there wasn't a foul church like yours here on the Strip my daughter would have no place to run to. You and your dirty hippies. The country is going to hell and you're helping. I hate you and everything you stand for."

She threw open the door and grabbed Evelyn, the stepfather following docilely.

I shuddered at the thought of the girl's future.

A few months later I was with the His Place staff for a two-day retreat at Forest Home, a Presbyterian mountain camp outside Los Angeles.

O. J. was at the piano and all of us were singing.

I felt a pair of arms curl around my neck.

I turned and saw Evelyn, her face wreathed in smiles.

"How is it at home?"

"Just like it's always been. But I've been going regularly to Bel-Air Presbyterian Church and I'm happy living for Christ."

Later Evelyn brought a large group of kids with her to my cabin. The staff and I witnessed to them, and all gave their hearts to Christ.

Through Christ Evelyn had surmounted the environment of her home. Her mother still treats her brutally, but she's living in the sunshine of Heaven.

It is that kind of hope—that a rose of Sharon can survive, grow and blossom from bad seed—that gives me the courage to urge kids to return to homes of gall and wormwood.

Larry was sixteen, tall for his age, well dressed, no hippie. In his voice was the sound of the Oklahoma prairie as we rapped one night at His Place for more than an hour. He was uptight and seemed completely indifferent when I asked him to give his life to Christ.

With no place to crash, he was still there at closing. I drove him to Norm's restaurant below Sunset Boulevard.

We ate breakfast together, but Larry wouldn't tell me why he left home.

He spent the remainder of the night at the restaurant and came back to His Place the next evening.

"I believe you're sincere. I want to be saved."

After bringing him to Christ, he told me the obscene circumstances that had led him to the Strip.

His father, a $65,000-a-year vice-president of a helicopter manufacturing company, had raped Larry's fourteen-year-old sister!

Wild with outrage, Larry knew it was either leave home or kill his father.

Larry's father was aware that his son knew about the rape. Nevertheless, we later learned that while Larry was gone his influential father was given free air time on television stations throughout the Southwest. He made a tear-jerking plea for Larry to return home. "All is forgiven," he said straight-faced.

Larry finally went back home when I convinced him that his

mother and sister desperately needed his help. And so did his sick father.

A few days after leaving Los Angeles airport, Larry called me to say he was doing fine. His mother and sister, considering the circumstances, were bearing up as well as could be expected.

He had one other bit of news.

The father who had raped his daughter had sent *Larry* to a psychiatrist for an examination. "Arthur, my father said he couldn't understand why I ran away. He couldn't understand what was wrong with *me!*"

Jerry, seventeen years old with a straight haircut and sharp, expensive clothes, walked into His Place one day and introduced himself.

He was a wonderfully saved Christian, yet he had run away.

"I left," he explained, "because my mother and dad don't need me. We have a home you wouldn't believe. Big and beautiful, but always filled with people. Parties almost every night. My folks ask me to leave the house whenever they give a party.

"They think I don't know what goes on. It's one big orgy after another. The upper crust of our city, politicians, lawyers, doctors, corporation big-shots. Everybody gets drunk and every man tries to make out with somebody else's wife. From what I've seen, they don't have to try very hard.

"It made me ill. I couldn't stand any more of it.

"I came out here to be a hippie. I wanted to get away from the money and the hassle."

But Jerry had been on the Strip a couple of weeks and was just as nauseated by the hippie scene once he saw it for the bummer it was.

"I'm going back," he said. "Becoming a hippie isn't going to solve my problems. The church is the only thing I have at home. I'll try to talk sense to my parents and plead with them to change their lives and accept Christ."

I've never learned if Jerry's parents—his mother was a Philadelphia Main Line socialite and his father a venerated Pennsylvania superior court judge—became born again. I have prayed often for them and for Jerry.

I was preaching at a church in Long Beach, California, and after my sermon I gave the customary invitation. Alfie, a darling sixteen-year-old girl, was one of several dozen who came forward to live for Christ.

When all the others had left the counseling room, Alfie lingered. With a great deal of embarrassment she told me that she had been released from Juvenile Hall the day before after being busted as a runaway.

Alfie's parents had seen my picture in the local paper, and her father insisted she come to hear me.

"So I hated you even before you got up to preach."

Alfie was a habitual runaway. She'd split at least a dozen times, and had been picked up on each occasion.

"My dad's a policeman and when he comes home he's still a policeman. He slaps the tar out of me almost every day. All I have to do is say something he doesn't agree with and pow! He treats me like I was a hood in a line-up.

"He's had a girl friend for over a year. My mother knows. She and Daddy never sleep together. Now Mother has her own boy friends.

"The happiest time of my life is when I'm with a bunch of kids and we're all stoned. I first started popping pills from those I found in my folks' medicine cabinet.

"I rode with the Hell's Angels for a couple of months, but it was a bad scene, so I took off.

"Every time I run away they catch me sooner or later. It's always the same. They put me in Juvenile Hall but since my dad's a policeman he goes and talks to them and they let me out."

Alfie's folks were waiting for her in the vestibule of the church.

"Maybe you can do something with her. Can she stay with you for a while?" her father asked.

Sherry and I took Alfie into our home. Alfie and Sherry became very close and Alfie confided that she was pregnant and afraid to tell her parents.

We went with Alfie and helped break the news to her astonished folks.

Alfie had the baby and married her boy friend.

They have their own small house now. It is a Christian home, and the future looks rosy.

Alfie's father, an ex-Baptist preacher turned policeman, was grateful for the change in his daughter. He said he wanted to come down to our Halfway House and talk to the kids about law enforcement.

"Our kids know quite a bit about law enforcement," I said. "What they need is more Bible study and prayer to keep them strong for the Lord."

The face of Alfie's father spread in a mile-wide grin. "That gives .me an idea. I can still deliver a pretty good sermon. I'll come down and preach."

"About what?"

Answered the man who used his daughter as a punching bag and lived in sin with another woman: "I want to preach to those kids on a subject very close to my heart, 'How to Live the Perfect Christian Life.'"

19

Busted and Evicted

> Congress shall make no law respecting an establishment of religion or prohibiting the free exercise thereof; or abridging the freedom of speech, or of the press; or the right of the people peaceably to assemble, and to petition the Government for a redress of grievances.
>
> —First Amendment to the Constitution of the United States

Seminal to America's survival as a democracy are those forty-five soaring words.

After the Bible, they are the most cherished, hallowed words I know. But as far as the Los Angeles sheriff's department was concerned, they might never have been written.

A confluence of behind-the-scenes power, its instrument the snappily uniformed sheriff's deputies, was gathering for the destruction of His Place.

Intimidation, harassment, threats against my life, bribes, Draconian laws, and conspiracy were being marshaled against our church in an effort to drive us from the Strip.

I hadn't made the Strip a hippie haven; the Strip had turned rancid before I arrived. Although I would have been as euphoric as the businessmen and the sheriff's department to see every hippie won for the Lord and leave the area, those who should have been my friends and supported our work became instead enemies bent on destroying us.

But in the meantime I was determined to stay.

The campaign to annihilate His Place and send me packing was fierce and dirty and in my mind unconstitutional.

The first bust came while I was witnessing on the Strip between the Hamburger Hamlet and Mother's, a combination pool room and coffee house. I was sharing Christ with two interested passers-by. We were standing only a foot from the wall of a building, leaving the wide sidewalk clear for uninterrupted pedestrian traffic.

"You have to keep moving," said one of the two sheriff's deputies who approached me as my two prospects walked on with the Bibles and Gospel tracts I had given them for study.

I knew the law. The California State Penal Code, Section 647C, says a person can't "maliciously block the sidewalk."

Since I wasn't blocking the sidewalk, maliciously or otherwise, I refused to budge.

"You have to keep moving," the deputy said again.

"Congress shall make no law respecting an establishment of religion or prohibiting the free exercise thereof; or abridging the freedom of speech . . . or the right of the people peaceably to assemble."

Did the vengeful no-loitering law, which was enforced no place in Los Angeles County except on the Strip, supersede the First Amendment to the Constitution of the United States?

In my opinion, no.

In the opinion of the sheriff's men, yes.

"You're under arrest!" said the officer, jackknifing my hands behind my back and slapping handcuffs around my wrists.

Handcuffs as a penalty for telling people about Jesus. It didn't seem possible. I wasn't a homicidal maniac. A would-be presidential assassin. An escaped killer. Man, I wasn't even a bellicose, drunken straight weaving down the street, as many do every day along the Strip, looking for a fight or propositioning women in the foulest language.

I was shoved into a squad car and taken to the sheriff's lock-up, the West Hollywood County Jail.

I was searched and manhandled by a deputy. I couldn't imagine what he was looking for. What he found were three Bibles and about two hundred Gospel tracts—nothing but the word of God all over me.

The handcuffs were removed and the deputy ordered me to take off my wedding ring. I refused. He shimmied it from my finger.

The deputy and a couple of other officers standing around were aggressive, impolite, rough, and nasty. There wasn't an ounce of dignity or even routine courtesy in their behavior.

One deputy mocked me. "You ain't no ordained preacher. You're just a kook and a Communist. Whoever heard of a real preacher in jail? You ought to be ashamed of yourself. The Bible says you should cooperate with the authorities and not disobey the law."

"Man, don't you tell me about the Bible. Peter and John got busted, too." I flipped to the Book of Acts and read aloud from 4:2–3: " 'Being grieved that they taught the people, and preached through Jesus the resurrection from the dead. And they laid hands on them, and put them in custody.'

"You're the ones who should be ashamed," I said, my anger rising. "Jesus and his first followers were all busted." I turned to Acts 5:18. I read it loud and clear. " 'And laid their hands on the apostles, and put them in the common prison.' "

A deputy snatched my Bible from my hand and hustled me into a small, barred retaining section of the jail.

I asked the guard, "May I please have my Bible?"

He ignored me.

I sat against the wall and began singing hymns and quoting Scripture from memory.

"Shut up," the guard said.

In song and verse I kept singing His praises.

Exasperated, the guard came back and said, "If we return your Bible, will you shut up?"

I nodded.

And the Book was handed to me.

Soon the guard ordered me to remove my shoes, and I was transferred to a large, crowded bullpen. We were packed together like peanuts in a vacuum-sealed can. There wasn't even room to lie down.

I knew half the guys in there from the Strip. A doper I'd witnessed to many times called out, "Arthur, what in the world are you doing in here?"

I told him the circumstances of my arrest and then said, "I believe I'd like to preach."

My doper pal quieted everyone down and gave me the floor. "Preacher, go ahead and do your thing."

It was easier to reach the prisoners with the Word than it was to reach the police.

The text of my sermon was obvious: How to Be Happy in Jail. I told them they were as sad-looking a bunch as I'd ever seen, that none of them were happy except me and I was happy because I was saved. I added that by coming to the Lord they could find out what real happiness was all about.

When I gave the invitation, two prisoners stepped forward and they prayed without shame in front of everyone.

About three in the morning a teen-ager spaced out on STP was brought in and I worked with him through the night, gradually bringing him down.

I was released at noon the next day. Bill Gazzarri, the Hollywood-A-Go-Go entrepreneur, gave Sherry the bail money. I had tried unsuccessfully to win Bill for the Lord, but his gesture of friendship in standing bail for me showed that while he wasn't saved he was still serving God.

My trial was to be the initial court test of the no-loitering law. If the statute was upheld, our ministry would suffer a crushing blow since street-witnessing was crucial to our work of winning souls.

Though I had no money, my most pressing need was a first-class lawyer. I phoned several preachers and they gave me a list of twenty eminent Christian attorneys. I was assured that any one of these good, God-fearing lawyers would take my case without fee. Each would be overjoyed at the privilege of defending the Gospel.

I called every one of them—a disheartening experience. The least expensive said he would charge me five hundred dollars, and that provided he had to appear in court only once.

There was no way I could raise the bread.

So I went ·to the Los Angeles headquarters of the American Civil Liberties Union. Without a moment's hesitation I was told the ACLU would be honored to represent me in court because they agreed that my rights under the First Amendment had been trampled.

I asked for a Christian attorney, but was told I would have to accept whichever lawyer was available to donate his time and skill.

Martin H. Kahn was the attorney assigned to me. He was young, likable, brilliant—and Jewish.

I didn't care one whit that he was Jewish. What concerned me was that he was unsaved. "Be ye not unequally yoked together with unbelievers," 2 Corinthians 4:14 said. That verse had been pounded into me at church, college, and seminary, and because it was in the Bible, I accepted it without question.

I wondered if a person who didn't know Christ the way I knew Him could defend me. Could he understand my passion for the Lord? Could Jew and Christian be compatible?

Martin was tremendously interested in my pending trial and eager to go into court on my behalf.

"I'm not a Christian," he said when I told him the nature of my doubts. "But I appreciate and respect your beliefs and I believe in your right to express them. That's why I've taken your case."

I was still troubled. Everything about Martin appealed to me except that he hadn't given his heart to the Savior.

"I think I'll be my own attorney," I said.

"If you want to defend yourself," Martin replied, "I'll help all I can. There are a lot of legal technicalities you'll need to know. And it could get very complicated."

I was overwhelmed by his generosity, and suddenly I was ashamed of myself. The thought of those twenty so-called Christian lawyers flashed to mind. Their attitude didn't seem very Christian at all. Just a bunch of lawyers interested in a fee. And here was a man not getting a dime for the case and he was far more concerned with my rights than people who passed themselves off as Christians.

"Martin, my anxieties are over," I said. "Forgive me for hesitating. I apologize for doubting you. It had nothing to do with your religion or you as an individual. It was just something I had to battle in my mind. I had to decide if I could be defended in court as a Christian evangelist and minister by someone who hasn't had a conversion experience."

"I understand," Martin said, his face breaking into a huge smile.

We shook hands and prepared to do battle.

The trial testimony of the sheriff's officers virtually destroyed the last small hope I had in police integrity. Incredibly, the deputies testified that a crowd varying in number between 30 and 150 had been gathered around me at the time of my arrest! That was as far from the truth as the sun is from the moon.

In his cross-examination of the deputies Martin didn't dispute the size of the alleged crowd. He went right to the heart of the issue, drawing from the deputies the admission that pedestrians were able to navigate the street, that I hadn't prevented the free movement of anyone, that I was not in fact blocking the sidewalk.

The charge against me was so weak that Martin didn't trouble to put me on the stand. In view of the deputies' testimony that I wasn't blocking the sidewalk, he asked the judge for a dismissal.

The judge said that whatever the size of the supposed crowd there was no evidence introduced that I held or forced anyone to listen to me, that foot traffic had not been impeded, and that no pedestrian had made a complaint.

"The case is dismissed," the judge declared.

I was elated with the verdict, but it proved a short-lived victory. Our street ministry and the survival of His Place were still threatened as the sheriff's department stepped up its intimidation. Without search warrants they swept through His Place almost every night, checking kids out and indiscriminately arresting many of them. Those arrested were innocent of any wrongdoing. They were taken to headquarters, questioned, and released.

The culmination came on a night when His Place was raided three times! The sheriff's men fanned through the building, saying they were looking for runaways, curfew violators, and kids without proper I.D.'s.

"In your patience possess ye your souls," Luke wrote in 21:19.

Yet patience would play directly into the hands of those who wanted us off the Strip.

A line had to be drawn.

A stand had to be made.

Prayer had to be reinforced by action.

I walked to the commander of the sheriff's raiding party and said, "Sir, I'm placing you under citizen's arrest. I charge you with illegal search and seizure and trespassing."

"Shut up," he spat out. "We'll come in here anytime we want."

"No! Not unless you have a search warrant or a plausible reason. Your men use profanity. We have a rule that says no guns are permitted in God's house. Your men are wearing guns. You are welcome to come in, take a Bible, and pray. Otherwise, this is a private building, and you are not permitted in here."

"You're just harboring degenerates, prostitutes, dope addicts, and pushers," he said. "The scum of the Strip."

"If you catch anyone committing an act of prostitution or dealing on our premises, arrest that person and make a specific charge. What you're doing is persecution, no different from Communist Russia or Nazi Germany."

I asked for his name and badge number, but he laughed and walked out the door where a flotilla of squad cars were parked. A stranger would have thought we had a hundred Jack the Rippers inside the building.

Completely fed up, I decided to pursue my constitutional guarantee of freedom of religion. Quicker sought than found, I rapidly discovered.

I went to the sheriff's department and attempted to consummate my citizen's arrest against the officer who had led the raid. The deputy I talked to wouldn't even give me the form to fill out. He said the department wasn't in the habit of accepting charges against its own men who were merely carrying out orders. He told me to take my complaint to the district attorney.

I called Los Angeles County District Attorney Evelle Younger, but I couldn't get through. His chief assistant said in any case there was nothing that office could do.

I phoned the Civil Rights Commission in Washington, D.C.
"It's not within our jurisdiction."
"But it's discrimination."
"Sorry."

I called the U.S. Marshal's office in Los Angeles. I was told to call the U.S. Attorney, who told me to call the FBI, who told me to call County Supervisor Debs. ("You're running a hog wallow down there. Anything the sheriff's office wants to do to clean up the mess on the Strip, I am for," he said smugly.)

I called Governor Ronald Reagan. His office told me to call Senator George Murphy. Senator Murphy's office brushed me off.

I called Senator Edward Kennedy's Washington office and got my first and only polite, sympathetic hearing. Senator Kennedy was out of town making a speech, but one of his aides said he would be willing to investigate the matter, though it should more properly be dealt with through my own congressman.

I called my congressman and several other Southern California representatives. None of them was interested.

It all added up to one long merry-go-round ride with no brass ring.

I again took my complaint to the ACLU. Yes, they would go to court on my behalf.

But courtroom action might take forever. And even if I won a verdict in court, His Place might no longer be in existence by then. If the sheriff kept raiding us, the kids wouldn't come and any hope I had of reaching them for Christ would be lost.

I gathered the staff and told them we were going to stage a demonstration, a demonstration for freedom of religion. It was a spur-of-the-moment idea.

We asked that night's His Place crowd, about two hundred kids, to join the demonstration. With the exception of a few who were totally spaced out, everyone volunteered. If we had planned the demonstration, passed out handbills, and held back for a week we could have raised an army of thousands of kids. But I decided to go with those on hand. I was anxious to bring the issue directly to the doorstep of the sheriff.

We quickly rounded up a couple of walkie-talkies and a bullhorn, and assigned monitors to keep the crowd in check and make certain there was no violence or disobedience of the law.

We met in front of The Classic Cat, which featured topless girls. Little Gina carried a sign that read, "WOULD YOU WANT YOUR DAUGHTER DANCING TOPLESS?" Tiny Joel held up his sign: "POLICEMEN, WHAT'S WRONG WITH MY DADDY?" Mine read, "WOULD YOU ARREST JESUS FOR LOITERING?"

A sheriff's squad car rolled up and a deputy asked me to call off the demonstration. "You're supposed to be a Christian, and you're having a demonstration."

"There's nothing un-Christian about a demonstration. This is for Jesus."

We marched up and down the Strip for two or three hours, being careful not to block the sidewalk and obeying the traffic lights. Then we massed in the parking lot of the Sheriff's Department.

Waiting for us were hundreds of officers, all with guns.

I got on the bullhorn and explained why we were there, and I preached the Gospel. Several kids who'd been saved at His Place gave their testimony. Soon the crowd started chanting: "We want to talk, we want to talk, we want to talk."

But no one from the sheriff's office would meet with us. The officers stood firm. When I heard some of the kids shout "Pig," a term for the police I despise, I decided to break it up. Both sides were getting edgy and tense. I led the crowd back to His Place.

The news of our demonstration was broadcast over radio and

television and for our second peaceful protest more than three hundred kids turned out.

Again we massed in the sheriff's parking lot. Again the "We want to talk" chant went up.

A deputy finally emerged and said they would meet with three of us. I went in with one of my staff members, Barry Sparks, and a friend named Barry Woods.

We talked with the sheriff's community relations officer. The meeting was short and to the point. He would make no concessions, no direct promises that the department would stop hassling His Place.

"I'm going to call this demonstration off," I said.. "But I want you to know that if your men ever raid our church again without a search warrant or proper cause I'm going to organize the biggest demonstration in the history of Sunset Strip. We'll blow the lid off in the name of Christ."

I went outside and dispersed the crowd.

The next day I got a call from the ACLU's Bruce Margolin. He said he was prepared to file a restraining order against the sheriff plus charges of assault and disturbing the peace. Bruce said I was also in a position to file a personal damage suit for $100,000 for defamation of my name, character, and reputation.

I told him to hold off. I wanted to see how the sheriff's department would react now. I had no interest in a courtroom vendetta if it could be avoided.

The demonstration tactics worked. His Place was never rousted or raided again. The sheriff's men came by from time to time and if they had a justifiable reason for entering we gave permission without a warrant.

But now they were always polite!

Although His Place at last had become an acknowledged sanctuary of God, the streets of the Strip were still a battleground. I had to be free to witness anywhere, anytime, as Jesus did. I considered street-witnessing as important to our ministry as His Place and the Halfway House. The timorous, the troubled, the suspicious could often be reached in no other way. Some of the most gloriously saved Christians I knew had their first interest in Christ generated in a sidewalk contact. The Lord doesn't mind where a soul is won. He offers salvation and everlasting life to those who come to Him in a church, a stadium, a topless nightclub, a brothel, skid row, a jail cell, the private office of a corporation executive, as well as the sidewalk. The paramount consideration is leading the lost to Christ wherever contact can be made. And the sidewalks of the Sunset Strip offered abundant opportunity for such contacts.

My acquittal under 647C had in effect destroyed that statute in the State Penal Code. But the ever-resourceful county had passed a fresh, equally obnoxious law, Ordinance No. 9648.21, which said: "A person shall not loiter or stand in or upon any public highway, alley, sidewalk or crosswalk or other public way open for pedestrian travel or otherwise occupy any portion thereof in such a manner as *unreasonably* to annoy or molest any pedestrian thereon or as to obstruct or *unreasonably* interfere with the free passage of pedestrians."

The italicization of the adverb "unreasonably" is mine. Could a minister unreasonably witness on a public sidewalk as long as he did not "annoy or molest" or use force? Could the Bible be unreasonably quoted to an interested passer-by who chose of his own accord to listen?

The answers to those questions were as obvious to me as the answer to the question: Does God exist?

What was unreasonable was the broad, free, and easy enforcement of the ordinance, which was only the old law dressed in new verbiage. It was simply another power play to drive the young people from the Strip. The Establishment had not yet learned its lesson.

I collided head-on with the new ordinance while I was standing against the wall of the Hamburger Hamlet with a friend, the Reverend Mitchell Osborn, education director of the Highland Avenue Baptist Church of National City, just outside San Diego. Mitch had come up to help me witness on the Strip, and we were passing out Gospel tracts when the inevitable sheriff's men arrived. Said one: "You've got to move."

"We are not obstructing pedestrians. You can see the sidewalk is clear."

"Are you going to move, or are you going to be arrested?"

"I hate to have such a choice. But since we are doing nothing wrong, we are not moving."

The deputy busted me, ringing my wrists once more with handcuffs. Looking at Mitch he said, "Do you want to go, too?"

"Might as well," said Mitch. He was also handcuffed.

In less than thirty minutes I was back in the bullpen and preaching again. Two of the inmates were brought to the Lord as the result of our jail service.

After twenty-four hours in the sheriff's bullpen we were transferred to the big county jail downtown. They lined us up—about a dozen prisoners all in handcuffs with a chain running through the cuffs from man to man, binding us all together.

I sighed and took it in stride. Nothing the sheriff's men might do would surprise me. But I felt burdened for Mitch. He was a straight and a conservative minister, nothing hip about him. A graduate of Golden Gate Theological Seminary and the California Baptist College, Mitch had a wife, two children, and a passion for winning souls. This was the first time he'd been arrested. I don't believe he ever had so much as a traffic ticket before.

The police van gave us a wild ride downtown. The driver, his foot pushing the accelerator to the floor, was purposely making it uncomfortable for us, taking the corners on two wheels, jostling all of us in the back of the van. The handcuffs were so tight my wrists were beginning to bleed. Through it all, I tried to witness to the fellow sitting next to me.

"Man, I don't feel like hearing it," he said. "Will you please leave me alone?"

At the jail we were stripped, shoved through a cold shower, deloused (presumably), fingerprinted and photographed, and moved into a cell, the whole dangerous convict bit.

I suddenly remembered that I was scheduled to preach in a few hours at the Mount Zion Baptist Church in Watts, the largest Negro Baptist church in the West. And here I was in jail.

Unexpectedly, a deputy came up to our cell and said we were free to go. Mitch's wife had bailed him out. My bail money came from a highly unlikely, unexpected source, my old friend Richard, the pusher who had given His Place one of its more memorable episodes the night he outsmarted the sheriff's men by pretending he was a narc.

I ran home, changed and zipped out to the church in Watts. Man, it was a powerful service. I preached about my getting busted and hassled by the police, and those were facts of life that everyone in the Watts ghetto thoroughly understood. Amens soared through the air like angels.

News of my latest arrest hit the papers and the TV and radio newscasts. The ACLU called, asking to represent me. This would be the first court test of the new ordinance.

Another extraordinarily gifted Jewish attorney volunteered his time and skill, cost-free. All my attorneys have been Jewish. Only too aware of the terrible price that has been paid for the right to worship freely, these men are in the forefront of the struggle to guarantee the sanctity of the First Amendment.

When we went to trial, my attorney, Bennett Kerns, challenged the law on grounds that it was, on its face, unconstitutional.

The jury was composed of upper-middle-class straights from Beverly Hills, Bel-Air, Brentwood, Westwood, Santa Monica. They were all over-forty Gold Coast Establishmentarians. How could they understand my work with young people whose life-style and values conflicted so starkly with their own? I would have appreciated at least one under-thirty long-hair in that jury box.

However, there was no cause for concern. Bennett destroyed the prosecution witnesses, and after all the evidence had been heard Mitch and I were acquitted. And the jury's verdict was unanimous! . Coincidentally, that day I was scheduled to speak before the well-fed, well-entrenched sachems of the West Hollywood Chamber of Commerce. When the invitation had come, I was surprised beyond words. But the Chamber's program chairman was an eminently fair man. A spokesman for the sheriff's department had addressed the group and given a vehement antihippie speech. Now the Chamber wanted to hear an opposing view.

Four representatives of the sheriff's department, including the West Hollywood station commander, were in the audience. I felt like a lamb in a lion's lair.

The Chamber president, prior to my talk, made an announcement that the group had just raised a sizable amount of money for the support of blind children.

This gave me the springboard for my message. There was so much to say. I had been wondering how I could extract the essence of my position in a short talk.

"I commend you for your contribution to the blind," I began. "But what about the thousands of walking blind who pass your business establishments every day and to whom you so heartily object?

"These are the blind who have eyes but do not see. They need direction, someone to show them the light so they might see for the first time in their lives, someone to bring them hope, strengthen their souls.

"Sure, they're kids hung up on the needle and pills. But how many in this room have sons or daughters strung out on drugs? It seems so easy to condemn a kid who's rejected his parents until one of your children becomes a runaway. And if he runs away to a strange city, who will be there to help him?

"When you think about that your condemnation of the young people of the Strip must be mixed with a little compassion.

"It's not only the kids on the Strip who are blind, but many adults who come out of your fancy restaurants staggering and blind drunk.

"What difference is there between a kid blinded by speed, acid, or pot and a businessman blinded by Scotch, bourbon, or vodka?

"The generation of the young and the generation of straights both must come to God and live for Him.

"I ask every businessman in this room: Are you blind to your responsibilities, your responsibilities to God and your fellow human beings?

"I ask you: What should really count on the Strip, the dollar or people?

"Why have I had to fight tooth and nail for the survival of my church, a church where many of the blind have been taught to see? Why have I been arrested for preaching on the sidewalks the same message of Christ you hear in your own churches on Sunday mornings?

"I leave the answers to your own consciences."

I sat down. Had I convinced the alliance of businessmen and the sheriff's representatives to take the pressure off the kids, off His Place, off my witnessing in the streets? Was all the hassle over at last?

I didn't have to wait long to find out.

In eight hours I knew.

In eight hours I was busted again.

About ten o'clock that evening I was in front of the Sunbeam Market witnessing to a young doper known as "Trip," a fitting cognomen. He swallowed acid like jelly beans.

"When are you going to start tripping out on Jesus?"

Trip shrugged.

I began to share Christ with him. If ever a soul needed Christ, Trip did. Only in his early twenties, the dissipated countenance, unhealthy pallor, and emaciated body so often seen in hard-core addicts made him look twice as old.

A sheriff's car drove up.

"Keep moving," a deputy shouted.

I was stunned with disbelief. It couldn't be happening again.

At the sight of The Man, Trip took off like an Apollo rocket. I was alone on the sidewalk. I stood there, unmoving.

The deputy scrambled from the squad car and said belligerently, "Are you going to move or not?"

"Officer, don't you know I won this thing in court only this morning?"

"I'm under orders to keep everybody walking. Now walk or else!"

"I have my orders, too—from God, and He says I should stay here and witness. As you can see, I'm not obstructing traffic."

Out came the handcuffs. Manacled again. Busted for the third time. Though I put up no resistance, the deputy shoved me hard against the steel exterior of the squad car.

When Bennett Kerns heard of my new arrest, he nearly split a gut. We agreed there could be no reason for the continuing arrests other than harassment.

At the trial we introduced testimony that the sidewalk was thirteen feet wide, making it impossible for one person to obstruct it.

Two ladies on the jury went down to the Sunbeam Market and measured the sidewalk. Their figure tallied exactly with ours.

I was not only swiftly acquitted, but every member of the jury stepped up and congratulated me. Several said they were in favor of my work. One well-dressed matron told me, "It's humiliating and disgraceful that you were even brought to trial."

Three trials. Three acquittals.

Unless the county now passed an ordinance outlawing breathing on the sidewalks of the Strip, perhaps I could safely assume I was free to continue my street-witnessing.

Then came the most punishing blow of all.

Two days after my third acquittal, my landlord notified me that he would not renew the lease on His Place!

The pressures against him were not to be believed. There had been a meeting among the largest property owners on the Strip and an agreement struck that no one would rent to any business catering to teen-agers, His Place included.

The straights were hurting. His Place had put a neighboring liquor store and nightclub into bankruptcy. Other businesses in our immediate area threatened a rent strike until His Place was closed.

My landlord was visited by sheriff's representatives and encouraged not to renew my lease.

All of this was a last-ditch attempt on the part of the Establishment to sweep the Strip clean of hippies and turn it back into a happy hunting ground for straight drunks.

But though His Place might vanish like a vapor that didn't mean the hippies would disappear. In fact, we were the only ones effectively weaning the hips off the Strip. Some kids had been busted a dozen times by the sheriff and warned to keep away from the Strip, yet they returned like homing pigeons.

I visited my landlord, an elderly, wealthy man free of malice and completely in accord with my work.

"I like you," he said. "I know you're doing a good job, but I just can't stand the pressure. I'm an old man and I don't want problems. I want to live in peace. Everyone's on my neck because I rent to you. I've even had calls threatening my life if I let you stay in the building."

On the floor of his living room I fell to my knees at his feet. I begged without shame. "You can do so much to help people and help God's work. Please, please don't put us out."

Gently, the landlord said, "I'm sorry. I just want peace."

The news that His Place was closing spread rapidly along the Strip.

Our final day in the building inevitably arrived. A few moments before the midnight deadline for vacating, I preached and told the large crowd, "His Place is *not* closed, only temporarily transferred."

The last thing we did was unbolt our cross, which by now had become the symbol of His Place. I hefted it to my shoulder, went through the door and marched down the Strip, a public declaration that I had no intention of silently folding our tent and disappearing.

We moved His Place into the street, re-gathering our church in the parking lot of a dry cleaning establishment. The owner had given us permission to use his property at night after he closed.

We were still witnessing, praying, helping to save souls, still serving Bibles, tracts, Kool-Aid, coffee, bagels, and sandwiches.

During the day I hunted for a building. Many were vacant, but none were available to me. If, using my own name, I phoned an owner or a real-estate office and expressed interest in renting an empty building, the answer was always no. To prove collusion, I would have members of the staff call back without identifying themselves as my associates. The answer was always that the building was for lease.

Our parking lot ministry lasted a month. Then Bill Harris managed to rent a building in his name, which he sublet to me.

We moved down the street from 9109 Sunset to 8913 Sunset.

The new His Place flourished as never before. Our crowds were running from five hundred to two thousand a night. We had no problems with the sheriff. But then the complaints began rolling in from the landlord—we were violating the building rules by bringing "degenerates" into the area; His Place was offensive to the neighboring establishments and not in harmony with the surrounding area.

We certainly weren't in harmony with the surrounding area—His Place had no topless dancers, we didn't serve booze, we didn't permit prostitutes or pushers to deal their wares.

Unharmonious too was the fact that at His Place the cross, not the cash register, was our guiding light.

We were at our second location only two months when the eviction notice came. We went to trial and lost.

Because there was no other choice I then made the decision to chain myself to the cross.

20

At the Cross

WAS MY MINISTRY FINISHED?

Could a third His Place rise somewhere along the sin-swollen lanes of the Strip?

Was there room for a tower of faith amid a slum of sacrilege?

Was there room on the Strip for God to compete with the godless?

More than ten thousand souls, young people and many straights, had been saved and pointed toward Heaven since I had come to the Strip. Yet there were legions of others who needed the life-changing experience of being carried over God's threshold. Without His Place, who would get them high on Jesus instead of junk, cleanse and heal them as Christ had cleansed and healed the leper?

Would the combined power of the straights and their supporting shock troops from the sheriff's department prove insurmountable?

The kids vastly outnumbered the straights on the Strip, but they prevailed only in body count, not influence. Could I somehow keep working with the majority and yet make peace with the potent minority?

Would the kids themselves in this showdown witness for Christ stay the course? Would they care enough about a new His Place to make the run for the roses with me and give me their moral support?

Even with the support of my dropout flock, could the heart of even one property owner be moved to rent us a building?

Though I had put it all in God's hands, the questions nagged at me.

I decided to take the adventure at the cross a heartbeat at a time, praying constantly for Him to sustain me and lead us to victory, as David had been led to triumph over Goliath.

What ensued at the cross cannot be recounted minute by minute, hour by hour, nor even day by day. It was too panoramic, a cyclorama of swirling, constantly shifting events, people, and patterns.

The emotional reactions to one of God's ministers foursquare on a sidewalk along a border of gutter, sitting, standing, or sleeping against a telephone pole with a garbage can a few feet away, ranged from the sacred to the sacrilegious. There were those who understood, and there were those who considered the stand at the cross the obsessive act of a crank or a madman.

Time yawned, time fled swiftly. Time was a watched pot and a winged chariot.

My memories of the experience are like slides flicking on and off in my brain, stereoscopic snapshots, captured photographs, many still in perfect focus, unforgettable and alive, many blurred and fuzzy.

Some, but by no means all, of the slides:

—I managed a short nap during the first night at the cross, and when I awoke early on the morning of June 28, summer heat was already scorching the pavement, and a giant swatch of smog quilted God's blue-white skies.

I hadn't thought to bring an umbrella to protect me from the furnace-hot sun.

—An elderly lady in a Thunderbird drove up beside me with a squeal of brakes.

"Brother Blessitt," she said, "I've got a surprise for you. I shopped all day for it."

From the trunk of her car she removed an expensive, adjustable lounge chair, a large beach umbrella, and a table.

"This will make you more comfortable." She smiled.

"Ma'am, I'm sorry, but I don't think it would be proper for me to sit out here with all the frills of a movie star at the pool of the Beverly Hills Hotel."

—Three friends, Mrs. B. J. Edwards and her sons, came by and nailed a hand-lettered sign to the top of the cross: "DOES ANYONE CARE?"

—My appetite was ravenous as a result of my fast. The hunger pangs were so great that I was beginning to feel weak and dizzy. As the day wore on and the merciless sun beat down, I began to feel sick. I could barely stand on my feet. I dropped off to sleep for a few hours.

—The first night turned into a street revival, though the staff was careful to keep the sidewalk clear. Two sheriff's men were standing a twenty-four shift a few yards from me near Sneaky Pete's restaurant. My staff was also working in shifts, and O. J., Ed Human, Dale, and Jim McPheeters were strung out along the street witnessing to passers-by. They had already won dozens of people for the Lord.

Thousands of reds, our symbolic stickers, had been dealt to the passing throngs. I laughed seeing half a dozen reds gummed on a frisky black French poodle.

—A nurse from the UCLA Medical Center stopped by. "You won't last two days," she said.

—Roy, the young boy I had rushed to the hospital as an OD, turned up and knelt on the sidewalk. He asked me to bring him to Christ. Then he showed me his Army enlistment papers. He was scheduled to leave the next day for boot camp.

—Another old friend appeared, the college student I had talked down from his STP trip. "I never thanked you," he said. I led him to the Lord, too.

—Dale brought me the first of many rumors that a new location for His Place was available, this one an abandoned motel across the street from the Playboy Club. Man, what a spot for a church. We could turn them on to the Bible instead of the Bunnies. When Dale checked it out the next day the location was suddenly "unavailable."

—A moonbeam-faced girl from Miami, in Los Angeles on a tour sponsored by the Campus Crusade for Christ, told me she was saved.

"Before I came to Christ," she said, "my parents would have bought God for me if it was possible. Now I've got the Lord's manna instead of my dad's money."

—Little Britches, a diminutive ex-addict that I had led to the Lord some time back, said she was planning to get married and live in a hippie commune in New Mexico. In order to obtain a license, Little Britches had to undergo a routine blood test.

"You know how it is with a clean head, Arthur. I'll blow my mind if they put a needle in me."

I prayed with her to have the strength to handle the needle. "This one's harmless, just a little blood out instead of a lot of speed in." I knew God would strengthen her to face the needle, a mental block a lot of former dopers have.

—By the third day, I was no longer hungry. Now even the thought of food repelled me. A man can survive much longer without food than without liquids. I'd been drinking nonbulk liquids—water, orange crush, and Cokes. Some wonderful Christians came to the cross with gallons of soft drinks, more than I could possibly consume. Among them was Hazel Colson, a serene, God-loving, titian-haired widow from Kansas, who voluntarily called one of the television stations, which resulted in the news of our witness at the cross being broadcast over the local ABC channel to all of Southern California.

—Joe Pyne sent one of his aides to ask me to appear again on his TV show. "Tell him," I said, "I'm all tied up."

—On the fifth day there was another rumor that a building was available, not one hundred yards from my perch. But this, too, proved to be hearsay.

—It was difficult to believe a week had swept by. It was even more difficult to believe that the sheriff hadn't hassled me once. I'd seen squad cars cruising by a dozen times a day. Either the sheriff's men had come dramatically under conviction or were waiting me out until I starved to death or until my strength had ebbed to the point where I'd have to be carried from the cross.

—Visitors at the cross included preachers, ministers, deacons, evangelists, churchmen from all over the country. Jess Moody, pastor of the First Baptist Church of West Palm Beach, Florida, a tall, confident, conscientious man of God, sat with me for hours. Jess stormed through a half-dozen real-estate offices on the Strip, lending his prestige to my witness and ministry. His passionate pleas to brokers and agents for a site for His Place resulted in soaring hopes and promises, but Jess, too, learned the hard lesson of what it meant to be an outlaw minister on the Strip. Jess and I prayed together for continued strength.

My good friend Jack Taylor from Castle Hills Baptist in San Antonio also helped buttress my faith. Jack said, "What you're doing is having an impact all over the country." We shared prayer and Jack expressed faith that His Place would open again on the Strip, no matter how discouraging things looked at the moment. "Jesus is smiling at you," he said.

—I was urged by friends at least to take vitamins to keep going. But in my mind vitamins were capsuled food, and that would be breaking the fast.

—"You're fantastic!" said a girl with dark roots at the crown of her blond hair as she handed me a daisy.

"You're a nut," said a straight early on a Sunday morning. "If you're a minister, why aren't you in church where you belong?"

"Sir, if *you're* a Christian, why aren't *you* in church where you belong?"

—Sherry was back from Bogalusa with our new baby, three weeks old. We named her Joy for the passage in Galatians 5:22: "But the fruit of the Spirit is love, joy, peace, long-suffering, gentleness, goodness, faith."

There wasn't much Sherry and I could say to each other. She, above all others, understood why I was at the cross. Though I knew it was torturing her emotionally, Sherry spent all her spare time with me, though she herself needed more rest.

—A sergeant from the sheriff's department was stopping by three or four times a day. To my delight, he was civilized and friendly.

"Are you making it?" he asked. "If there's anything I can do, let me know."

"Pray, man, pray."

He seemed genuinely sympathetic and caring, a welcome relief from the previous attitude of the sheriff's department.

—Looming up two blocks from me, dominating the Strip like Gulliver among the Lilliputians, was the 9000 Sunset Boulevard building, the black multi-tiered, prestigious headquarters of lawyers, businessmen, agents, and many movie and television stars.

A Negro singer, tears flowing down his cheeks, walked up and said, "I saw you from my agent's office. The whole building is shook up. I want you to know everyone's pulling for you. You're all together, man. Would you say a prayer with me?"

Paul Webb, an angular young man in a gold suit who runs an advertising agency that services Christian clients, was also a tenant in the 9000 building. He offered me an office to think, pray, meditate, and prepare my sermons, a refuge away from the hurly-burly of His Place. At least I now had an office waiting for me even if I still had no church.

—A newsman from KABC radio interviewed me, his Telefunken tape recorder whirling.

"When do you think you'll find a building?"

"When God wills it."

"Why are you doing this?"

"Because we have to keep Jesus on the Strip."

—Dale: "It's two weeks tonight, Arthur. Happy anniversary."

—A spaced-out hip asked me if I wanted to buy a rattlesnake. He wasn't joking. He opened the lid of a cardboard box and I saw the searching, darting tongue.

"Groovy, man," I said. "I'll trade that snake for your soul."

He melted into the crowd.

—"You're on a tough trip, man," said a pusher I knew. "How about some uppers to see you through?"

—Bob Friedman, a young reporter for the Los Angeles *Herald-Examiner*, interviewed me and I asked him if he knew Jesus in his heart. "No, but I'm okay. I'm Jewish and I'm together without Christ." The next day his story appeared in the paper. It helped churn up a bigger crowd of the faithful as well as the curious.

—"Arthur, there's just been a killing down the street," said a girl with buck teeth. "A black man's dead. Started over an argument in a psychedelic shop. The owner, a white dude, pulled a gun and shot him. I feel sorry for him. You just don't get trigger happy on the Strip. That dead cat's buddies are going to even the score. I hope the dude has sense enough to split."

—"You're a false prophet. The hell with you," said a downer-drowned chick. "I don't believe in God, my trip's flying saucers and men from Mars. I dig Vulcan. He's my God."

—The nights on the Strip were cold. Sherry brought a stack of blankets.

"How are Gina, Joel, and Joy?"

"They miss their daddy."

"Good night, darling."

"Good night, darling."

—Saturday, July 19. Twenty-three days have passed. No building. No hope for a building. But I feel strong and well. At the moment I feel strong enough to last indefinitely.

—The street was tumbling with humanity, the usual mixture of straights and hips. "You need a freaky chick," laughed a head sauntering by.

—A girl in a rainbow-hued blouse ran up breathlessly. "Arthur, the Bible you gave me after I was saved . . . I gave it to a prostitute. . . . She's coming down to be saved, too. . . . She wants to get off the Strip."

"Groovy."

—Angry, dark, intense, a seventeen-year-old boy who had been in Juvenile Hall until a few hours ago on a shoplifting charge refused my invitation to come to Christ.

"Who needs it? All I want is a joint, a woman, and some bread, and I don't care how I get them. Pretty soon you're going to see the biggest fire of your life. I'm going to burn down Beverly Hills."

—One of the kids from the Halfway House decided to spend the night with me. A lucky survivor of dozens of acid trips, he said, "Man, Proverbs, chapter three, verses five to six, made me want to live again. I was on a death trip." Aloud he recited the Scripture that gave him new life: "Trust in the Lord with all thine heart, and lean not unto thine own understanding. In all the ways acknowledge him, and he shall direct thy paths."

—July 21. Twenty-five days at the cross. Fasting still. Praying still. Believing still. Hoping still.

—A pleasant man in his sixties, glint in his eyes, purpose in his bearing, a Rotary pin in his lapel, said, "I've been down here several nights watching you. I believe you're sincere. But this riffraff you're ministering to—well, I just don't understand."

"Sir, are you saved?"

"I haven't missed church in thirty years."

"Let me share with you the witness of Jesus when He ate a festive meal with outcasts, prostitutes, and tax collectors."

I read to him from Matthew 9:11–13: " 'And when the Pharisees saw it, they said unto his disciples, Why eateth your Master with tax collectors and sinners? But when Jesus heard that, he said unto them, They that are well need not a physician, but they that are sick. For I am not come to call the righteous, but sinners to repentance.' "

I talked with the man for more than an hour. He had racked up thirty years of faithful church attendance, but like millions of other churchgoers who tithe, sing the hymns, amen the sermons, he didn't understand the teachings of Jesus. I led him gently to the

Promised Land, and Christ truly entered the heart of the man for the first time in his life.

—Dennis Hopper, co-star and director of *Easy Rider*, visited the cross and we discussed Christ and the Gospel. He invited me to dinner to talk about the Lord to some of his Hollywood friends.

—Sherry, Gina, and Joel passed out tracts and reds along the Strip. Sherry was holding Joy, who had a red glued to her forehead.

—Maxine Wagner, a dedicated straight from fashionable Toluca Lake, left the quiet confines of comfortable suburbia to join me at the cross almost every evening. She became a devoted friend of my ministry. One night she challenged three men who emerged from Sneaky Pete's and looked me over skeptically.

"Whatever he's for, I'm against," said one of the men.

"He's for Jesus Christ," Maxine said. "Are you against Him?"

The men turned red-faced with embarrassment as Maxine witnessed to them vigorously. They walked away stunned, reds pasted to their suits, tracts and Bibles in their hands.

Maxine's alert, brown-eyed twelve-year-old daughter, Rayne, brought a handsome young University of Georgia Law School dropout to me. "Virgil needs your help," Rayne said. "He's been wandering along the Strip lost and lonely."

I offered Virgil the fellowship of Christ and convinced him to knock off his first experiments with downers.

He didn't come to the Lord, but promised he would go home and return to school.

—July 22, 7 P.M. Sherry, our children, and a group of kids from USC circled me at the cross. A Volkswagen ground to a halt beside us, and a twentyish hippie hopped out. He came up to me, his fists clenched.

"I've got to kill someone. It might as well be you!"

He went for me, but one of the college kids grabbed him. My unknown assailant was obviously on a trip.

Sherry latched onto the children and stepped aside as the doper broke loose and went berserk, smashing his fists senselessly against the shuttered door of His Place. He fortunately seemed to have no other weapon than his angry hands. One of the parking lot attendants at Sneaky Pete's, a judo expert, brought him to the turf with one swift chop.

The head picked himself up in a moment, and in a spinning whirl, took off down the street, leaving his car behind.

A couple of hours later the sheriff's men towed the Volkswagen away. I later learned it was stolen. The doper was never apprehended.

—Barry Woods, my friend and pastor of the First Baptist Church of Beverly Hills, led three ragged young men to the Lord. They had hitchhiked from Orange, Texas, and were broke and hungry and already disenchanted with the Strip. Barry arranged for them to spend the night sleeping under his pulpit.

—July 23. I was tiring. I wasn't sure how much longer I could last.

—"I'm offering you a building rent-free on Santa Monica or Hollywood Boulevard," a hefty stranger said to me.

"No, thank you, sir. I'm not leaving the Strip."

"I've got enough guys with muscle who say you are."

"I have one who says I'm not. He's got muscle, too. His name is Christ. The only way you're going to get me off this cross is in a casket."

With a scowl and a curse, the man shoved off.

—A brother and sister from Michigan, eighteen and sixteen years old, whispered to me that they were turned on with CTL, Christmas Tree Lights, a murderous amalgam of speed and acid. Both were hallucinating. Their parents were standing less than three feet away with ear-to-ear smiles, probably thinking how wonderful that their kids were talking to a preacher beside a cross of God. The parents had no idea their kids were heads.

—"I'm the reason my boy ran away," said a desperate father from Kansas City. He showed me his son's picture and left me his address and phone number in case I spotted the boy. Sadly, he wandered down the street on a trip of his own, burdened by guilt, shame, and fear.

—For two days a quiet dude squatted near me, never saying a word. Suddenly he got up and asked, "When are you going to die?"

—Listening to KHJ, I heard a disc jockey say, "Man, if you don't see that preacher on Sunset Strip, you're not tripping out."

—Bob Friedman, the young Jewish reporter, visited me several evenings on his own time. Tonight he came joyfully to the Lord.

—The Hi-Sonics, a Negro quartet, were harmonizing moving spirituals as a crowd gathered and listened. "I Need Jesus," they sang gloriously. That's what it's all about, people who need Jesus.

—More rumors of available buildings, more disappointments.

—I led a girl from Tacoma, Washington, to the Lord. She is a prostitute hung up on speed; her father is a minister.

—Someone dropped a book into my lap, and I couldn't help but smile at the title, *Fasting Can Save Your Life*.

—A hippie I knew gave me a bulletin on the international drug scene. "The action's bad in Iran. They stand you in front of a firing squad there just for possession. In India and Pakistan heads from the States are begging rupees on the streets, taking bread from those fakirs. In Greece the heads are living in caves. The freaks pay their way over by selling their bodies. Prostitution, man. The chicks and guys go any way the dudes dig it."

—"Have you seen Tony?" a freckle-faced chick asked me. "He was supposed to meet me here last night at seven."

I led her to the Lord, then told her, "Tony died three weeks ago, OD'd on acid."

—July 24. My mouth was dry. The heat and smog were still tandem tortures.

I had talked to thousands of people. With the aid of the staff, hundreds were saved, dozens of runaways sent home, lives rescued, rededicated, uplifted. And all of it accomplished on a Sunset Strip sidewalk. How much more effective we could be with a new His Place.

My physical stamina was fading fast, the tension of the joined battle tugged at my nerves. Then suddenly, unexpectedly, dramatically, a man came up and whispered in my ear.

I had waited a month to hear those words, and I no longer felt tired or taut.

"I have a building I'll rent to you," the man said.

21

His Place Again

I ENDED MY VIGIL at the cross at one-fifteen in the afternoon on July 24.

Faith had sired victory.

Belief had bred triumph.

Prayer sown. Answer reaped.

Four weeks of witnessing, supplication, and fasting had proved too mighty a sword for all the weapons in the Establishment's arsenal.

A determined soldier at the cross had defeated the generalissimos of greed who commanded the Strip.

A vision glimpsed in a Beverly Hills courtroom—seemingly so long ago—had been fulfilled.

The third His Place on Sunset Strip was a promise delivered, an exultant reality, a gift from Christ.

As O. J. unchained me, the television, radio, and newspaper reporters, alerted by the staff to share our moment of thankfulness, snapped pictures and tossed out a garland of questions.

For the men of the media it was a story that had come full circle. They had recorded the beginning of the witness at the cross and now they were writing a happy ending.

For me, however, the acquisition of the new His Place was another beginning, another opportunity. So much work yet to do, so many souls yet to be saved, unbridled sin yet to be overthrown and destroyed, the psychedelic sea yet to be transformed by the pure blood of Christ, shed so long ago in sacrifice for mankind's transgressions.

Still standing at the cross, my arm no longer shackled, surrounded by the smile-wreathed faces of the staff and several dozen kids, I ate my first meal in twenty-eight days.

Never had fried chicken tasted so good.

Sherry and some friends insisted I visit a doctor for a checkup. He pronounced me completely fit despite the loss of thirty-five pounds.

Physically, emotionally, spiritually, I never felt better.

A moment's walk from the Playboy Club and across the street from the balcony-jawed Continental Hyatt House and Ciro's nightclub was 8428 Sunset Boulevard, our new home. We were still in the heart of the Strip, still in the middle of the action. We were exactly where I wanted us to be. We signed an unbreakable lease to rent the building, formerly the site of two forgotten nightclubs, The Renaissance and Stratford-on-Sunset.

My new landlord was fifty-nine-year-old William Penzner, a walking history of the Strip. He has owned property on Sunset Boulevard since 1942. Tough, independent, compassionate, and sensitive, he was yet another man of Jewish heritage who helped at a critical point in my life. The Old and New Testaments had again been interwoven.

Mr. Penzner was one of the few Strip property owners, perhaps the only one, who would not knuckle under to the organized pressure of those who wanted to see our ministry murdered.

He told me frankly, "The insurance on my building has been canceled and I've had letters and phone calls, complaints from everybody on the Strip about my renting to you."

A widower with no children, he was also frank about the kids who had taken over the Strip.

"I don't approve of the hippies," he said. "They have no morality. Their way of life would destroy us."

However, William Penzner understood our mission.

"I've seen the results of your work, how you get the kids off the Strip, bring them to God and help them build better lives. I believe God is spelled g-o-o-d. If everyone believed in God there would be no murder, killing, or stealing."

With His Place once again in business for the Lord, I received an overwhelming surprise. The Sheriff's Department invited me to explain our work and ministry to their officers!

"Thank you for your recent assistance to Sergeant Roderick A. McLendon and your presentation to his Police Community Relations Class at West Hollywood," Sheriff Pitchess wrote me after I talked to the deputies who once had been so implacable in their opposition to His Place. "It is cooperation of this kind between individuals and agencies that helps us all to do a better job. Surely your time and efforts will add to the success of our program. My kindest personal regards and please be assured of our continuing cooperation in all matters of mutual interest."

An understanding landlord and a cooperative Sheriff's Department.

God at last had put it all together for us on the Strip.

22

Soul Session

Iт's MIDNIGHT at His Place, and slim shafts of light play on our wooden cross.

It's time for a Soul Session, another His Place tradition.

The Soul Session sums up the core of my belief and expresses the essence of what His Place is all about and the certainty of His return.

The words come from deep inside me. It's not a conventional sermon—that would turn the kids off in a flash.

It's the gospel at His Place, the only gospel thousands of kids have ever heard, a gospel to which they can relate.

The Soul Session tells it like it is and tells it like it's going to be to the hundreds of kids jammed into the building.

Except for the muted, reverent accompaniment from our musicians all is silence as I walk to the stage.

It's late and a lot of us feel we're all alone, that no one seems to care.

Your hearts hurt and inside your soul it seems that you're going to break apart. It seems like you could just cry . . . cry . . . cry all night.

But you know, brother, whenever you feel like that and you think there's no hope for you in this whole world, let me just ask you, friend, to open your heart to God and pray, really pray, man.

You'll suddenly realize that the shadows and darkness have turned to a thrilling gold. The clouds are gone, replaced by God's brilliant sunshine.

And, man, you really feel free and one with Him.

It's like when you walk along the beach and a cool wind braces you and the freshness of the water makes you feel everything is new and clean. It's like running through a field of clover and you see the birds, the green trees, and the flowers.

That's the way it feels when Christ comes into your heart.

You've walked into His Place from the Strip tonight, some of you for the first time. And when you came through the door you found something halfway between a church and a nightclub.

You had a cup of coffee or some Kool-Aid. You began to chew on a bagel or a peanut butter and jelly sandwich. You sat down and saw a little sign that said, "Smile, God Loves You."

And it all made you feel a little better.

Suddenly, you saw people going upstairs and maybe you walked upstairs yourself. You saw an open Bible and a little prayer altar and a burning candle. And when you stood in that upper room it seemed like you found what you needed. You realized you needed Him in your life.

Tonight you've been listening to the music and the singing and you've seen hundreds and hundreds come in and out the door. And now you sit here at midnight at the Soul Session. And your own soul cries out and in tears you want to say to God, I've been turning on every way I can, but every trip's been a bummer. It just isn't real.

You're spaced out on acid, some of you are high on speed, or you've been smoking grass. Some of you are loaded on downers or maybe you've hit up and felt the rush of heroin.

Let me tell you, brother, if you really want to get turned on, I mean, man, where the trip's heavy, just pray to Jesus. He'll turn you on to the ultimate trip. He'll give you a high that will keep you for eternity.

Man, you don't have to drop downers; all you have to do is drop a little Matthew, Mark, Luke, and John. I mean you can start dealing Bibles and Gospel tracts, and you can tell everyone about the love of God.

There's hope for you, man.

There's still hope.

Don't cry.

Stand and look up.

Don't die.

Don't wallow.

Don't moan.

God loves you.

The Bible says, "For God so loved the world, that he gave his only begotten Son, that whosoever believeth in him should not perish, but have everlasting life." Christ said, "Behold, I stand at the door, and knock: if any man hear my voice, and open the door, I will come in to him."

Tonight I want you to hear that knock. Just come and kneel at the altar and open your heart and soul to Him.

I want you to say that name, that precious, matchless name.

Jesus.

Just say that name.

Jesus.

Say, Jesus come into my heart and take away all my sin. I give my heart to God.

Now say His precious name again.

Jesus.

Lift up your head, just open your soul and say . . .

Peace and love,

Sent from above,

Fill my heart with love.

Jesus.

And you know, brother, one day Jesus is going to come again, and on that day when Jesus comes it's going to be so wonderful, so great.

Man, how different things are going to be.

I mean Jesus will really make the scene, and He'll be the best friend you've ever had.

Like tonight, if you walked out the door of His Place and looked up and down the Strip, you'd see hippies and bikers, teeny-boppers and movie stars, pushers, straights, and hookers.

But when Jesus comes, that's all going to change.

Close your eyes for a moment. I want you to take a trip with me.

You look down the Strip and you see guys and chicks, men and women, boys and girls. They're on their knees all along the street, and they're praying.

And there's peace.

And there's love.

There's no more hassle.

No more hurt.

No more pain.

No more sorrow.

No more fear.

You look up at Whisky-A-Go-Go, and the sign's been changed to Jesus-A-Go-Go.

Sneaky Pete's says, "We're Not Scared Any More."

The Classic Cat is now The Saved Cat.

Brother, can you dig it?

The Phone Booth has been transformed to The Prayer Booth.

Mother's is The Heavenly Father's.

The Body Shop is The Soul Shop.

The marquee of The Losers reads, "Everybody's a Winner Now."

Dino's says, "Jesus Knows."

The Playboy Club is the Psalms and Proverbs Club.

Brother, do you believe it?

The Palladium says, "Revival, You All Come."

The Hollywood Bowl has a new name—The Salvation Bowl.

There are bumper stickers all over town: "Come to Griffith Park and Get Saved."

Can you imagine what it's going to be like in Las Vegas when they cut the crap tables down low enough for prayer altars? And the slot machines will be in front of the churches to receive the offering.

In Washington the Pentagon will be open to everybody, and they'll sing a song, "We Ain't Goin' to Study War No More."

And back here on the Strip, man, I can't describe how different things are going to be when Jesus comes.

Groove on the scene when the sheriff's men are carrying Bibles in their holsters instead of guns. Instead of police radios squawking "Roger ten, four over and out," they'll be broadcasting "John, chapter three, verse thirteen, over, out, and saved."

That's the day I want to see.

That's the day I'm going to see.

But right now it just isn't that way.

We're going to have to wait a while longer until He comes again.

When He does return, I'm going to fall on my knees and give Him the key to His Place.

I won't need it any more.

All the world, when Jesus comes, will be His Place.

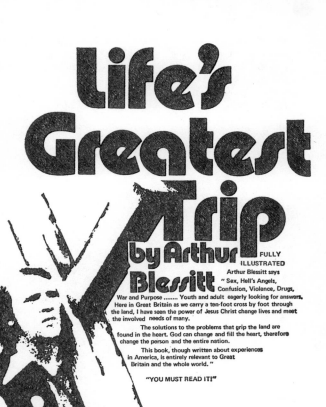

Life's Greatest Trip

by Arthur Blessitt

FULLY ILLUSTRATED

Arthur Blessitt says

" Sex, Hell's Angels, Confusion, Violence, Drugs, War and Purpose .... Youth and adult eagerly looking for answers. Here in Great Britain as we carry a ten-foot cross by foot through the land, I have seen the power of Jesus Christ change lives and meet the involved needs of many.

The solutions to the problems that grip the land are found in the heart. God can change and fill the heart, therefore change the person and the entire nation.

This book, though written about experiences in America, is entirely relevant to Great Britain and the whole world. "

"YOU MUST READ IT!"